The Science of Stories

The Science of Stories explores the role narrative plays in human life. Supported by in-depth research, the book demonstrates how the ways in which people tell their stories can be indicative of how they construct their worlds and their own identities.

Based on linguistic analysis and computer technology, László offers an innovative methodology which aims to uncover underlying psychological processes in narrative texts. The reader is presented with a theoretical framework along with a series of studies which explore the way a systematic linguistic analysis of narrative discourse can lead to a scientific study of identity construction, both individual and group.

The book gives a critical overview of earlier narrative theories and summarizes previous scientific attempts to uncover relationships between language and personality. It also deals with social memory and group identity: various narrative forms of historical representations (history books, folk narratives, historical novels) are analysed as to how they construct the past of a nation.

The Science of Stories is the first book to build a bridge between scientific and hermeneutic studies of narratives. As such, it will be of great interest to a diverse spectrum of readers in social science and the liberal arts, including those in the fields of cognitive science, social psychology, linguistics, philosophy, literary studies and history.

János László is professor of social psychology at the Institute for Psychology of the Hungarian Academy of Sciences, Budapest and the University of Pécs, where he is currently head of the Institute of Psychology and of the Doctoral School in Psychology.

British Library of Political
and Economic Science

**Please return this item by the
date/ time shown below**

If another user requests this item, we will contact
you with an amended date for return.

Fines are charged for overdue items.

Renew via the Library catalogue at www.library.lse.ac.uk
or Tel: 020 7955 7229 (10am–5pm Monday–Friday)

Thank you

The Science of Stories
An Introduction to Narrative Psychology

János László

Routledge
Taylor & Francis Group

LONDON AND NEW YORK

First published 2008 by Routledge
27 Church Road, Hove, East Sussex BN3 2FA
Simultaneously published in the USA and Canada
by Routledge
270 Madison Avenue, New York, NY 10016

Routledge is an imprint of the Taylor & Francis Group, an Informa business

© 2008 Psychology Press

Typeset in Times by Regent Typesetting, London
Printed and bound in Great Britain by TJ International Ltd, Padstow, Cornwall
Paperback cover design by Design Deluxe

British Library Cataloguing in Publication Data
A catalogue record for this book is available from the British Library

Library of Congress Cataloging in Publication Data
László, János.
    The science of stories : an introduction to narrative psychology / János László.
        p. cm.
    Includes bibliographical references and index.
    ISBN 978-0–415–45794–1 (hardcover
    ISBN 978-0–415–45795–8 (pbk.)
    1. Psychology--Biographical methods. 2. Discourse analysis, Narrative--
Psychological aspects. I. Title.
    BF39.4.L37 2009
    150.72'2--dc22
                                        2008002878

ISBN 978-0–415–45794–1 (hbk)
ISBN 978-0–415–45795–8 (pbk)

Contents

Illustrations

Figures

Tables

Preface

An old Latin proverb says 'Habent sua fata libelli' – each book has its own fate. The story of this book goes back to 1996, when with Wendy Stainton-Rogers we organized a small group meeting in Budapest under the auspices of the European Association of Experimental Social Psychology. The aim of this conference was to introduce the narrative approach into empirical models of social psychology. When we wanted to publish the conference papers in a volume, we found that no international publishers were interested . Eventually, the book came out with the help of a small Hungarian publishing house Új Mandátum (László and Stainton-Rogers, 2002). This moderate success did not discourage us and we went on to find new ways of studying empirically the interrelations between narrative language and human psychological processes. The first study performed with narrative psychological content analysis was published in 1997 (Stephenson, László, Ehmann, Lefever and Lefever, 1997), and a comprehensive outline of this methodology appeared in 2002 (László, Ehmann, Péley, Pólya, 2002). From 2001, two major research grants supported our work (NKFP 2001/5/26 and NKFP 2005/6/74). The original team with Bea Ehmann and Tibor Pólya of the Institute of Psychology of the Hungarian Academy of Sciences, and Bernadette Péley of the University of Pécs continued to work in collaboration with young psychologists of the University of Pécs (Rita Hargitai, Melinda Pohárnok, Ildikó Somogyváry, Orsolya Vincze), computer linguists Balázs Kis, Mátyás Naszódi and Gábor Prószéky of the leading Hungarian language technological enterprise, Morphologic Ltd. Tamás Váradi of the Institute of Linguistics of the Hungarian Academy of Sciences, Zoltán Alexin and János Csirik of the Institute of Informatics of the University of Szeged joined to the project later. Without the contribution of this enthusiastic team this book would have never been written.

The scope and intensity of research in this area has been broadened and strengthened in the past decade and the intellectual climate around application of quantitative methodologies in narrative psychological research has also become more favourable. Lucy Kennedy as editor of the Psychology Press/Routledge not only appreciated, but facilitated this change when she kept urging me to write this book. She has devoted considerable energy to getting the book into the best possible shape. I am particularly grateful to her.

It is not possible to mention all the people to whom I owe gratitude for their contribution. I have already mentioned all those involved in the research, but I ought to add that practically all of them also read and commented on the manuscript. Their comments helped to eliminate some of the flaws. I owe special thanks to three of my readers: Joe Forgas, Csaba Pléh, and Jamie Pennebaker and with each of whom I have been sharing dialogues for decades. Our conversations and correspondence, just like their comments on the manuscript have given me a lot of inspiration and encouragement.

English is not my first language. It's not even my second or third language. I started to learn it when I was over twenty and turned to an academic career. As a consequence, I will never command this language with the perfection that native speakers or bilinguals do. Theresa M. Lillis of the Open University has been running a program for many years in academic writing for scholars of my type. She has not only polished my papers and books, but, in the course of the years she has become my intellectual partner, who keeps pressing me to express my thoughts clearly and explicitly, even providing me with editorial comments and advice. I do not want to suggest that any obscure sentences remaining in the book are her fault. Rather I want to express my gratitude for her significant contribution. Some parts of the book were first written in Hungarian. András Bocz, a linguist of the University of Pécs helped me with the translation. His assistance was reassuring to me not only because he produced a smooth translation, but also because Theresa could find and correct mistakes even in this professional work. I hope that as a result of our joint efforts the text is clear and readable.

Anyone who has ever written a book, knows that the preparation of the manuscript is a tedious and time consuming task. I am grateful to Ildikó Kántor and Ilona Molnár who helped me to carry this out. Christine Firth (freelance copyeditor) took care of the manuscript after submission and I have to admit that there was plenty of work for her to do. She did her job with extreme kindness and cooperation.

I have already expressed my gratitude to my wife, Bernadette Péley as coworker, co-author, and reviewer. It remains 'only' for me to thank her for being my companion in all matters of my life and thereby enabling the birth of this book.

János László
Budapest and Pécs
February, 2007

Introduction

Narrative psychology evolved in the late twentieth century. It has had at least five different strands or paradigms since its inception. The term 'narrative psychology' was introduced by Theodor Sarbin's influential book (Sarbin 1986b), which declared narrative to be the 'root metaphor' for psychology, and suggested that qualitative studies exploit this metaphorical value. Another book from the same year, Jerome Bruner's *Actual Minds, Possible Words* (1986), explored the 'narrative kind of knowing' in a more empiricist manner. Around the same time, Dan McAdams (1985) developed a theoretical framework and a coding system for interpreting life narratives in the personological tradition. By that time, stories, their production and comprehension became one of the central targets of mainstream scientific psychology (e.g. Bobrow and Collins 1975; Mandl et al. 1984; Rumelhart 1975; Thorndyke 1977) as opposed to their earlier sporadic occurrence (the most notable classic example is Sir Frederick Bartlett's (1932) work on remembering). And last but not at least, the linguistic qualities of narratives such as structure and word selection became objects of personality and social psychological research in James Pennebaker's works (Pennebaker 1993; Pennebaker et al. 1997a). I will deal with all of these approaches in due course. However, the major objective of this book is to outline a project of narrative psychology, which draws on the scientific traditions of psychological study, but adds to the existing theories by pursuing the empirical study of psychological meaning construction. Our contention is that *scientific narrative psychology* opens a new perspective on complex phenomena such as cultural and evolutionary dimensions of personality, personal or social identity and group life.

The nature of narratives

Narratives are generally conceived as accounts of events, which involve some temporal and/or causal coherence (Hoshmand 2005). Narrative is not the only possible form of human communication. Communicative manifestations are characterized by a boundless diversity of speech acts, and even if we consider the discourse genres of monologues alone, we have, in addition to narrative, argumentation, description and explanation, just as we have a wide range of mental constructs for analysing the organization of observation and experience besides episodic or story schemas. Nonetheless, as Barthes (1977) writes:

> narrative is present in myth, legend, fable, tale, novella, epic, history, tragedy, drama, comedy, mime, painting, ... stained-glass windows, cinema, comics, news item, conversation. Moreover, under this almost infinite diversity of forms, narrative is present in every age, in every place, in every society; it begins with the very history of mankind and there nowhere is nor has been a people without narrative. ... Caring nothing for the division between good and bad literature, narrative is international, transhistorical, transcultural: it is simply there, like life itself.
>
> (Barthes 1977: 79)

More cogently, Hardy (1968: 5) has written: 'we dream in narrative, daydream in narrative, remember, anticipate, hope, despair, believe, doubt, plan, revise, criticize, construct, gossip, learn, hate and love by narrative'.

This 'omnipresence' of narrative is explained by the fact that narrative accounts are embedded in social action. Events become socially visible through narratives, and expectations towards future events are, for the most part, substantiated by them. Since narratives permeate the events of everyday life, the events themselves become story-like too. They assume the reality of 'beginning', 'peak', 'nadir' or 'termination'. This is how people experience events, and we all record them in this way. Thus, in this very important sense, our life goes on its way in terms of stories, whether we simply tell our self or create it in an active fashion.

In the past few decades it has been recognized more and more intensively in the social sciences and the humanities that social knowledge and social thinking are characterized by some sort of distinct type of *narrativity*. One of the leading representatives of the narrative approach in psychology, Jerome Bruner (1986, 1990, 1996) makes a distinction between two natural forms of human thinking. These two cognitive modes organize our experiences and construe reality in different ways. One of them is the *paradigmatic or logical-scientific mode*, which works with abstract concepts, construes truth by means of empirical evidence and methods of formal logic, and while doing so, it seeks causal relations that lead to universal truth conditions. The other, more 'mundane' mode of thinking is the *narrative mode*, which investigates human or human-like intentions and acts, as well as the stories and consequences related to them. What justifies this mode is life-likeness rather than truth, and it aspires to create a realistic representation of life. Bruner (1986) illustrates the two types of causality as follows:

> The term then functions differently in the logical proposition 'if x than y', and in the narrative recit 'The king died, and then the queen died.' One leads to a search for universal truth conditions, the other for likely particular connections between two events – mortal grief, suicide, foul play.
>
> (Bruner 1986: 11–12)

In other words, narrative thinking aspires to make sense or to establish coherence.

The most obvious forms of narrative thinking are stories told by professional authors and the man in the street. With a subtle sense Bruner (1986: 14) notes that there are two kinds of psychological domain, or, as he puts it, two land-scapes emerging concurrently in stories. The landscape of action comprises the arguments of action: actor, intention or goal, situation, means, etc. The other domain, the *landscape of consciousness* expresses what the participants of the action know, think and feel, or what they do not know, think and feel. At the same time, the concurrent presence of these two landscapes of narrative assumes that fully fledged stories do not merely give an account of what has happened but they involve a lot more than that: they also outline the psychological perspective of events. The ability to elaborate action, the inevitable presence of time (see Cupchik and László 1994), perspective (László and Larsen 1991) and the way time and perspective are handled make narrative a kind of a 'natural tool' for making a distinction between action, emotion and thought so that these compon-ents can be reintegrated (see Bruner and Lucariello 1989: 77–79).

For the same reason, Bruner and Lucariello (1989) stress the creative nature of narrative:

> a developed narrative, then, is not simply an account of what happened, but implies much more about the psychological perspectives taken toward those happenings. Accordingly, one deep reason why we tell stories to ourselves (or to our confessor or to our analyst or to our confidant) is precisely to 'make sense' of what we are encountering in the course of living – through narrative elaborations of the natural arguments of action.
>
> (Bruner and Lucariello 1989: 79)

In essence, we make sense of our life by telling stories, because 'There is no such thing psychologically as "life itself"… In the end it is a narrative achievement' (Bruner 1987: 13). Like Ricoeur (1984–1989) and Flick (1995), Bruner construes the interrelationship of life, construction and interpretation as a circular mimetic process: 'Narrative imitates life, life imitates narrative' (Bruner 1987: 12).

Narrative analysis

Traditionally, narratives are analysed in social sciences in three distinct ways. *Formal-structural analysis* initiated by the Russian formalists focuses on the role that linguistic and discourse structures play in conveying meaning. In psychology this approach prevails in cognitive studies of story production and comprehen-sion. *Content analysis* is directed to the semantic content and tries to quantify it. In psychology, of course, psychological contents are classified and measured. Major limits of both analytic tools are, first, the uncertainty of the external valid-ity of the constructs derived from them, and second, blindness to the context where structures or semantic contents occur. This latter flaw prevents formal-structural analysis and content analysis to reconstruct pragmatic or psychological meaning of texts (see Chapter 7). However, the third type of narrative analytics, *hermeneutic analysis*, embraces the social, cultural and textual context of the narrative and interprets its meaning against this background. In psychology it mostly means interpretation of personal narratives with reference to identity. Validity of the interpretation, however, is not amenable to empirical testing.

The positivism versus hermeneutics or the sciences versus humanities controversy is clearly reflected in the above approaches. Whereas content analysis goes bottom-up, attempting to construct meaning from elementary pieces of narrative discourse, hermeneutics adopts a top-down strategy in which the interpretation horizon has absolute primacy. Attempts have been made to reconcile the two approaches with moderate success. For instance, Martindale's empirically aided 'quantitative hermeneutics' (Martindale and West 2002), which uses computer technology to unravel thematic lines in text corpora, has been by and large dismissed by positivists as too soft and by hermeneutic scholars as too reductionist. Nevertheless, as I will argue in Chapters 3 and 4, psychology is a discipline where the 'two cultures' of sciences and humanities (Snow 1993) can and should meet. Of course, we do not envision a merging between the two epistemological stances. We rather expect to emerge psychological issues in personality, social and cultural processes, where complexity of the phenomena both allows and requires concerted application of top-down and bottom-up methodologies. Narrative, by its undoubted structural organization, its material, empirical aspects, and its close relation to the broad issues of identity, seems to be the vehicle of these complex psychological processes. Scientific narrative psychology is an attempt to outline these domains and to facilitate the encounter between the scientific and hermeneutic methodologies.

Preliminary on scientific narrative psychology

Scientific narrative psychology takes seriously the interrelations between language and human psychological processes or narrative and identity. This is what discriminates the scientific narrative psychological approach from earlier psychometric studies, which established correlations between language use and psychological states (Pennebaker and King 1999; Pennebaker et al. 2003). It assumes that studying narratives as vehicles of complex psychological contents leads to empirically based knowledge about human social adaptation. Individuals in their life stories, just like groups in their group histories, compose their significant life episodes. In this composition, which is meaning construction in itself, they express the ways in which they organize their relations to the social world, or construct their identity. If we accept that people construct themselves and their psychological reality by stories in many substantial respects, then we are justified in assuming that the organizational characters and experiential qualities of these stories will tell us about the potential behavioural adaptation and the coping capacities of the storytellers. In order to study these experiential organizations and qualities we need an empirical methodology which has the capacity to reliably unfold psychologically relevant meaning from narrative discourse. Scientific narrative psychology has turned to narratology in order to develop such a methodology.

Narratology has described the limited number of elements and the limited number of variations of the elements in narrative composition. These compositional factors can be reliably identified in discourse. We assume that each narrative component corresponds to certain processes or states of experiential organization or psychological meaning construction. For instance, using a retrospective narrative perspective as opposed to experiencing or re-experiencing perspectives when telling a traumatic life event suggests emotional balance, i.e., that the storyteller managed to elaborate the negative experience and restore the integrity of his or her identity. In an experiment, Pólya, László and Forgas (2005) provided evidence supporting the above assumption. Traumatic life events, such as the failure of an in-vitro fertilization (IVF) treatment, were reported from different perspectives. The use of the different perspectives can be illustrated with the following excerpts: 'I was waiting in the doctor's office ... The doctor entered the room ... He told me that we had not succeeded ...' (retrospective perspective). 'It was in the doctor's office ... I see the doctor entering the room ... I don't remember how it could happen ...' (re-experiencing perspective). Subjects consistently evaluated the target person as having better emotional control, higher social value and more stable identity when they read retrospective stories as opposed to re-experienced ones.

Beyond the perspective, narratives contain other compositional devices such as time structure and time experience (the latter particularly in self-narratives), characters' agency, characters' mental involvement, coherence, evaluation, spatial and interpersonal relations of the characters, etc. This limited number of compositional 'slots' corresponds to a similarly limited number of psychological constructions, whereas the text can be endlessly variable on the surface level (i.e. linguistically). Based on the narrative compositional elements, algorithms have been constructed that are able to automatically detect and quantitatively process the linguistic features of each element (Ehmann et al. 2007; Hargitai et al. 2007; László et al. 2007; Pohárnok et al. 2007; Polya et al 2007). The reliability and validity of these algorithms for identifying the underlying psychological constructs are continuously tested. The principles and procedures of the narrative psychological content analysis are discussed in Chapter 9. Some results concerning social (national) identity are also presented in Chapter 10. But before arriving at the results, here is a brief summary of the 'story of this book'.

In Chapter 1 narrativity in the broadest sense is discussed. Beyond cognitive studies, which focus on narrative structures or canons, many aspects of narrative are analysed and rethought from the perspective of potential integration into the narrative psychology. Chapter 2 draws an epistemological context around narrative psychology contrasting analytic and narrative philosophies. In this chapter we argue that the complexity level of many psychological phenomena requires research objects and research methodologies which correspond to this complexity. We claim that narrative represents a complexity level, which allows for meaningful empirical investigations. We also discuss the potential of narrative psychology in the study of personal development and cultural evolution. Chapter 3 is built on contrast again. It demarcates scientific narrative psychology's quest for meaning from hermeneutic studies of narrative identity, also from cultural anthropological and psychoanalytic approaches. There is one major area, perhaps the largest in psychology, which has a long record in dealing with narrative phenomena. This is cognitive psychology. Chapter 4 relates scientific narrative psychology to existing cognitive studies also in a contrastive manner. In Chapter 5 we bring together all the previously discussed rival approaches around the concept of representation. In this chapter, it should become clear why and how we conceive narrative as a representational form. Chapter 6 is devoted to Moscovici's social representations theory, primarily because this theory resembles narrative psychology in several respects. Not only is it engaged in studying meaning construction, but also it studies the process of social meaning construction through empirical methodologies. This theory also has deep insight into the relation between representations and identity, which is a major interest of narrative psychology as well. The chapter also discusses the actual and potential contributions of narrative psychology to social representations research. Chapter 7 deals with earlier psychological approaches to the relation between various forms of life narratives and various forms of self and identity. Theories which have also developed empirical methodologies in order to infer different qualities of identity from narratives or to trace the process of identity construction through narratives are presented in detail. This chapter points out that earlier concepts and methodologies focus almost exclusively on narrative content and neglect the formal, compositional aspects of narratives. The chapter also discusses the social constraints on life narratives and the role of narrative in psychotherapy, particularly in trauma elaboration.

From Chapter 8 on we turn in depth to methodology. Starting from the more general issues of the interrelations between linguistic forms and psychological processes, this chapter leads the reader through the intricacies of psychological content analysis and into the history of the automation of the content analytic methodology. Chapter 9 outlines the principles and the scope of narrative psychological content analysis, a method which has been developed for scientific narrative psychology. For readers who are interested in methodological details, the process of automation of this analytic tool and validity studies of the programs are presented in the Appendix.

Whereas earlier chapters revolve around construction and expression of personal identity in individual life narratives, Chapter 10 expands the boundaries of scientific narrative psychology to the study of social identity by relating social psychological phenomena to historical representations. This chapter presents empirical studies on national identity which demonstrate the application of the new methodology in social psychological research. The concluding Chapter 11 summarizes the main arguments and contribution of the book to narrative psychology and considers future directions.

1 Foundations of narrative psychology

The narrative nature of human knowledge

When modelling cognitive and memory processes, though by no means on the basis of some social constructivist position, Schank and Abelson (1995: 1) argue for the narrative nature of all human knowledge. They state that 'Virtually all human knowledge is based on stories constructed around past experiences', and 'New experiences are interpreted in terms of old stories'. With intuitive insight Schank and Abelson derive nearly any knowledge – from facts to beliefs – from storytelling and story understanding. In this framework, lexical items, words, numbers, even grammar itself can be investigated in the context of stories. Schank and Abelson (1995) question the traditional cognitivist model of human consciousness (cf. Newel and Simon 1972), in which humans work as information-processing machines, and the task of the human mind to prove theorems and solve problems. They point out how atypical these phenomena are in everyday life: 'very few people spend time trying to prove theorems ... and when they do, they don't ordinarily talk about it' (Schank and Abelson 1995: 15). However, this idea again implies a semantic distinction between an abstract, theoretical argument and everyday thinking, which precisely reflects the difference between *natural and communicative logic* mentioned by Moscovici and Bruner's *paradigmatic versus narrative thinking* mentioned in the Introduction. Without doubt, Schank and Abelson (1995) explicitly give preference – at least as far as everyday human things are concerned – to the latter type of thinking. Schank and Abelson's new theory can be viewed as a further refinement of their earlier model of human memory and understanding based on episodes or scripts (Schank 1975; Schank and Abelson 1977), which was essentially meant to question Tulving's (1972) dual memory system (an episodic, story-like, or semantic, conceptual model) that was fairly influential at that time. Although these two authors are interested in the cognitive construction of stories and the memory effects of storytelling, their observations concerning the *social context of storytelling* and the concept of *narrative framework* have far-reaching social implications. When they state that understanding means 'mapping your stories to mine', they actually refer to a cognitive constraint that 'we can only understand things that relate to our experiences' (Schank and Abelson 1995: 17). However, this cognitivist statement, which is somewhat trivial in this narrow sense, implies that people can tell only stories that are in some relationship with relatable experiences of other people. It does not simply suggest that stories should be *shared socially*, but it also addresses the issue as to how stories change in a given society or culture and how they are distributed in them; or even, what is the relationship between story and reality. Referring to the famous scene in Woody Allen's film *Annie Hall* (1977), in which the male and female leading characters tell their analyst two different stories about how energetically, frequently or regrettably infrequently they make love, Schank and Abelson do not simply state that 'we and our audience shape our memories by the stories we tell', but they hasten to add that stories interpret the world, and we can see the world only as is allowed by our stories (Schank and Abelson 1995: 60).

Nevertheless, our stories are not merely our own personal – mental or verbal – narratives. Common experience in a culture or society takes shape in common stories or story frames. Every society has its own *'historically crystallized stories'*, and although individuals may view them from different aspects and create different stories out of the same experienced event, culture informs all its members of the set of possible story frames. This fact has been proved by several decision-making experiments which have shown that selection among the possible sets of decisions is closely related to making a choice from the set of possible stories that can be spun around an event or action (Abelson 1976; Pennington and Hastie 1992; Wagenaar et al. 1993). Even autobiographies are social constructs (Gergen and Gergen 1988; Nelson 1993), and they are created in the light of local conditions as a function of several different narrative possibilities. It is hard to see this set of story frames in any other way other than as a culturally valid naive psychology, everyday thinking, or – as Bartlett (1932) viewed it – the *social framework* of rationality. The role of narrative in psychology as a meaning configuration that has some significance beyond associative organization has been raised by several outstanding scholars of the twentieth century. For Bartlett, Binet, Janet or Blonsky, narrative represented the fundamental non-associative organizing principle of mental life. They viewed the logic of these stories as social logic and story memory as social memory, though in different ways. For them, narrative was a metatheory of theoretical assumptions on mental life, as well as the subject matter and the means of carrying out research work on memory processes.

Heider's (1958) naive psychology assigns goals to the movement of objects and shows the role of intentionality in perception. Heider applied the categories of intentionality and other perceptual categories arising from the tale entitled *The Fox and the Raven* (for instance, the raven *possesses* the cheese, the fox is not *able* to get the cheese – for more on this, see Heider 1958: 53–55) in his cognitive balance theory, and explained action in his attribution theory in a way that he was at the same time trying to find out what sort of rules are used to create 'conceptually good forms' or, as would be stated today, coherent stories. A decade later, when writing a critique of reductionist and homeostatic approaches to the Heiderian theory, Abelson (1968) suggested that we should return to Heider's naive psychology, and he outlined the foundations of an independent *psycho-logic*. A close descendant of this psycho-logic, the theory of narrated knowledge proposed by Schank and Abelson (1995) (see also Harvey and Martin 1995) comprises all the advantages of this earlier train of thought, but it also exhibits some of its shortcomings. One of the shortcomings is that although he acknowledges that stories can give rise to constructs, he denies that stories themselves have a construed nature.

Another reductionist element in the model proposed by Schank and Abelson (1995) is that they simplify narratives to stories. As a result, they introduced the metaphor of an *information-generating machine*, though they did suggest that human consciousness should not be viewed as a problem-solving machine. The former lacks any experience-like aspect that is made possible, however implicitly, by Bruner's narrative approach. This is a rather ironic development, for it was precisely Abelson (1975) and Schank (1986) as scientists doing work in artificial intelligence theory that played a leading role in having experience-like representations 'carried' by narrative recognized by others.

It has to be emphasized here that the *narrative paradigm* not only can offer a special kind of cognitive logic for intentional actions, thoughts and emotions but also is capable of handling experiences such as emotions, images, time or perspective that have not been treated conceptually thus far. When we read a story, not only can we understand the time and place of actions but also we can imagine the scene and the protagonist. And when we read, for instance, that the protagonist's wife has died, we do not simply understand that he is in mourning for her but we are also caught up by the feeling of mourning (see Oatley 1992). Jerome Bruner (1986) explains reader involvement by linking the mental states of the characters of a narrated event to the reader through perspectivization. This kind of ability to involve the recipient is utilized most effectively in literature. As noted by Vygotsky (1971), literature captures unconscious, floating, undefined emotions in social relationships, and thereby it can be regarded as the 'social technique of handling emotions'.

However, this capacity of narrative is not limited to literary narratives; they are equally valid for the real life of social groups when they perform joint activities and view their own actions as experience. Consider the notion of *collective experience* and *allusion* introduced by Mérei (1949). As the imitation of the sound of a fire-engine among kindergarten children evokes the entire experience of the firefighter game played the day before on the basis of a certain part for whole mechanism, literary narratives can also create the direct intimacy of collective experience in a conscious dimension through reference.

However, narratives can be defined not just in the way discussed so far, that is, as the carrier and the ingredient of creating meaning and reality on a social-cognitive basis. In psychology, the research on narratives covers the way in which stories work on the one hand, and several psychologically interpreted forms and functions of narratives on the other, which can be derived from the role that narratives play in people's lives.

Psychologists interested in narratives insist that the psychology of man can be fully unfolded from stories (Bower 1976), or rather, there is no human experience that could not be expressed in a narrative form (Jovchelovitch 1995).

Other authors maintain that narrative is the most important tool for integrating practical experience in life and creating coherence (Stein and Policastro 1984; Sutton-Smith 1976). In the psychological literature, Bruno Bettelheim's *The Uses of Enchantment* (1976) demonstrates the idea very well that stories provide a structure, a form for the unconscious desires and anxiety of individuals, thereby fostering the development and integration of the self. The story of Little Red Riding-Hood for instance includes all the characteristic fears and the basic dynamics of the Oedipus complex in 3–5-year-old children. Children who live through similar stories of power and love unconsciously in their own life identify with Little Red Riding-Hood, and may experience oedipal struggles. As a result of overcoming their troubles together with Little Red Riding-Hood they may be able to strengthen their selves that have been shattered by the oedipal tragedy (Bettelheim 1976). In experimental psychology the classic work of Bartlett (1932) shows that a story can give meaning to an otherwise nonsensical detail, and the comprehension and memory-based reconstruction of stories are governed by the quest for sense.

Narratology

Psychology can borrow a number of notions and analytic methods from the research project of *narratology* for the study of narratives. Narratology was organized as an independent research school in structuralist literary theory in the 1960s, so for quite a time its subject matter comprised the structural analysis of narrative forms of representation. In the past few decades narratology has become a so-called multidisciplinary field at the intersection of several branches of science where, in addition to structural analyses, special attention is given to the interpretation of stories and to the analysis of their cognitive and ideological functions. The emergence of narratology was symbolically marked by the 1966 special issue of the journal *Communications*, in which Roland Barthes argued for the universality and omnipresence of narrative.

In order for a representation to qualify as a narrative, be it mental or linguistic-semiotic, it must have two basic properties: it must have some sort of a *reference* and some sort of a *temporal structure*. Labov and Waletzky (1967, 1997) have recognized that simple narratives told by everyday people can be used to derive the formal features of narrative and to establish its individual components. In a series of interviews they had their subjects tell some episodes of their lives in which their life was in some danger. Although the original goal of the authors was to find a correlation between the social features of the narrators (their social status, residence, age, nationality, etc.) and the structure of the narrated story, the analysis led to some apparently general conclusions.

Labov and Waletzky (1967, 1997) view narrative from the point of view of a referential function, that is, they conceived of narrative as a procedure to put past personal experience into words in which narrators coordinated linguistic sequences with the sequence of events that had taken place. They derive the property of narrative that they believe to be the most important one, *temporal order*, from this referential function. Their minimal criterion for narrative is that it should include at least two consecutive, temporally related event sequences. In their view the term narrative can be used only to describe a sequence of events, in contrast to any other arrangement of events, which includes stories told in a way that is compatible with the original chronological order of the referred event. Needless to say, the world of narrative is richer by far than this narrow, one could say, minimalist definition. We do not even need to turn to the narrative theory of great storytellers like Dostoyevsky or Kafka or the Russian formalists to see this; it is enough to recall our own everyday stories in which we present events in an order that is different from the original sequence, using temporal leaps and returning back to earlier events, so that we can arouse interest and maintain tension. Obviously, Labov and Waletzky were also aware of all this. The definition they used in their research reflects their endeavour to trace more complex narrative forms back to simpler, basic cases, to fundamental components, so their analysis was aimed at basic cases. However, even this rather limited definition of narrative leaves a number of questions open. For example, it does not include any rules as to the boundaries of narrative. When there are several episodes in a story, we have to rely on our intuition to decide whether it comprises one single narrative or several narratives that are linked in some way.

The logical consequence of placing the focus on the relationship between narrative and the told events, on linear temporal order, was that Labov and Waletzky, unlike Propp (1968) who analysed the structure of Russian magic tales by identifying units of plot, or Colby (1973) who used the word as the unit of analysis in investigating Eskimo folk tales, took the clause as the smallest unit of analysing narrative. In their method they distinguished three types of clauses or narrative units. Certain sequences, so-called *free clauses*, can be moved freely within the text without affecting the meaning or the course of events of a given story. There are *restricted clauses* that can be moved forwards or backwards within their immediate context as long as the displacement does not violate the temporal order of the original semantic interpretation of the event. Finally, Labov and Waletzky distinguish *narrative clauses* proper, sequences that are closely tied to the temporal course of the event, and are thus not displaceable without changing the original semantic interpretation. Labov and Waletzky divided narrative into five large structural units in which each sequence type has a different frequency of distribution. *Orientation*, that is, the introduction of the story's circumstances largely includes free sequences. *Complication* and *resolution* are built up from bound or partially limited displaceable sequences. With the criterion of displaceability, Labov and Waletzky identified another component, as compared to traditional components of story structure, *evaluation*, which has proved to be especially productive in further studies of narrative.

The referentiality of narrative

According to Scholes (1980: 205) narrative is a text that refers, or appears to refer, to a set of events outside itself. In the latter case, for instance in literature,

narrative refers to an imagined reality. It is not problematic for narrative referentiality, as the imagined reality itself is not created in vacuum. The imagined,
possible worlds are all related to the outside world. However, the problem of the
reference of narrative, not merely of fictitious narrative, is not so simple.

Bruner (1996) contrasts the categories of philosophy with those of narrative.
The reference of the former is clear, while that of narrative is always ambiguous, whether narrative refers to facts or it is fictitious. Narrative always creates
its own 'reality', the thing that it refers to, as the categories of narrative in the
sense of Propp are always functional. It is like the meaning of a word, which is
determined by its place and function in the sentence. This is what decides, for
instance, whether we think of a financial institution or the land alongside a river
when we use the word 'bank'. This is true not only of fictitious stories. When
public events, for instance complicated social scandals, are interpreted, narrative
functions prove to be extremely powerful.

Bruner uses the scandal concerning the former Irish Taoiseach, Albert Reynolds to show how originally ambiguous events gain their canonic narrative form.
The scandal broke out when Reynolds, at that time as Minister of Industry and
Commerce, undertook a guarantee on behalf of the government for a shipment of
beef that had been delivered to Iraq by a rich contractor who was known for some
rather suspicious transactions. How could Reynolds have spent public funds on
this transaction when everybody knew that the beef that had been shipped to Iraq
was not from Ireland but from different countries of the European Union? In the
following years, the scandal grew bigger and several aspects of it were explored
by journalists, but even a special committee of inquiry was unable to find a narrative form for the event. After the report of the committee had been published,
the Taoiseach was content and made a statement saying that the committee had
cleared him of the charges. Still, the final word was claimed by narrative reality.
A few days after the committee's report had been published, a newspaper leaked
out some rumour about a considerable amount of money paid to experts invited by
the committee for participating in the investigations. Here we have got the narrative that contrived the events into a story: the story of 'corruption taking place in
high positions'.

Albert Reynolds resigned from office, and his resignation was caused by an in-
defensible corruption narrative rather than by established facts. It will be the task
of historians to find out whether Reynolds was a corrupt politician or just a plain
dupe. In Hungary one could experience the same in connection with the so-called
Tocsik scandal. A lawyer working for the State Privatization Agency transferred a
huge amount of money to mysterious bank accounts. Although several contradictory judgements were made in this case, and probably even historians will not be
able to find out what exactly happened, we are not likely to be mistaken when we
attribute the fall of the socialist cabinet largely to the Tocsik scandal a few months
before the elections.

Narrative, while creating its own reference and making it real, makes contact with reality in several other ways as well. Openly fictitious literary or film
stories often have consequences which are far too real; we have known this at

least since a wave of suicides swept through young people after Goethe's *The Sorrows of Young Werther* had been published in 1774. A more ordinary example is that after seeing Steven Spielberg's *Jaws* (1975), many holidaymakers kept away from going into the sea (Gerrig 1993), or after the horror movie *It* (1990, based on Stephen King's novel) had been shown, the turnover of clown toys fell sharply in toy shops (Cantor 2004). In 2004 a special issue of *Poetics Today* was devoted to the discussion of this type of relationship between real life and fictitious narrative.

The reference of therapeutic narratives

The question of the reference of narratives is raised especially sharply in connection with stories told in psychotherapeutic conversations, for example when childhood traumas are recalled. From the point of view of the main goal of the therapy, which is restoring the mental health of the patient, it seems to be of minor importance whether the story told in the therapy is 'historically true'; in other words, psychoanalysis is not archaeological research. It appears to be much more important that by the end of the therapy a narrative should be established with the help of the therapeutic expert which the patient can accept without any conflict (Schafer 1980; Spence 1982). According to Spence (1982: 31) this narrative should be compatible with the conditions of narrative truth; that is, it should evoke an experience that is usually evoked by good stories, convincing explanations and genuine resolutions of mysteries.

History as narrative

According to Hayden White (1981) 'Historiography is an especially good ground on which to consider the nature of narration and narrativity because it is here that our desire for the imaginary, the possible, must contest with the imperatives of the real, the actual' (White 1981: 4). Historiography is known to have three consecutive forms. In *annals* events that are worth mentioning are recorded one after the other in chronological order, but the individual events are not related to one another. A *chronicle* has certain properties of narrative, it has a central subject (for example, in Gesta written by Anonymus it is the Hungarians), a geographical and social centre, but in modern terms it cannot be regarded as historical text because it follows a strict chronological order; that is, it creates a chronological order between the events only, and instead of providing a conclusion it simply comes to an end, shifting the task to the reader to figure out retrospectively all the possible relationships between the beginning and the end of the chronicle. On the other hand, a true *historical text* recounts events in terms of their inherent interrelations in the light of an existing legal and moral order, so it has all the properties of narrative. The consequences of this is formulated by White as follows:

> Common opinion has it that the plot of a narrative imposes a meaning on the events that comprise its story level by revealing at the end a structure that was

immanent in the events all along. What I am trying to establish is the nature of this immanence in any narrative account of real events, the kind of events that are offered as the proper content of historical discourse. The reality of these events does not consist in the fact that they occurred but that, first of all, they were remembered and, second, that they are capable of finding a place in a chronologically ordered sequence.

(White 1981: 19)

In order for an account of events to be considered a historical account, however, it is not enough that events be recorded in the order of their original occurrence. It is the fact that they can be recorded otherwise, in an order of narrative, that makes them at once questionable as to their authenticity and susceptible to being considered tokens of reality. In order to qualify as 'historical', an event must be susceptible to at least two narrations of its occurrence. Unless at least two versions of the same set of events can be imagined, there is no reason for historians to take upon themselves the authority of giving the true account of what really happened. The authority of the historical narrative is the authority of reality itself; the historical account endows this reality with form and thereby makes it desirable, imposing upon its processes the formal coherency that only stories possess.

According to Ricoeur (1981), historiography is not merely added to historical knowledge from the outside but is an integral part of it, and what makes it acceptable is that historical writings mimic the types of spinning a plot in the literary tradition. To intensify a sense of reality and truthfulness to real life, it makes use of rhetorical figures and relies heavily on the dimension of consciousness; that is, on what historical figures might have known, thought and felt. The reconstruction of stories is based, even tacitly, on the presumed subject of the person in question that is produced on the basis of psychological rules governing everyday human behaviour. In historiography, a special kind of reconstruction of experience takes place in which the experiences of characters receive meaning in terms of the interrelationship between causes and consequences. The political stories embedded in a biography that have been published in recent years all support the above claim very clearly. The historiographer as narrator willy-nilly takes up a narrative position, that is a historical narrative is not in the position to evade the functionality of narrative, the need for a 'usable' story. The origin of modern historical science itself is also closely related to the national history that was demanded by nineteenth-century nationalism.

Science as narrative

Using ethnographical research on Native Americans, the American anthropologist Edward Bruner demonstrated how the subject matter and the results of research are determined by the story model that is created for the ethnic group being studied. In the 1930s and 1940s the dominant story about Indian culture was progressing from an idyllic past to present disintegration and towards future assimilation. The endpoint of this process was full assimilation. Several excellent anthropologists believed that their main task was to describe Native American cultures before they totally disappeared for good. They rated the investigated Indian cultures as to how close they were to inescapable total assimilation. However, a new story started spreading in the 1970s that saw exploitation in the past, resistance against assimilation in the present and ethnic revival in the future. This ethnic revival came to be the subject matter of description, and as a result the key notions of anthropology also changed. Notions like assimilation or acculturation were replaced by colonization, liberation, independence, identity or ethnicity. Informants were asked to give information in connection with these concepts, and the information collected in the research was interpreted through these concepts (E.M. Bruner 1986).

Not only these 'storytelling' disciplines like ethnography but also other social sciences that follow the logic of paradigmatic thinking, like psychology or sociology, cannot be free from elements of this social construct, narrative either. Sociologists of science (for instance Haraway 1984, 1989; Latour 1988; Mulkay 1985) have shown that the world of science is just as sensitive to 'good' stories as any other field of social communication. According to Donna Haraway (1984), in any given age there is a limited set of possible worlds in human society. These possible worlds as recognized systems of meaning have a strong influence on what can be told in what way in a scientific discipline at a given age, that is, what counts as a good story. Haraway (1984) uses the example of primatology to illustrate the point. When taking a look at the history of research on apes, it can be established that early research was mostly concerned with dominance hierarchies and questions of rivalry and defending territory; in other words, with questions that are related to masculine values. When the role of women gained more value and recognition in the world, and in science too, new topics emerged that were related to feminine values, such as care for offspring, cooperation or the attachment of offspring to the mother.

In psychology Wendy Stainton Rogers tracked the changes in the evaluation of narrative in studies of external and internal control related to personality. While in early research an individual with internal control was clearly viewed as a positive hero, the new approach intends to avoid making a distinction between different types, or at least it makes an effort to provide a more balanced description of types (Stainton Rogers 1991, 1996).

Narrative causality

The actions of characters in a narrative are not defined primarily by cause and effect relationships. These acts are motivated by beliefs, desires, values, in other words, by 'intentional stances'. A narrative action always implies intentional stances. However, intentional stances never define the course of events fully; there is no unbroken causal chain; there is always action in events and action always presupposes choice. The omnipresence of human choice in narrative is the factor that questions the applicability of scientific causality in the human world. Intentional stances do not cause things. Nobody can be held morally responsible for something that was caused by some other thing. Responsibility implies choice. In narrative we seek intentional stances that underlie action; they are *motives* or *reasons*, not *causes*.

Hermeneutic composition

From the above it follows that there is no unambiguous narrative. There is no rational procedure which could be used to determine that a particular reading is necessary, like logical truth is necessary, and there is no empirical method which could be used to justify a particular reading. The main task of hermeneutic analysis is to provide a convincing and consistent interpretation for the meaning of narrative that is in harmony with all the constituents of narrative. This is the famous hermeneutic circle – in other words, it is the view that a particular reading of a text is justified in terms of other, alternative readings rather than with reference to the outside world or the rules of logic. This task is performed within a text in the following way according to Charles Taylor (1979):

> We are trying to establish a reading for the whole text, and for this we appeal to readings of its partial expressions; and yet because we are dealing with meaning, with making sense, where expressions only make sense or not in relations to others, the readings of partial expressions depend on those of others, and ultimately of the whole.
>
> (Taylor 1979: 28)

Since the meaning of parts depends on the meaning of the story as a whole, but the story as a whole is dependent on the meaning of its component parts, hermeneutic interpretation is inescapable. This is even true of narratives called 'readerly' texts by Barthes (1977), for example in the case of pulp fiction, which mobilize routine-like, well-rehearsed narrative structures. In contrast to a 'readerly' text, a 'writerly' text calls upon recipients to become co-authors and create their own version of the text.

Another possible problem for hermeneutic analysis may be the question of why this particular story is told by this particular narrator in this particular situation. Narratives rarely get into our sight just by chance as 'found' texts. Every narrator has their own viewpoint, and it is the inalienable right of any reader to question the viewpoint of others, although in everyday life we usually show 'benevolent neglect' (Goffman 1959).

The role of time in narrative

Besides referentiality, the other essential property of narrative is *temporal structure*. Narratives are always about events taking place in time. Narrative time is not the same as calendar time. It is not segmented by the ticks of a clock or a metronome, but by the unfolding events. Narrative time is always the time that is relevant for people; the significance of time is given by the meaning of events

(Ricoeur 1984–1989). Ricoeur contrasts the temporal configuration of narrative (it always has a beginning, a middle and an end) with human experience, which flows without bounds. Articulation is always achieved by means of narrative tools, like condensation or omission. Labov and Waletzky (1967) distinguished *narrative nodes* within a story. They classify those sequences as narrative nodes which – contrary to other, displaceable sequences – are chronologically fixed within the story. These nodes constitute the backbone of narrative. At the same time, narrative genres can break up time and play around with the temporal boundaries of human actions that take place in time. Modern art has created numerous techniques for representing series of events taking place in time (Goodman 1981), whereby modern artistic forms move about in time practically without any limits.

The time of a narrated event and narrative time do not coincide. While certain narratives may compress entire eras into a single paragraph by telling only the most striking events, others may devote several pages to one single second, depicting the state of a particular character or representing the author's comments. As was described by the Russian formalists, by increasing the number of events or omitting several of them, narratives may delay or speed up the process that leads to the outcome of the plot; in both cases the result is increased tension. Sternberg (1978) derives principles of literary composition from the relationship between the time of narrated events and the duration of narration time, and directs attention to the psychological aspects of these compositional principles.

The story-emotion theory of Brewer and Lichtenstein (1981) points to the close relationship between the management of time and emotions. Their theory illustrates very well the emotional consequences of the diversions of events from normal, linear development in time and space, and demonstrates that the effects produced by narrative cannot be attributed exclusively to linguistic expression. Interestingly, the novel content of events also plays an important role. The theory of story-emotion distinguishes three basic emotional structures. If the first event in an event structure is one that is likely to have important consequences and the narrative precisely follows the events, it may produce tension. For example, a starting event like '*the servant put some poison in the glass*' generates suspense as to the outcome of poisoning, only to be intensified by further details like '*the servant served the drink to the count*' and '*the count gulped down the drink*'. Tension is then diffused by the closing event: '*the count dropped dead*'.

A story structure that is built on surprise rearranges the events. A certain element that is important for forthcoming events is left out at the beginning of the story. '*The servant served the drink to the count*', '*the count gulped down the drink*', '*the count dropped dead*'. Leaving out the bit about putting the poison in the glass reserves the surprise as a posterior explanation.

A story structure that induces curiosity places the most important outcome at the beginning, signalling, as it were, that further important pieces of information are missing. In this kind of structure, the story begins by '*the count dropped dead*', followed by 'rolling back' the events: '*the count gulped down the drink*', '*the servant served the drink to the count*', '*the servant put some poison in the glass*'.

Genre-specific particularity

Narratives can be grouped into types or *genres*. It has been a hotly disputed issue since Aristotle whether genres generate specific stories or whether they are merely posterior constructs produced by scientists to classify infinitely diverse stories.

The generative nature of genres is supported by an intuitive argument which says that certain stories are very similar, however different the details they might have; the *Iliad* is different from *Gilgames* in almost every detail, yet it is easy to see that they are also similar in many ways. Another argument for the view that genres are abstract schemas is that the constituents of stories, the heroes and their acts constitute a structure that is an instance of a more general structure (Propp 1968). A third argument concerns the possibility of playing around with formal conventions. When formal conventions are intentionally 'violated', for instance, standards of two different genres are juxtaposed, a novel meaning can be created. Literary caricature and irony in general presuppose formal skills and expertise. One semantic constituent of Voltaire's *Candide* (1759), for example, is the parody of the baroque picaresque novel. Following the line of the Greek novel of adventure, this genre, which ruled the sixteenth and seventeenth centuries, completely ignored biological and historical chronology as well as the chronology of life history. In *Candide*, Voltaire stuck to a time period that was necessary for experiencing an average dose of adventures stipulated by this novel type. As a result, when Candide and Kunigunda finally get married after overcoming all the obstacles, they are both rather old. The ironic message that passion is followed by satisfaction only when it is already unfeasible biologically can get across only if there is a formal rule which stipulates that passion is followed by satisfaction (Bakhtin 1981).

Genre is a particular text or a particular way of creating text; that is, genres do not only exist in literature but there are numerous discourse genres in everyday life from confessing to lecturing. It seems that no genre is coded in the genes, no genre is a cultural universal; however, as was stated by Jerome Bruner (1996: 136): genre itself is universal 'culturally specialised modes of thinking and communicating about human affairs'.

Nevertheless, genres do not in general set rigid boundaries against the diversity of stories. They are obscure, lifeless categories (László and Viehoff 1993; Prince 1990; Ryan 1981) whose tokens, individual narratives, are more or less typical instances of the category.

Genre archetypes

Some sort of a typology of the wealth of experience and the structure of narrative shows up even behind the diversity of literary genres. Frye (1957) describes four archetypical narrative forms. These forms, which he calls mythical archetypes, are related to natural processes, that is, to the four seasons, parts of the day and life cycles. *Comedy* corresponds to the archetype of dawn and birth. Comedy, which is not necessarily funny, is about creation, revival and the triumphant fight against dark forces. In typical comedies the young heroes long for each other, but their affection runs into difficulties. However, they overcome the difficulties and the story has a happy ending. The myth of summer, the sun at its peak, and of the age of full energy is *romance*. The most important constituent of romance is adventure, the test of strength. Amidst a series of dangerous situations the protagonist often makes risky journeys but eventually he comes out as a winner. *Tragedy* is the archetype of sunset and death. In a tragedy the fate of the protagonist is to restore the 'derailed' order of the world. He falls in the course of this struggle, but his fall at the same time means that the order of the world is restored. The fourth archetype is *irony* and *satire*, corresponding to the myth of winter, darkness and dissolution. Satire is militant irony. In this archetype there are no heroes in the classical sense; the plot does not lead to some sort of order but rather to chaos and confusion.

In addition to identifying formal archetypes, there have been attempts to define archetypical plot frames that recur from time to time in different eras. Elsbree (1982) maintains that at least five such plot archetypes can be distinguished: *establishing a home, rivalry or battle, travelling, prolonged suffering* and *consumption*. Elsbree's analysis offered important bases for establishing a typology of biographical plot frames.

Narrative canons

The structure of narrative – a series of actions suitable for achieving one or more main goals – does not in itself guarantee that a text is a story that can be narrated (that it commands interest). The literary or everyday form of narrative presupposes a knot, a clash between the story and expectations, although this clash is often as conventional as the 'normal' course of events. Narrative sees and displays the world either as canonic or as a world that is different from some sort of an implied canon.

The simplest forms of canonic narrative are scripts. The notion of scripts, defined by Schank and Abelson (1977: 41) as 'a series of stereotypical actions defining a known situation', or knowledge representations called scripts were developed to enable computers to understand texts that give an account of simple situations. These knowledge representations, or rather, the properties of somewhat boring narratives that use them, can help us draw conclusions about the properties of scripts. For instance, what turns out from the following short story, 'Peter ordered the meal. The waiter brought the meal. The bill was more than what Peter had expected', is that the restaurant script comprises standard situations to which standard characters (e.g. a waiter) and standard accessories (like a bill) belong that can be referred to by the definite article. It is also obvious that members of a particular culture have a good deal of knowledge about these situations on the basis of which they can fill in the missing details and have certain expectations as to further developments.

Scripts can be more specific as well as more general than the one presented above. There are several restaurants ranging from a small pub to a McDonald's and each can have a slightly different script. For instance, if Peter ordered a Big Mac with chips, we do not expect the meal to be delivered by a waiter nor do we expect to come across accessories like a tablecloth or red wine. At the same time the restaurant script is integrated into a more general script of delivering a service that includes elements ranging from placing an order to paying.

Scripts are stereotypical causal chains (Schank and Abelson 1977; Trabasso et al. 1984). Actions are organized in scripts not only in terms of time but also in accordance with a causal hierarchy. In general a script action cannot be executed until the previous action has been completed, and it has to be executed in order for the next action to take place. Of course, this does not mean that each and every script action has to be mentioned separately, it is enough if the audience know that it has taken place. Returning to the previous example, not only does the audience know that the waiter serves the meal because Peter has ordered it, but also they know that Peter first had to call the waiter to order the meal.

From the point of view of both specificity and causal chaining, interpersonal scripts, for example flattering or courting, constitute a separate class (László 1986). Although these actions are nearly as stereotypical culturally as restaurant visits, since they are not tied to a particular situation at all, they show an infinite diversity as far as actual actions, scenes and accessories are concerned. Similarly, these scripts appear in numerous versions depending on the type of relationship, and the charm of interpersonal behaviour lies in the fact that it is not possible to define with much accuracy the boundaries that are crossed when going from one script version to another. Therefore, it often appears as if the execution of an action did not require the execution of a previous action that makes it possible to happen (e.g. in the case of courting, physical contact does not require that the individuals involved in it first get acquainted with each other), though what in fact happens in most such cases is that instead of a conventional courting script a 'rapid' script comes into effect.

Script-based knowledge is also inherent in narratives, though generally not in an explicit from. Examples of how scripts are unfolded can be seen in classical epic and oral tradition, for instance Rubin (1995: 25) has shown that in Homer's epic the description of armament always takes place in the form of a script: first the tunic is mentioned, followed by the bow, the sword, the shield, the helmet and finally the spear.

The difference between a script-based narrative and a narrative or story proper is demonstrated with an example by Rubin (1995: 27). Like many of her peers, Rubin's daughter also liked to say over and over again to herself what she had to do as a routine activity. Once her father noticed that the little girl, who had just learned how to write, put down the following text on paper: 'When we get up in the morning, we make the bed, then have breakfast, then wash our teeth, and then get dressed.' When Rubin praised his daughter for writing a nice story, the little girl firmly protested: she said she had not written a story but had simply put down what she had to do after getting up. This example demonstrates not only that the girl could clearly distinguish a story from a script-based narrative but also that by using a first person plural subject and present tense that is devoid of a historical dimension, she could make the distinction obvious.

Story-like narratives necessarily contain some sort of a knot, a deviation from the natural, canonic course of events. Certain authors, for instance Prince (1973), maintain that any change of state is a sufficient criterion for constituting a story. In this view a story must have at least three constituents: a *starting state*, an *event* and a *modified state*. According to Prince the following text also qualifies as a story: 'It was hot. A cold front set in. The weather got bad.' However, most authors (see e.g. Brockmeier and Harré 2001; Pléh et al. 1983; Stein and Policastro 1984; Wilensky 1983) believe that storiness requires some goal-directed action of living or impersonated actors taking place in time. This latter view, which is not very different from the Aristotelian definition of drama, is related to another aspect of the canonic nature of narrative, the canon that involves the organization of stories called story grammar. In contrast to scripts that contain information both for form and for content and are valid exclusively for a given domain of knowledge, story grammars contain information, in principle, concerning only the form of stories, or rather, their structure and refer, again in principle, to any domain of knowledge. They can be conceived of as generative grammars consisting of re-writing rules that – like generative syntax, which is meant to describe all the possible sentences of a language – are meant to generate the structure of all possible stories (Mandler and Johnson 1977; Rumelhart 1975; Stein and Glenn 1979; Thorndyke 1977).

Just as sentence grammars divide the sentence into a noun phrase and a verb phrase (SENTENCE = NOUN PHRASE + VERB PHRASE), story grammars start out with a STORY = SITUATION + EPISODE structure. Situation and episode then have their own rewriting rules. For example, situation can be rewritten by using English words, while one way to rewrite episode is: EPISODE = INTRODUCTION + KNOT + CONCLUSION. Rewriting rules can be further specified by going into details of story structure, for instance INTRODUCTION = STATE + GOAL, GOAL = DESIRED STATE.

The starting point of story grammars was the work of the Russian formalist ethnographer, Propp (1968), who analysed the functional units of Russian folk tales and their interrelationships. Propp identified thirty-one 'functions' (e.g. 'a witch does harm or injury to a member of the family' or 'a member of the family is in need of something or has a desire for something') which appear in the surface structure of stories contained in tales as various texts, but altogether they represent a deep structure also shared by readers into which readers 'insert', as it were, the text on the surface and thereby interpret the stories.

Propp's analysis also points out that story grammars are tied to genres or to a particular corpus of stories. Rubin (1995) draws attention to the fact that genres of the oral tradition follow special rules. In folk ballads there is often no starting point, and the triple rule (three sons, three tests) consistently shows up in western folk tales, so instead of the EPISODE = TEST + GOAL rule the EPISODE = TEST + TEST + TEST + GOAL rule is valid in this case.

The idea that story grammars are content-free, and that stories are structured and interpreted by these abstract rules, is challenged by many researchers. Instead, they attribute more fundamental significance to event schemas. In experiments investigating story retention Black and Bower (1980) and Trabasso et al. (1984) obtained results which demonstrate that the understanding and retention of stories is dependent on causal chains created on the basis of the logical structures of world knowledge relating to social action rather than on cognitive structures presupposed by story memory.

Literature is a special terrain of both world knowledge and the violation of and compliance with narrative canons. The Russian formalists derive literary effect from the tension between fable (the narrated events) and sujet (events put into a linguistic form). The concept of diversion or de-automation is a central notion of several schools of literary theory. According to Shklovsky (1965 [1917]) the goal of art is to reflect the suggestivity and experienceability of the world for the everyday man who is deeply engaged in the daily routines of life, and this goal is attained by turning off automatisms through deviations from schemas.

The tension between canonicity and irregularity was used by Martindale (1975, 1990) for building an original aesthetic theory. Martindale took as his starting point Berlyne's activation theory. According to Berlyne (1971) there is an optimal activation level for an organism, and any higher (excitement) or lower level (boredom) than this optimal level evokes a somewhat less pleasant experience. The more complex (complicated and irregular) an object is, the higher the activation level is when it is perceived. According to Martindale the complexity of a text, or rather, the level of tension produced by it is determined by two factors: its content and form. Martindale defined the complexity of the content of a text as the ratio between a Freudian primary process (dreamlike, illogical thinking) and a secondary process (rational, logical thinking), while the complexity of form as formal innovations, grammatical complexity, etc. By analysing literary texts that have been produced in the course of many centuries – both poetry and prose – a very special literary history arises. The complexity of content and form proceeds in exactly the opposite direction. When the complexity of content increases, the number of formal innovations and the complexity of form decrease. However, when formal canons are violated, the complexity of form decreases; that is, thinking follows a more rationalistic line.

Narrative comprehension

An intriguing field of contemporary cognitive psychology and artificial intelligence (AI) studies is the research on how people and computers understand narrative texts. This research is largely focusing on semantic or conceptual processing. Surface structural (e.g. morpho-phonological and syntactic) information in the text should be transformed into concepts. The reader's task is to connect adjacent sentences semantically, thereby establishing a coherent text representation. The interpretation of individual sentences and the establishment of coherence relations between successive sentences proceed with the help of information already transformed into conceptual-propositional micro-structures. However, interpretation proceeds not only locally, but also on a more general level concerning the theme, topic, or gist of the text. As a result, semantic macro-structures evolve which consist of generalized macro-propositions (Just and Carpenter 1992; Kintsch and van Dijk 1978). Both *local* and *global* interpretation draws heavily upon semantic structures or schemes of world knowledge which are sources of several kinds of inferences. Even if one assumes, as story grammar theorists did, that a syntax for stories existed, the effect of these narrative super-structures is made explicit again on the semantic level, namely in semantic macro-structures. As a consequence, the function of higher ordered knowledge structures came to the forefront of research on narrative comprehension. This type of study became very popular among scholars working on text understanding at the interface of cognitive psychology and AI research. Story understanding machines such as SAM (Cullingford 1978), PAM (Wilensky 1978), FRUMP (DeJong 1979) and BORIS (Lehnert et al. 1983) all apply scripts, plans, plot units or thematic structures so as to model the process of comprehension. A rich body of experiments supports the psychological reality of the participation of the assumed knowledge structures in narrative comprehension (Bower et al. 1979; Bransford and Johnson 1972; Graesser and Bower 1990; Graesser and Nakamura 1982; Graesser et al. 1991; Seifert et al. 1986; Zhang and Hoosain 2005).

The most general super-structures are themes. The theme of a narrative is its main point or moral, which can be formulated in a declarative sentence (see Graesser et al. 2002), but some themes can be grasped by a single concept. For instance, the adage of Aesop's tale *The Tortoise and the Hare* could be 'slow and steady gets ahead', whereas the concept 'race' also expresses the theme of the story. Thematic knowledge cannot be arbitrarily employed to stories. For Aesop's tale also 'mind overcomes power' would work well, whereas clichés such as 'a stitch in time saves nine' or 'hard work will bring happiness' would not fit into the constraints of the text. As Graesser et al. (2002) writes:

> the psychological process of constructing a theme during comprehension is a constraint satisfaction mechanism that evaluates how well any given theme (T) resonates with the cumulative constraints of the explicit text (E), the discourse context (C), and the reader's knowledge base (K).
>
> (Graesser et al. 2002: 21)

Simple, straightforward stories invite themes with relative ease. More complex stories, particularly literary narratives, may be characterized with various degrees of *thematic aboutness* or ambiguity, that is a wide range of themes can be applied to the text. When real readers cope with the thematic aboutness of a story, in order to arrive at possible analogical meanings, they command an enormous store of historical incidents, other stories and personal experiences. Mobilization of this type of information is hard to model on computers. This is one of the reasons why Abelson (1987) thinks that computers will never arrive at literary appreciation.

Narrative speech acts

Iser (1978) offers an explanation for the ambiguity of narrative, especially literary narrative on the basis of speech act theory. He starts out on the premise that narrative is not a copy of something that has previously existed but it creates its own subject, the 'reading'. As a result, it cannot have the definiteness that is characteristic of philosophical or literary writings. Indefiniteness originates from the dual structure of narrative. The verbal aspect of structure governs meaning reactions, restricting the possible range of meanings. As for the emotional aspect, however, the language of the text merely provides a preliminary structure for it, leaving a considerable degree of freedom for the reader or the listener to create meaning. According to Iser (1978), instead of shaping the meanings themselves, literary texts set the formation of meaning into motion. Thus, literary narrative is a speech act whose intention is to launch a process of seeking meaning among the set of possible meanings.

Texts give special signals to set the formation of meaning in motion. Following Jerome Bruner (1986) these signals can be divided into four groups: signalling that a particular story will be told; signalling whether the story is real or fictitious; signalling the genre of the story (e.g. biographical event, scandal, tale, parable); and signalling the style of the story.

The language of literary texts shifts the emphasis from explicit meaning to implicit meaning, thereby opening the way for interpretation. Placed in a literary context, even strongly explicit texts are interpreted with presuppositions for implicit meaning, like István Örkény's one-minute short story 'All the things we need to know', which contains directions for use of a tram transit ticket, or Primo Levi's short story 'The Periodic Table', which evokes a set of implicit meanings that can be interpreted by introducing chemical elements.

In addition to *presuppositions for creating implicit meaning*, the subjectivization of the presented events also 'calls for' meaning formation; that is, the events are linked to a person in a way that the world depicted in the story does not unfold as impersonal, omniscient truth independent of personal knowledge but rather, it is filtered through the mind of the narrator or the heroes. This effect is further strengthened by a *multiple perspective* emerging in narratives; in other words, narrative represents the same reality from an equal but at the same time different perspective of several characters (J. Bruner 1986: 25–26).

Narrative perspective

Narrative always takes place from the perspective of somebody. It is the narrative perspective that carries mental states which characterize the narrator and the characters of the story in relation to the events, so the narrative perspective or viewpoint has a distinguished place in the narratological analysis of the introduction of events. Certain authors (e.g. Bakhtin 1981; Bal 1985; Friedman 1955; Genette 1980; Van Peer and Chatman 2003) treat it as the key to literary composition.

The possible effects of perspective and its psychological implications will be analysed following Uspensky (1974), who was especially receptive to psychological effects in his theory of perspective (László and Pólya 2002). Uspensky unravels a typology of the representation of possible perspectives along two dimensions. First of all, he makes a distinction between thematically delineated areas or planes of words and expression that refer to perspective. The *evaluative, phraseological, spatial-temporal* and *psychological* planes defined in his analysis are not joined together; the four planes and the areas that are sensitive to the representation of perspectives are described independently.

The evaluative-ideological plane involves the evaluation of the depicted world by the author or a character with a perspective. This is the plane that is the most difficult to define on the basis of formal criteria; still, this is the one that Uspensky believes to be the most important one with respect to the essence of works of art. By laying the emphasis on the evaluative plane he seems to follow the view that the goal of works of art is to educate readers by means of representing a system of values.

In contrast to the abstract definition of the evaluative plane, the perspective that manifests itself in spatial and temporal relations can be unravelled relatively easily. The definition of the spatial perspective is supported by the original spatial metaphor of perspective: if the text is seen as the description of a scene, the spatial position of the narrator can be inferred. In fact this inference presupposes the transformation of the text into an imaginative picture. The temporal perspective involves the grounding of events as they are seen as a sequence of events. This perspective has two distinct types: the synchronic and retrospective representation of events expressed in the use of different tenses (present versus past) and aspects (continuous versus perfective).

The perspective expressed on the phraseological plane is revealed by the analysis of linguistic composition. First, given and new information in a sentence can be separated by means of functional sentence perspective. If the character represents given information and his or her action is new information, then the sentence is formulated from the character's perspective; likewise, if the action is given and the character is a new element, then the author's perspective or the viewpoint of some other character gains dominance. The perspective expressed on the phraseological plane can also be analysed at the level of word choice. This is where the effect of perspective can be captured in the simplest way. The same character is called by characteristically different names by other characters or the author, so naming makes an unambiguous reference to perspective. The third level at which the phraseological perspective is represented can be related to the characters, and thus it is based on the use of text elements that are foreign to the author. Passages that are foreign from the author's perspective can be very short, one-word items, but they can also be longer phrases that represent the discourse world of the given character. As the phrase weaves the discourse world of the author or a given character into the text, any phenomena that are related to it are also in close connection with the psychological plane of perspective.

The psychological planes of perspective involve the way in which characters are introduced. The narrator – who is not necessarily the author, it can be one of the characters too – can choose from several options when introducing the characters. The characterization of heroes may be limited to the description of their behaviour. As an opposite alternative, there are omniscient narrators who may also introduce their readers to the inner world, the emotions, thoughts and experiences of a given character. As a further alternative, a special amalgamation of these two options, the narrator may also characterize the hero of a story in a way that although the inner states of the character are designated, the actual existence of a given mental state is only suggested, by formulating the perceptual actions of the observer (e.g. 'it seemed that he thought ...'). The abovementioned options of introducing characters that explore inner mental states and infer the existence of these states can be easily captured on the basis of linguistic formulation. The narrator uses action verbs to describe behaviour and mental verbs (verba sentiendi) to describe the mental states of a character. In the third combined form, the narrator uses so-called alienating expressions, which refer to the perceptions of the observer, to connect the contents of the character's mental states that are invisible from the outside (e.g. 'it could be seen that ...'). On the psychological plane there is another possibility for perspective to assert itself. This possibility emerges when the narrator – without giving any specific verbal signal – directly weaves the emotions and thoughts of a character into the text of a work of art.

Of course, the narrator's perspective also appears in non-literary texts and reveals a lot about the narrator's mental states and his or her relationship to the events, characters, etc. of a story. The psychological utilization of the narrative perspective has become quite common in the analysis of interviews that are used to study the self-reflexive function and attachment (Fonagy and Target 1997).

Psycho-narratology

A special psychological approach to narrative is *psycho-narratology*, which aims to understand the psychological processing of narrative form (Bortolussi and Dixon 2003). In theory, processing depends on three factors: the qualities of the reader, the special features of the text and the reading situation. Psycho-narratology frames these factors into experimental variables and investigates their joint effect on processing. Psychological and psycholinguistic research on text processing has examined basic processes of reading, such as the role of rapid eye movements or word recognition quite extensively, and a lot of attention has also been given to more complex processes like the identification of sentence structure, the role of working memory or the factors that influence the remembering of texts. As compared to these approaches, psycho-narratology studies how textual features of narrative, such as the position of the narrator in the text, influence the evolution of narrative representation. Systematically manipulated stimuli that are perceived as objective information are studied in these experiments in a cause and effect relationship with the subjective representations of the reader.

As in most cases when experimental and, in general, empirical studies are conducted, the critical question is the identification of textual features (the experimental variables in experiments). Psycho-narratology sets five criteria for textual features. *Objectivity* means that the definition of a feature should be clearly communicable and understandable. Intimacy, for example, cannot be used to characterize a text, for its interpretation, and as a result, its identification in the text largely depends on who means what by intimacy. If somebody wishes to study intimacy, special linguistic configurations should be chosen, such as the use of first person singular, which are straightforward and can be assumed to have something to do with intimacy.

Closely related to objectivity is the *precision* of the definition of textual features. For instance, in a study that investigates indirect speech, it is not enough to establish that it contains 'a lot of' or 'little' indirect speech. The amount of indirect speech should be examined quantitatively, in terms of the percentage of the total number of words.

A third requirement for textual features is *stability*. Only those features of texts can be studied that are independent of the reading situation or the readers. The emotional effects evoked by a text or their relationship with any subjective experience cannot be regarded as a stable textual feature. Instead, expressions that are related to the emotional states of the narrator of the characters in a story should be identified in the text.

The textual feature to be studied should be *relevant* from the point of view of text processing. The investigator may choose to precisely count the frequency of letter 'e' in the text or the words starting with a consonant, but this has very little impact on the evolution of the reader's representation of the text.

Finally, the selected textual feature should be manageable experimentally and systematically modifiable so that its effect could be traced back in the evolution of the reader's representation.

The set of criteria used by psycho-narratology, as we will see in Chapter 9, plays an important role in investigations that study the validity of content analysis in narrative psychology. Such analyses can be used to test whether the content analysis programs developed for coding linguistic patterns that correspond to psychological processes and states in fact measure those mental constructs that they are designed to investigate. Subjective impressions and interpretations that are evoked in readers who read texts in which linguistic features are experimentally manipulated may confirm or falsify the supposed relationship between linguistic patterns and psychological constructs.

Summary

This chapter reviewed various sources of narrative psychology from narratology to hermeneutics. It also discussed the consequences of the narrative approach in various disciplinary fields including historiography and sciences. The chapter introduced the twentieth-century psychological career of narrative, which by and large coincides with the ebb and flow of cognitive psychology. So as to preserve most of the methodological rigour of cognitive psychology and its sensitivity to narrative schemes, still further the boundaries of narrative psychology, we need a brief overview of the place of narrative in psychology from an epistemological perspective. This is provided in Chapter 2.

2   The place of narrative in psychology

what testing could be done to measure storytelling?

Psychology: natural and/or social science

Conceiving psychology as natural science, we deal with human biological faculties. We search for universal laws between the physical or social environment and forms of human adaptation that enlighten human nature. Environmental variation and individual differences reflect conditions that govern particular occurrences of universal laws. We search for causal relations between changes in the external or internal environment and human behaviour, transform these changes into experimental variables, form hypotheses, and test these hypotheses in experiments.

Psychology as social science starts with the social determination of human beings. In explaining human behaviour, it relies on collective representations or symbolic systems such as social structure, culture or language. This approach is present primarily in personality and social psychology, but attempts were made as far back as the first decades of the twentieth century to describe relations between forms of thinking and forms of social-cultural organization (Levy-Brühl 1926; Vygotsky 1978). The psychological tradition, which builds upon the Durkheimian Standard Social Sciences (cf. Cosmides and Tooby 1992; Pléh 2003a), conceives the social environment as a complex structure of social facts. It assumes that psychological processes and the behaviour of individuals from similar social positions are influenced in the same direction by this structure. Thus, Standard Social Sciences-type psychology tries to establish causal explanations between an external, objective reality and internal states or behaviour. There were, of course, attempts to reconcile social scientific and natural scientific approaches. Perhaps the most notable among these theories is symbolic interactionism (Mead 1934), which derives both social system and individual mind from social interaction.

The duality of natural scientific and social scientific psychology was already evident at the crib of scientific psychology. Wilhelm Wundt, founder of the first psychological laboratory and author of the first monograph on experimental psychology, carries this duality in his work. Wundt delimited the competence of natural scientific, experimental psychology to individual processes, whereas he approached the psychological phenomena of social life with procedures of description and interpretation in his *Folk Psychology*, published from 1900 on in ten volumes.

Knowing reality and/or understanding narrative

There are, however, other dualities in the epistemological roots of psychology. Psychology cannot be indifferent toward the opposition between the Platonic and Hegelian philosophy, and also should take a stance in the debate between atomist and holist conceptions of analytic philosophy (Rorty 2004). For Plato, the capacity to know reality is the specific attribute that discriminates humans from animals. Analytic philosophy, led by Russell, tries to follow this principle by understanding *relations between language, mind and reality*. In contrast, Hegelian philosophy puts *becoming* or *self-realization* into the centre of human existence. It tries to give meaning to the unfolding story. Analytic philosophers, although they agree that mind and language are specific to humans, and none of them challenge the idea that an explanation of mind and language should be made on materialist grounds, split into two camps when it comes to explanation. As Rorty (2004) points out, atomists believe that if we break down mind and language into bits, we may arrive at a neurologically underpinned psychology in the same way that chemistry has been brought together with physics and biology with chemistry. Their aim is to trace back non-physical concepts such as belief or meaning to the processes of central nervous system, in other words to correspond the work of the mind with the work of the brain. They often use a computation metaphor for solving the Cartesian problem: how can non-physical objects, such as belief or desire, cause physical consequences such as behaviour? According to Pinker (1997), for instance:

> The computational theory of mind resolves the paradox. It says that beliefs and desires are *information*, incarnated as configurations of symbols. The symbols are the physical states of bits of matter, like chips in a computer or neurons in the brain. They symbolize things in the world because they are triggered by those things via our sense organs, and because of what they do once they are triggered. If the bits of matter that constitute a symbol are arranged so as to bump into the bits of matter constituting another symbol in just the right way, the symbols corresponding to one belief can give rise to new symbols corresponding to another belief logically related to it, which can give rise to symbols corresponding to other beliefs, and so on. Eventually the bits of matter constituting a symbol bump into bits of matter connected to the muscles, and behavior happens. The computational theory of mind thus allows us to keep beliefs and desires in our explanations of behavior while planting them squarely in the physical universe. It allows meaning to cause and be caused.
>
> (Pinker 1997: 25, italics in original)

Holists, in contrast, following the later Wittgenstein and Ryle, believe that the major accomplishment of mind and language as human essences is rationality and this is not a biological but a social phenomenon. They claim that understanding mind and language presupposes understanding social practice and understanding how it evolves.

Explanations of human behaviour that tie in either with neurology or with evolutionary biology, will tell us only about what we share with chimpanzees. It will not tell us what we, not the chimpanzees, share with creatures who painted pictures on the walls of caves, nor with those that built the ships that sailed to Troy. We can learn about the processes that mediated between those organisms and ourselves only by constructing a narrative, telling a story about how they become us.

(Rorty 2004: 5)

The story should tell us about cultural evolution. It should enlighten us about how cultural evolution takes over biological evolution. These storied explanations do not make claim to universal validity, rather they try to expand the boundaries of understanding human existence by comparing the social practices of the present with those of the past and the future.

Accordingly, cultural evolution could start only at a particular phase of biological evolution. But since its inception, cultural evolution runs independently and the historical-interpretative method, that is the narrative approach, is the only adequate method for understanding it. Narrative philosophy denies that philosophy could be put on the secure path of a science. This could be made possible, if concepts and meaning were isolated from social practices and history. We know since Wittgenstein's *Philosophical Investigations* that it is not possible (Wittgenstein 1961). As Rorty (2004: 8) writes, the metaphor of the jigsaw puzzle where the right pieces are found and fit together may work in palaeontology, particle physics and philology, that is in areas of culture in which it is plausible to think that we may eventually get things right, but this metaphor is not valid for studies of social life. Here the 'particles' are not determinate, nether are the structures formed by the particles.

What do all these problems entail for human psychology? Do Descartes's thoughts on the representation of the real world, which were also taken for granted by Locke, Hume and other stars of empiricist epistemology, lead into dead-end streets? Is empirical knowing sufficient only to understand chimpanzees, and when dealing with human meaning should one turn to narratives and their analysis? Should physical causality be eliminated from the psychological explanations of social life? In other words, should we exclusively accept the criteria of narrative causality, for example coherence, verisimilitude or credibility, as the only salutary measures?

Before we outline our answers to the above questions, it should be remembered that psychology has been formed not only in the philosophical departments of nineteenth century universities as positive, experimental epistemology. Knowing psychological phenomena proved to be indispensable also for medicine, for healing mental illness or correcting developmental disorders. For instance, the first psychological laboratory in Hungary was established by Pál Ranschburg at the neurological clinic of Budapest University, and it soon became part of the institute for the education of 'defective' children. In pragmatic American psychology, measurement of individual differences and learning theories instrumental for influencing behaviour had already been foregrounded at the turn of the twentieth century. Thus, psychology was from the beginning expected to produce knowledge that served the adaptation of people living in a certain time and under certain social conditions. Given that human functioning and performance is non-detachable from the human nervous system, it was plausible for an individualistic, ahistoric and universalistic psychology to emerge, which was quite successful in its applications. This constraint on psychology is pervasive to the present day. It strengthens the functionalist attitude, the study of immediately observable, individual phenomena even in areas, such as personality development or social psychology, where the direct application of natural scientific methods is not or not always justifiable.

In this book we present a version of narrative psychology, which accepts that mind and meaning cannot be disassembled into stable particles. However, we also challenge the idea that the analysis should stop at 'stories' tailored to social practices. *The critical question for us is the unit of analysis.* We will try to prove that narrative is a sufficiently stable, but equally flexible entity that can serve as a basis for a scientific cultural and evolutionary psychology.

The problem of complexity of phenomena: narrative as complex pattern

As opposed to Popper (1957), who declared the unity of the method of natural and social sciences, another scholar from the Vienna circle, the economist Hayek (1967) argued that in complex social processes, for instance the economic market, there are several immediately non-observable factors. These factors cannot be operationalized and measured and they can be taken into account only by the mediation of a theory.

> Perhaps it is only natural that in the exuberance generated by the successful advances of science the circumstances which limit our factual knowledge, and the consequent boundaries imposed upon the applicability of theoretical knowledge, have been rather disregarded. It is high time, however, that we take our ignorance more seriously. ... We have indeed in many fields learnt enough to know that we cannot know all that we would have to know for a full explanation of the phenomena. What we must get rid of is the naive superstition that the world must be so organized that it is possible by direct observation to discover simple regularities between all phenomena and that this is a necessary presupposition for the application of the scientific method. What we have by now discovered about the organization of many complex structures should be sufficient to teach us that there is no reason to expect this, and that if we want to get ahead in these fields our aims will have to be somewhat different from what they are in the fields of simple phenomena.
>
> (Hayek 1967: 39–40)

Hayek stresses the distinction between complexity along one single or on a few variables and the complexity of the phenomenon itself:

It has occasionally been questioned whether the phenomena of life, of mind, and of society are really more complex than those of the physical world. This seems to be largely due to a confusion between the degree of complexity characteristic of a peculiar kind of phenomenon and the degree of complexity to which, by a combination of elements, any kind of phenomenon can be built up. Of course, in this manner physical phenomena may achieve any degree of complexity. Yet when we consider the question from the angle of the minimum number of distinct variables a formula or model must possess in order to reproduce the characteristic patterns of structures of different fields (or to exhibit the general laws which these structures obey), the increasing complexity as we proceed from the inanimate to the ('more highly organized') animate and social phenomena becomes fairly obvious.

(Hayek 1967: 25–26)

Hayek claims that we may not know as much about certain complex phenomena as we can know about simple phenomena, but the boundaries can be pierced by deliberately cultivating a technique which aims at more limited objectives – the explanation not of individual events but merely of the appearance of certain patterns or orders. The understanding of the general mechanism, which produces patterns of a certain kind is not merely a tool for specific predictions. It can be important in its own right, and it may provide important guidelines to action. Hayek (1967) calls this type of prediction scheme-like prediction or prediction of schemes.

In our book we will argue that the Hayekian epistemology seems to apply in certain areas of psychology, and narrative psychology is an attempt to handle phenomenal complexity in the psychological domain. Complex psychological phenomena such as thinking, personality and group processes are embodied culturally and also in an evolutionary sense in narrative. Therefore, scientific narrative psychology when striving for cultural and evolutionary explanations, rejects both atomistic and holistic approaches. Instead, it stresses that the narrative represents a phenomenal level where only *patterns are meaningful. Psychological phenomena are expressed in narratives at a high complexity level, which enables meaningful diagnosis and predictions, although both can only be scheme-like, because of the phenomenal complexity.* There are, of course, opportunities to pierce the boundaries towards more detailed analysis converging towards biological reduction, just as paths may lead towards broader cultural or social conditions, interpretation and theorizing (we will meet these issues when talking on cultural evolution or transmission of historical representations). However, narration as a human specific mode of meaning construction is amenable to scientific study in itself, because narratives are such language games that can frame themselves to a certain extent. They embody such complex processes as thinking or personality, so their complexity carries a lot of the cultural heritage, as well as of the capacities of the human mind.

We can illustrate what was said above with a preliminary example. The often used category of identity refers to a complex psychological phenomenon, which has vital importance in social life or human functioning. When introducing this concept in his psychosocial theory of personality, Erikson (1968) defined it as integration of conscious and unconscious experiences which arise in interactions with the social world. Identity changes with human ages and with social environments. The integration is represented for the individual by his or her life story. In Erikson's identity theory, qualities such as *continuity, security and integrity* receive particular stress. Each of them is relevant for self-regulation, and therefore from the functional point of view of social adaptation. Knowledge about these qualities, however, does not predict actual behaviour, rather ways of adaptation, which can be evaluated against the background of the social environment and culture. Nevertheless, the above psychological contents of identity take such a form in life story, which is amenable for scientific study.

The issue of complexity in the theory of evolution

When arguing for methodology and theorizing that correspond to the complexity of the phenomena under study, Hayek (1967) often refers to Darwin's theory of evolution as the best illustration of theories of complex phenomena. The basic proposition of the theory of evolution is that a mechanism of reduplication, with transmittable variations and competitive selection of those which prove to have a better chance of survival, will in the course of time produce a great variety of structures adapted to continuous adjustment to the environment and to each other. The validity of this general proposition is not dependent on the truth of the particular applications which were first made of it. The fact that structurally similar species such as *marsupial* and *placental carnivores*, which were first thought to be evolved from a comparatively near common ancestor, turned out later to have different evolutionary roots does not refute Darwin's general theory of evolution but only the manner of its application to the particular case.

Thus, the theory of evolution takes an intermediate position between the atomist directions of analytical philosophy or simple positivist theories and theories that are derived from narrative philosophies. Evolution is doubtlessly a story that unfolds in time, but a story with conditions, with scheme-like rules, and these rules or principles can even be falsified. Evolution does not stop with humans, just as history does not end with a particular social formation (Prussian state in Hegel or bourgeois democracy in Fukuyama). However, for self-conscious people living in society, evolution means primarily cultural evolution, that is faculties necessary for human adaptation, which develop and function in relation to cultural objects and means, to language, to social institutions and practices, etc. In this sense culture, not a particular culture, but *the* culture is completing the evolution, or as Jerome Bruner (1996) puts it, the last trick of the evolution. The major mistake of social Darwinism was that, instead of the selection of institutions and social practices, it focused on the selection of individuals (i.e., on the selection of innate faculties), rather than on faculties that are passed on by culture.

Evolution and cultural evolution

Some protagonists of social sciences see something diabolic in an evolutionary perspective, which leads directly to racism. Even the metaphorical use of cultural evolution may seem dubious for them. On the one hand, psychology, although it has the capacity to study human faculties in relation to cultural practices (cultural psychology is based on this assumption), cannot entirely be detached from the individual (this holds true even for cultural psychology). On the other hand, psychology needs historical knowledge that locates the relation between social practices and human faculties in the context of their development and transmission. Here we are thinking not simply of faculties, which evolved tens or hundreds of thousands of years ago in the course of transforming apes into humans, for example better spatial orientation of males as compared to females, which is probably a consequence of the hunting activity of males as opposed to 'domestic' activity of females (Silverman and Eales 1992), or of the relation between growth in group size and the evolution of language (Dunbar 1996, 2004). Cultural systems such as writing (Olson 1977) or audiovisual media (MacLuhan 1968) and more recently the computer and internet (Winograd and Flores 1987) substantially transform human communication and thinking. In this sense, Vygotsky's idea that culture is a tool, which is produced by humankind so as to evolve its own mind seems to be perfectly right. This is a literal, non-metaphorical conception of cultural evolution, where human faculties and cultural practices are related to each other.

Space and narrative

This kind of cultural evolutionary view is valid for the institutions of social life too. Assmann's (1992) theory of cultural memory is a fascinating example of how this view can be put to work. This theory derives the significant institutional and social-psychological changes that lead to the emergence of the state in Egypt, religion in Israel and disciplinary thinking in Greece from the appearance of literacy and the evolution of collective identity.

The Egyptologist-archaeologist Assmann (1992) – following Halbwachs (1980) – assigns a distinguished role to human memory and the institutionalization of memory in the study of the development of culture. One way of organizing memory is related to space, to places that can be designated in space. It is an ancient method of mnemotechnique, the so-called method of places, when we assign things to be memorized to places of a well-known space, such as in a church, and in a memory situation we 'gather together' these things for recollection by taking an imaginative tour, as it were, in the church (Neisser 1976). It was pointed out by the French historian Pierre Nora how important a role the scenes of memory, natural spaces and marks or monuments placed in space played in historical memory (Nora 1989). Halbwachs himself discusses the legend-like topography of the Holy Land as an outward form of collective memory.

Time and narrative

Another possible way of organizing memory involves time. In his work on the history of civilization, when analysing the meaning of line patterns of a bone fragment from a Mesolithic era, another excellent archaeologist, Alexander Mar-shack (1972) concluded that it was a primitive moon calendar. The marks were in accord with the seasonal schedule of agricultural activities, the cultivation of land, plantation, harvesting; in other words, pre-historic people engaged in agriculture had to take time into consideration, for which he used the above-mentioned 'story-like' calendar.

By proposing a relationship between memory and temporal organization, we are directly involved in narrative. Ricoeur (1984–1987) devoted a three-volume mono-graph to this issue, stating that present, past and future, that is, the human experience of time is closely related to the narrative ability. Heidegger's (1971) hermeneutic philosophy also stresses that it is through narrative that we are able to bring past ex-periences or future events into the present and make them part of present existence. Although for philosophers the issue as to how the anthropological ability to use narrative developed does not come up as a problem, in the psychological analysis of cultural evolution the emergence of narrative itself is an interesting scientific ques-tion. The reasoning behind Marshack's (1972) agriculture-time-memory-narrative model suggests that the cognitive ability to use narratives evolved under a particu-lar ecological and cultural pressure in the process of adapting to these conditions, while Assmann's (1992) concept of memory-narrative-collective identity describes the process of adaptation to changing social conditions and the organization of ethnic groups. Sarbin (1986a) is right in saying:

> A developed narrative, then, is not simply an account of what happened, but implies much more about the psychological perspectives taken toward those happenings. Accordingly, one deep reason why we tell stories to ourselves (or to our confessor or to our analyst or to our confidant) is precisely to 'make sense' of what we are encountering in the course of living – through narrative elaborations of the natural arguments of action.

(Sarbin 1986a: 4)

Universal narrative ability raises a number of questions concerning the psychology of humans. Typically, some of these questions, especially the one concerning the development of mental abilities needed for narrative, justify a scientific, biological evolutionary attitude both from a phylogenetic and from an ontogenetic point of view. At the same time, the diversity of narratives from culture to culture can be explained from a psychological perspective in a cultural evolutionary context.

Intention and action in narrative

Pioneers of narrative psychology, like Sarbin (1986b) and Jerome Bruner (1986), have clearly recognized that narrative is based on action and on the interpretation of action. MacIntyre formulated this principle as follows:

in successfully identifying and understanding what someone else is doing we always move towards placing a particular episode in the context of a set of narrative histories, histories both of the individuals concerned and of the settings in which they act and suffer. It is now becoming clear that we render the actions of others intelligible in this way because action itself has a basic-ally historical character. It is because we all live out narratives in our lives and because we understand our own lives in terms of the narratives that we live out that the form of narrative is appropriate for understanding the ac-tions of others. Stories are lived before they are told – except in the case of fiction.

(MacIntyre 1981: 197)

Michotte (1963) and Heider (1958) believe that the principle which produces meaningful and rational action-based events out of mere physical movements can be identified in the attribution of causes and intentions. In an experiment, Heider and Simmel (1944) presented a short animated cartoon to subjects in which geo-metrical figures – a big triangle, a small triangle and a circle – were moving inside a square, one side of which was at times open. Subjects were asked to describe what they had seen. The accounts given by the subjects, as shown by the example below, were not about the movement of geometrical figures but about human ac-tions that were integrated into a story:

> A man has planned to meet a girl and the girl comes along with another man. The first man tells the second to go; the second tells the first, and he shakes his head. Then the two men have a fight and the girl starts to go into the room. ... She apparently does not want to be with the first man. The first man follows her into the room after having left the second in a rather weakened condition leaning on the wall outside the room. The girl gets worried and races from one corner to the other in the far part of the room. ... The girl gets out of the room in a sudden dash just as man number two gets the door open. They chase around the outside of the room together, followed by man number one, but they finally elude him and get away. The first man goes back and tries to open his door, but he is so blinded by rage and frustration that he cannot open it.
>
> (Heider and Simmel 1944, quoted by Sarbin 1986a: 12)

The subjects 'animated' the moving objects, attributing goals to them and turning the event into a story.

In present-day psychology a lot of attention is devoted to research on naive theories of the mind or metarepresentation (knowledge about the mental states, desires and beliefs of partners) (Leslie 1987; Wimmer and Perner 1983). It has been demonstrated in a number of experiments in the framework of developmental psychology that intentionality, the perception of causing appears in very early in-fancy, which means that our ability to perceive environmental changes in a cause-effect order and to attribute goals and intentions to objects is innate (Gergely et al.

1995; Leslie 1991). The role of metarepresentational abilities in the development of the narrative mode, that is, the ability to tell and understand stories, is also studied extensively (Astington 1990). Mentalization is given a strong emphasis in evolutionary psychology too. The experiments of Tomasello and colleagues with chimpanzees and infants (Tomasello 1999; Tomasello et al. 2005) show that in addition to this metarepresentational ability there is another ability which played an important role in the evolution of the human capacity to create culture, namely, the development of the ability to share intentions, utilize collective attention and achieve joint goals in the framework of joint plans cooperatively.

The metarepresentational ability shared by all humans – whose impairment can be seen, irrespective of different cultures, in autism (see Győri et al. 2004), which is not contradicted by the fact that autistic symptoms may be respected like features of a saint in certain cultures – thus provides a solid foundation for the narrative ability. (Naturally, it is also a foundation for the evolution of language. As has been argued by Tomasello, et al. (2005), the metarepresentational ability and the ability to share intentions are primary with respect to language; these abilities are preconditions for the evolution of language.) However, what narrative forms and functions develop as a result of the narrative ability and what sort of reality construct or meaning system is created through narrative is most likely determined by the laws and principles of cultural evolution. Cultural anthropologists have taught us that the western canons of narrative are not valid in several other cultures. For example, Ben Amos (1976) presents more than a dozen narrative forms valid in a particular culture. (Readers trained in psychology may be reminded here of Bartlett's (1932) research, who used the Indian folk tale *The War of the Ghosts* in his studies on memory with the explicit goal of exploring how subjects of a European origin searched for meaning and created schemas when recalling stories based on foreign modes of meaning construction.) These narrative modes differ, among other things, in the way temporal relations are handled. According to advocates of the strong version of the theory of linguistic relativity, language by itself determines world view (Whorf 1956). For example, Whorf maintains that in the Hopi language the missing grammatical past gives priority to present time, process-like thinking. Although the theory has been weakened significantly in the past few decades, it has also been shown, among other things, that Hopi does have past tense; the handling of time and space and what counts as a canonic or natural story in a given culture are an integral part of that culture, as it bears witness to what players of a culture highlight in an event and along what dimensions they attribute meaning to it. Sol Worth and John Adair visited the Navajo people in the 1960s and taught them how to use a film camera. The films shot by the Navajo were rather uneventful. They produced lengthy shots of a work process, such as the digging of a hole, without ever presenting the result or outcome of the act, as is usual in western-type stories (Worth 1972). Thus, Navajo narratives, similarly to the mental patterns of the Hopi, give priority to the process of an action over its temporal structure or result-centred action structure.

The archaeological paradigm in psychology

Finally, there is another reason why narratives are especially attractive to psychology. Earlier we have seen that it was archaeologists – Assmann and Marshack – who reconstructed the emergence of narrative in the process of cultural evolution and drew conclusions from written narratives concerning processes of institutionalization in social life. Archaeology as a metaphor has already been utilized once by the history of psychology in its past. It was Freud who likened the work of a psychoanalyst to that of an archaeologist. In the sense of this comparison, a psychoanalyst brings sunken traumatic memories out of the unconscious of a patient in the course of therapy pretty much like an archaeologist removes each layer of soil from the material remains of ancient times. Freud's perhaps most monumental work concerned with the interpretation of literature is about the novelette *Gradiva* by Jensen, a German author long since forgotten. The protagonist of the novelette is an archaeologist who is working hard on deciphering the puzzles of Pompeii. From the dreams and fantasies of the protagonist, Freud infers childhood experiences of the author. According to his biographers Freud liked to refer to the analogy between the burial and excavation of Pompeii and the burial of memories through suppression and their exploration by means of analysis. In his second temptation theory Freud modified the archaeological metaphor, recognizing that the subjective experience of patients is more important than the actual occurrence of a given traumatic event. Narrative theories of psychoanalysis stress precisely those aspects of psychoanalytic therapy which maintain that independent of the reality of the events experienced as a trauma there emerges a self-story during the dialogue between analyst and patient which is acceptable for the patient as a present reality. The therapeutic effect is produced by the very act of creating a story (Schafer 1980; Spence 1982).

Though not in a Freudian sense, the archaeological parallel of psychology came to the foreground again with the introduction of narrative. From time to time psychology, and especially social psychology, is strongly criticized for its chronic preference for present time and its insensitiveness to change (e.g. Gergen 1973). What we propose is that by seeing narrative as a fundamental tool for constructing meaning, in other words, as a mode of organizing experience rather than as mere knowledge construction, we should expand the horizon of scientific psychology in time. Through narrative we should not only study the development of personality, the invariance and the changes in personal identity but also look at the meaning patterns of social life that take shape through history as a tradition and can be interpreted as cultural change, constituting an equally vital social identity for humans that determines social orientation. One precondition for this kind of approach is historical in a dual sense: the historical accessibility of narratives has been available in libraries and archives since the advent of literacy, and as far as present research is concerned, it can be easily established, as we will see in Chapters 9 and 10, even in a verifiable manner. In this sense the psychological approach proposed here is also very much like the work of an archaeologist in that the researcher wants to extract information out of narrative texts concerning earlier states and interpret this information both in the context of other pieces of knowledge about historical states and in the context of present knowledge. The other precondition is more complicated. To avoid the danger that our psychological approach might become a pure interpretative 'understanding' psychology, we need a scientific method which, in addition to making sure that the data inherent in a narrative are relevant, enables us to control the selection of data and verify the validity of their interpretation. The method of content analysis in narrative psychology (László et al. 2002b) and its procedures for computerized content analysis (Ehmann et al. 2007; Hargitai et al. 2007; Pohárnok et al. 2007; Pólya et al. 2007), which will be introduced in Chapter 9, serve exactly this purpose. The use of a scientific method allows us, in fact makes it necessary for us, to distinguish the narrative approach advocated here, scientific narrative psychology, from any other version of narrative psychology that relies exclusively on hermeneutic interpretation, viewing personality and identity as social practice.

Narrative as medium of historical-cultural psychology

Tomasello (1999) suggests studying human cognition in three diachronic perspectives:

> from a metatheoretical perspective, my claim is that we cannot fully understand human cognition – at least not its uniquely human aspects – without considering in detail its unfolding in three distinct time frames:
> - in phylogenetic time, as the human primate evolved its unique ways of understanding conspecifics;
> - in historical time, as this distinctive form of social understanding led to distinctive forms of cultural inheritance involving material and symbolic artifacts that accumulate modifications over time; and
> - in ontogenetic time, as human children absorb all that their cultures have to offer, developing unique modes of perspectively based cognitive representation in the process.
>
> (Tomasello 1999: 202–203)

Tomasello criticizes cultural psychology, which pays little attention to the processes of sociogenesis in different domains of activity in human history.

> Cultural psychologists who should be concerned with this problem, have mostly not spent great effort in empirical investigations of the historical process by means of which particular cultural institutions in particular cultures have taken shape – for example, processes of grammaticization in the history of particular languages or processes of collaborative invention in the history of mathematical skills characteristic of a particular culture. Perhaps the most enlightening investigations of these processes are studies by intel-

lectual historians concerned with such things as the history of technology, the history of science and mathematics, and language history.

(Tomasello 1999: 209–210)

The cultural world of humans is not detached from the biological world, as human culture is a very recent product of evolution that has, in all likelihood, been in existence for a mere few hundred thousand years. The fact that culture is the product of evolution does not mean that each of its traits has a genetic counterpart, for there has not been enough time for them to develop. It is more probable that every human cultural institution is based on the biologically inherited social-cognitive ability to use social conventions and symbols. However, these do not turn the cognition of a non-human primate into human cognition by some magic touch. The cognition of adult people nowadays is the product not only of genetic events that have taken place in the several billion years of evolutionary time but also partly of the cultural events that have taken place in the many thousands of years of historical time and partly of the individual events that have taken place in the many thousands of hours of ontogeny too. There is a strong temptation to try to avoid having to do some hard work of exploring the mediating processes between the human genotype and phenotype, which often results in some sort of an easy genetic determinism so widespread in present-day social, behavioural and cognitive sciences. Genes play an important role in the development of human cognition, from a certain aspect they are perhaps the most important factors, since they triggered the process itself. However, a lot has transpired since the beginning. In other words, the good old philosophical categories of nature and society, innate and acquired knowledge, genes and the environment are simply unsuitable for the task, as they are too static and categorial for a dynamic, Darwinian explanation of the evolutionary, historical and ontogenetic dimensions of human cognition.

In this view narrative psychology can be seen as a tool for the task of reconstruction in the historical and ontogenetic dimension of the development of the human mind. We say the human *mind*, not mere *cognition*. What is at stake here is that from the point of view of the historical and ontogenetic study of culture it is impossible to separate clearly *cognitive* processes from processes of *constructing meaning*, the latter being realized in *emotionally saturated experiences related to individual and collective identity*. Both historically, through oral tradition and written records, and by the changes that take place in the course of ontogeny and the saturation of experiences that is manifest in life stories, narrative appears to be suitable for the study of the system of conditions and the alteration of construction of cultural meaning.

Narrative psychology as cultural and evolutionary psychology

From this perspective, narrative psychology is the means to build a bridge between human genotypic and phenotypic constitution by uncovering complex historical and ontogenetic intermediate processes. Narratives already occurred in prehistoric times, narrative thinking might even have preceded the evolution of language (Donald 1991). The archaeologist Marshack (1972), when deciphering the marks on a bone fragment from the Mesolithic period, concluded that the marks depicted a lunar calendar, which was in accordance with agricultural activities. So as to become agriculturalists, early humans had to take into account time, and the storied symbolic system of the marks was the tool, which helped them to perform this task. Similar archaeological findings, for instance the paintings in prehistoric caves, provide raw material for studying complex historical and ontogenetic intermediate processes.

The above example not only enlightens the intimate relationship between time and narrative (see also Ricoeur 1984–1989) but also illustrates that narrativity grows out of human activity. Narratives have rendered the world of actions intelligible and manageable from prehistoric times.

Summary

This chapter reviewed the apparently non-reconcilable debate between atomist and holist philosophies. Based on Hayek's (1967) theory on phenomenal complexity we rejected both extremist positions. We argued that certain human affairs can be approached only by conceptual and methodological tools, which allow for scheme-like interpretation. Our major claim is that the narrative represents a phenomenal level where only patterns are meaningful. Psychological phenomena are expressed in narratives at a high complexity level, which enables meaningful diagnosis and predictions, although these can only be scheme-like, because of the phenomenal complexity. We also argued that narrative is a means of forging basic human faculties such as experiences of time, space and intentionality. Given that narratives have rendered the world of actions intelligible and manageable from prehistoric times, narrative psychology is the means by which a bridge can be built between human genotypic and phenotypic constitution by uncovering complex historical and ontogenetic intermediate processes of cultural evolution.

genotype - genetic material passed
          between generations

phenotype - observable ch. or traits
            such as behaviour

3 Narrative psychology and postmodernism

What scientific narrative psychology may owe to the postmodern and what makes it different

When considering the position of narrative psychology represented in our book from the point of view of the history of science, we need to say something about the relationship of narrative psychology and postmodernism. The concept of narrative has been so closely connected to postmodern thinking and fictionality that any psychologist with a scientific attitude and at least with some self-respect is inclined to relegate narrative psychology to the world of postmodern fiction and view it with some doubt. Of course, this aversion is not novel. Plato himself (*The Republic*, Book 7) did not have a high opinion of stories either. He believed that similarly to other forms of the arts, stories were merely imitations of the material world, and the material world was a copy of a higher-order reality. Thus, stories are imitations of imitations. Just like the prisoner of Plato's cave, who was chained and forced to view the shadow of people on the wall of the cave as they marched by, the listeners of stories are compelled to see the shadow of reality. In Chapter 2 we argued against Platonic thinking by referring to narrative philosophies. More recent aversion to fictionality, fed by a general rejection of the postmodern, can be challenged by taking a closer look at the modes of psychological cognition. The meaning of the term narrative includes elements like putting actions into a cause-effect order, the creation of figures and metaphors, inferences drawn from problem-solving that takes place silently in the actor, etc. Thus, there are several fictitious activities associated with the creation of the meaning of everyday objects and events. From Jeremy Bentham to Jerome Bruner several authors claim that fictions are part of the psychological reality in which we live our life.

Another group of worries concerns the fear that scholarly quality is threatened by the 'childlike' nature of telling stories. As was put by Pataki (2001):

> Stretching the narrative principle too far may result in setting psychology back to an earlier stage – the era before conceptual thinking. This is because if all our knowledge – concerning the self – can only be presented in a narrative fashion, we may soon end up in the realm of *archaic-mythological thinking*, where the only way of capturing reality – including psychological reality – was indeed by means of narrative. Little children or adults untrained in self-reflection are not yet able to process experiences about themselves

in a conceptual order. Instead, they readily resort to narrative, to telling stories. They do so especially because they wish to *illustrate and make concrete* permanent knowledge about themselves. However, this is perhaps not the state that should be viewed as the *exclusive* feature of normal adult personality!

(Pataki 2001: 245, italics in original)

As with any other form of exclusiveness, stressing the absoluteness of the narrative principle may also lead us astray when investigating personality. However, it would be equally mistaken to fail to recognize the long neglected significance of this principle in psychology and qualify it in advance as being childish or of a lower order. Sarbin (1986a: 12) originates this sort of opinion from a positivist world view which ascribes a unique value to positivism, technology and realism, sticks to the view that every experience can be processed conceptually and does not assign much value to imagination and playfulness. Once we recognize the proper significance of the narrative principle, we can gain knowledge about the psychology of humans that is not based on positivist empirical research and which is comparable to our previous psychological knowledge; that is, *we can reflect on experience-like processes conceptually.*

Representatives of postmodern thinking are at least equally wary in this respect. The term narrative raises expectations in them. In the light of these expectations, the *scientific empiricism, the adherence to a phenomenal level of mental representations, the evolutionary attitude, horribile dictu, the hypotheses testing supported by statistical procedures* propagated in the scientific narrative psychology are regarded as a stumbling block, since they all question the faith in the omnipotence of interpretation and the construction of meaning. In this respect it is worth quoting a longer passage from one of the referees of the reader entitled *Narrative Psychology* (László and Thomka 2001):

The occasional predictability of the studies in this volume is perhaps related to the sometimes almost brutal use of structuralist methods, which otherwise reminds me of an old pledge: it was about ten years ago that I decided I would never read a book which contains tables, diagrams and figures. Yet when I come across a book like this, the otherwise rather irrational strategy works surprisingly well; the two best studies of *Narrative Psychology* (Ricoeur and Spence) do not have any tables, and the other papers immediately lose interest when the first figures and diagrams appear. Emily's crib monologs are a thousand times more exciting than the statistical figures produced from them. But this is not surprising at all, as they are stories.

(Bényei 2002: 25)

Below we will attempt to show what scientific narrative psychology owes to postmodern thinking, and what special features distinguish it from postmodern trends.

Modernity and postmodernity

Our beliefs in the unity, comprehensibility and rationality of the world in the progress of humankind and science are traditionally connected to the intellectual achievements of the Age of Enlightenment. These beliefs or world concepts have been undermined, even shaken, by postmodern theories propagating the pluralistic nature of reality, the fallibility of our well-anchored terms, the peremptory role of dominance relations of society in scientific progress. Using the winged words of Lyotard (1984), in these theories even Enlightenment itself is conceived as only one of the several *grand narratives* of humankind.

The narrative metaphor in postmodern thinking implies two main inferences: first, given the fact that narratives belong to the realm of fictions, what the storyteller does is construct meanings and handle them as *reality* in certain cases, rather then simply making true or false statements about reality. Second, since language allows us to create or tell stories which are – in principle – endless in number, that is to create an infinite number of 'realities', and to provide the latter with an infinite number of interpretations, reality will be relativized and will stay within language according to the logic of postmodern philosophy.

Similarly, psychological schools having emerged on the back of the postmodern wave would also find their object of inquiry in language itself. This means that, at least from the viewpoint of psychology, they would deny the existence of extralinguistic psychological reality. Gergen's (1985) *constructivist psychology* goes as far as to announce the death of the subject, saying that the world created linguistically is not else than psychological reality itself, and this has a corollary that individual mind or mental life are mere epiphenomena. Similar principles are advocated by *discourse analysis*, following the traditions of the Oxford analytic school, Austin and Ryle (Harré and Gillett 1994; Potter and Wetherell 1987). The basic structures of the regulation of social behaviour are implied in samples taken from discourses and accounts – since both the activities and the accounts are of societal nature in the sense that they have to be societally shareable and meaningful. These have to be unravelled by deconstruction or qualitative analysis (which, again, means the analysis of meaning).

Although with somewhat different starting points, practically similar principles support *rhetorical psychology* (Billig 1991) or *feminist psychology* (Wilkinson 1997). A proliferating body of literature on *narrative identity* (e.g. Bamberg and Andrews 2004; Brockmeier and Carbaugh 2001; De Fina 2003; De Fina et al. 2006; Freeman 1993; Ochs and Capps 2001) attempts to uncover the role of the narrative in creating, maintaining and presenting various kinds of identity (individual, interactional, group, etc.). Based on discourse samples they describe various narrative means of identity construction. If we thought about narrative psychology in this manner, as some psychologists do (Crossley 2000; Hoshmand 2000; Polkinghorne 1997) then – with some simplification – we might say that by unfolding the meanings and uses of the narrative, by qualitative analysis, we may arrive at the psychology of the storytelling person. This psychology, however, avoids any individualistic flavour. It is highly contextual, relationship-oriented, and gives priority to the intentionality of narrative communication. The interpretation is performed against a possible wide cultural, social and historical background and extends to issues of authority, dialogicity and voice, as well as positioning (Hermans 1996). Some authors, for example Polkinghorne (1997), emphasize that qualitative narrative psychology need not even be dealing with narrative texts. The principal requirement for Polkinghorne is the narrativity of the interpretation of the data coming from any source. With other words, discussion should be a 'storied account'.

In the Introduction we argued that the view of narrative psychology advocated in this book sees narrative as an ability of individuals living in society to create and operate social life, including the ability to live as an individual with self-control or, put it slightly differently, with identity. We take narrative psychology to be a scientific enterprise which owes much to narrative philosophy and generally to the linguistic turn, but has its independent, legitimate subject matters, its own methods and systematically expandable and verifiable knowledge. It is an attempt to integrate the science of mind and socially embedded action; a project which many authors called for (Dickins 2004; Harré 2002).

Approaching narrative psychology from this perspective, let us see first the relationship between philosophy and science. In this respect, a very clear statement was made by Searle (1998):

> 'Philosophy' and 'science' do not name distinct subject matters in the way that 'economic history,' 'chemistry,' and 'Romance philology' name distinct subject matters because, in principle at least, both philosophy and science are universal in subject matter. Both aim for knowledge and understanding. When knowledge becomes secure to the point that we are confident that it is knowledge as opposed to mere opinion, we are more inclined to call it 'science' and less inclined to call it 'philosophy'. Much of philosophy is concerned with questions that we do not know how to answer in the systematic way that is characteristic of science, and many of the results of philosophy are efforts to revise questions to the point that they can become scientific questions.
>
> (Searle 1998: 157–158)

Postmodernism and psychoanalysis

We discussed the roots of scientific psychology in Chapter 2. For the perspectives of narrative psychology, it is equally important that we should speak about the relationship between postmodern thinking and psychoanalysis, because it may be a source of several misunderstandings. Despite Freud's natural scientific endeavours, this relationship is commonly taken for granted, not only because of the shared cradle in the intellectual atmosphere of the Austro-Hungarian monarchy at the turn of nineteenth and twentieth centuries, but also because of the incorporation of the irrational world of the Unconscious in the scientific sphere. Furthermore, which is perhaps even more important, because of the fact that psychoanalysis interprets narration (the patient's story) by narration (by the therapist's interpretation). One can concede that psychoanalysis is of storytelling or narrative nature in a double sense: manifest dream contents and autobiographical elements will gain meaning by being interpreted as projected onto another drama, onto the latent struggle between Id, Ego and Superego. That was why psychoanalysis became a favourite field of reference for postmodern thinkers. Freud himself was indifferent to empirical verification; he thought it irrelevant. On the other hand, psychoanalytic theory conveys good examples when conceptual analyses of postmodern theories become objects of scientific problem raising, that is psychoanalytic conceptions gain scientific confirmation.

When, for example, Ricoeur (1991) tussles with the ancient philosophical issues of the identity of humans, he relies on the narrative function. He refuses the essentialist concepts of the self (i.e. views advocating that personality has an unchanged component), and starts from the semantic equivocation of the notion of identity, signalled by the double nature of the Latin terms of *idem* and *ipse*. *Idem* is a synonym of the identical, the perfectly similar, the same, which implies temporal unchangedness. *Ipse* is related to the notion of 'selfness', which, in contrast, is not conditional upon any unchangedness or constancy. At the analytical level of scientific psychology, this basically philosophical question is raised in the social psychology rooted Social Identity Theory or SIT (Tajfel 1981; Turner 1975) on the one hand, and in the psychoanalysis rooted Personal Identity Theory or PIT (Erikson 1968) on the other. While SIT and its newer variants, such as Breakwell's Identity Process Theory (Breakwell 1986) or Turner's Self Perception Theory (Turner et al. 1987), analyse the sameness and changes of the self along categorial identifications, PIT departs from life story. Albeit the two identity theories represent a kind of dualism, giving the impression that we had a social and a personal self, and these two selves were created by different psychological processes (categorial identification and experiencing our life story), both theories investigate identity from the viewpoint of disposing power, operating power (i.e. from functional, and not from existential or ontological point). Which categories and groups does one have to identify with in order to maintain the positive feeling, continuity and valuableness of one's self? What life stories has one to 'compile' – or to 'put on' as Gergen and Gergen (1988) say – so that it may offer not only cognitive coherence, that is a content that can be communicated to and accepted by the external world, but also an identity with which one can live, which maintains the balance of one's internal conditions and life conduct?

Ricoeur built the identity of the storyteller (that of the Self) onto the sameness of the narrative. The Self will constitute and reconstitute himself by telling his own story, by creating his own plot, and by identifying with the fictitious or realistic stories of others (Ricoeur 1991). The identity of the self, and also the possibility of identification with others, and that of remaking and change are all borne by the narrative. In the Ricoeurian concept, the mode of action of psychotherapy is no more than a dialogic construction of a life story by the joint interpretative work of the therapist and the patient which will restore the damaged coherence of the patient's autobiography (Ricoeur 1965). This view is held by the critical psychoanalysts, such as Schafer (1980) and Spence (1982). Nevertheless, neither the application of the narrative principle for the construction and identity of the Self nor its transfer to the world of therapy will hinder us from speaking about Narrative Self as an entity with psychological features. It does not prevent us to speak about a subject in the language of psychology. In other words, we will not have to return to an essentialist Self-concept when we construct hypotheses and models for the development, structures, conditions or functions of the Self, or when we empirically test these models. The principle of (narrative) construction, changing from person to person, from situation to situation, does not necessarily have to lead us to the acceptance of a single universality, that of the interpretation; least of all it has to lead us to the view that any intuition or interpretation will be correct if it is coherent enough and 'works' in some sense, for instance it helps the patient. Projecting this to psychology would be an extremist enforcement of the postmodern concept of science, an arrangement into an all-absorbing, general, interpreting social science, the cessation of the Feyerabendian criteria of scholarship (Feyerabend 1997), giving the impression that there was no scientific continuation of problems alleged to be solved by postmodern philosophy.

In therapeutic practice, this appears as if the patient had a biological body, which produces symptoms, and which can be affected, via causal effects, by biochemical means. It is as if, irrespective of the former, the patient had a soul, which is expressed by the symptoms, and which, considering that the matter is only a subjective meaning, can be interpreted only within itself. The healing effect is exerted by interpretation, by meaning-giving itself, but neither mental activity nor the symptoms, nor the causal relationship between the therapeutic effect and the fate of the symptoms can be revealed. Empirical generalization is neither necessary, nor possible. All that exists is a series of cases, with alleged or real repetitions, with experiences shareable through mysterious paths.

Narrativity as constraint on meaning construction

When accepting the principle of narrative construction, narrative psychology will use this principle by no means for eliminating the subjective, psychological phenomenal level, or for 'wrapping it up' in the linguistic world of interpretation. It proclaims not only that the meanings of the world and the self are really socially constructed, but also that the most important tool and process – a basic principle revealed by Ricoeur – of construction is narrativity. Narrativity, however, will not only generate, but also limit construction. This limitation is seen at least at three levels: first, structurally, which can be demonstrated in the simplest way that the story has a beginning, a middle and an end; second, functionally, which means that the story represents an economical arrangement of meanings, and third, on content level, which means that the story has to be socially shareable. As a basic experiential and existential mode, as an anthropological feature of humans, the capability of narration had existed even before the appearance of the language or the story, and played a primary role in the development of human thinking, personality and culture. When making meanings, the narrative mode will not produce fictions, it will create reality. This recognition is used by narrative psychology for the unravelling of the psychological reality of humans, who are able to live and function in their society or culture: the aim is to understand how this reality is created, which forms it may take, and how it may function or dysfunction.

Narrative literature and narrative psychology

Naturally, narration allows for creating fictitious worlds, as well. These worlds, as with literature, will refer to human reality only in an indirect manner. However, both the narrator and the recipient may use narration as a tool for understanding themselves and external reality. Moreover, by incorporating the story in their own autobiography, they may use it for creating their own psychological reality (through the world of the characters, through the Ricoeurian double reading, through observation and introspection when the reader will read the character's mental state and his own mental state simultaneously).

The psychologizing work of literature has attracted the attention of some prominent psychologists. However, the voice of acknowledgement is sometimes interspersed with the criticism of scientific psychology. John Dewey, for example, wrote the following:

> The novelist and the dramatist are so much more illuminating as well as more interesting commentators on conduct than the schematizing psychologist. The artist makes perceptible individual responses and thus displays a new phase of human nature evoked in new situations. In putting the case visibly and dramatically he reveals vital actualities. The scientific systematizer treats each act as merely another sample of some old principle, or as a mechanical combination of elements drawn from a ready-made inventory.
>
> (cited by Sarbin 1986a: 11)

But is it really necessary for psychoanalysing work to be limited only to literature narratives? Is human mental life really made grey by scientific abstraction and by scientific methods? At least a partial answer can be found in this passage quoted from Ricoeur:

> A character in a drama or a novel well exemplifies that observation and introspection are of equal rank in the double reading of the mind. ... from where the hidden paths of jealousy, the tricks of hatred, and the different kinds of desire are created if not from persons created by artistic pieces? And it is not all too important whether these are written in first or third person singular. A significant share of the treasures of our mind is to be owed to the psychological work performed by narrators and creators of fictitious characters.
>
> (Ricoeur 1991: 42)

Speaking about the 'psychologizing' and 'soul-building' work of literature, Ricoeur undoubtedly implies a typology; he speaks of 'hidden paths of jealousy' or 'different kinds of desire'.

What calls against us to investigate mental states related to the characters in the narrative by scientific methods? Surely not the claim for generalization, characteristic to science, and so to psychology. Moscovici (1986) says that each story, novel or drama contains the author's observations about types of people, about important social events, about thinking patterns of the given era. Each artistic piece can be regarded as an 'Observational Protocol' which implies a psychological and a societal theory which is not exposed by the writer in detail, but may be a good starting point for rational evolving. The writer's theory and the scientist's theory are two different kinds. Moscovici (1986) illuminates this difference by that of the content and the form:

> The scientist's theory is a *form,* which arrays the facts in as general on order as possible. The artist's theory is a *content*, the very stuff of which he makes up his characters and situations so as to dispose them in a peculiar order that makes us say: This is Stendhal's or Balzac's world, Dickens's or Hemingway's. You can, however, rationally reconstruct, as we say, the artist's theory. And by doing this discover a prospect, problems, and solutions which had not been thought of before by scientists.
>
> (Moscovici 1986: 25)

In our efforts to generalize the writer's theory to the furthest extent by rational tools, we may perhaps encounter issues which have been unmet by science in the earlier phases of development. The case is not that we discover and describe existing psychological theories in the writers' works, something like an implicit personality theory by Dreiser (Rosenberg and Jones 1972); on the contrary, what the psychologist does is to unravel the writers' theories which refer to the nature of psychological forces that propel the plot. In this sense, literature undoubtedly goes ahead of psychology, since, as Vygotsky (1971) says, as a social technique of emotions, it is also able to articulate processes that are inaccessible for rational thinking. Until now, psychology has progressed along two routes. Positivist psychology has made emotions a decontextualized test object, uprooting them from the context of life history and social background, from that of identity. This kind of psychology cannot do much about 'great' human emotions, indeed. On the one hand, it is obvious that the relationship between cognition and emotional states may be studied even under laboratory conditions (see Forgas 1998), since the case here is moods and low-intensity emotions. On the other hand, however, it would be awkward for someone to investigate the relation between identity and emotions, since identity-related emotions and feelings (safety, anxiety, self-confidence, etc.) are organic parts of identity, undetachable from it either conceptually or empirically. It is not an accident that these emotions are studied in contemporary social psychology as emotions driven from group membership (Branscombe 2004; Doosje et al. 1998).

In contrast to positivist psychology, psychoanalysis has translated the human dramas of literature into a drama of instincts; the most obvious example of this is the Oedipus complex, where human conditions correspond to stages of a hypothetical instinctual development, and appear as if mere illustrations of the latter. In classic psychoanalytical theories, an empirically non-graspable but very effective hydraulic-topologic metaphor mediates between the biological and the socio-cultural levels. Many modern or postmodern theories emphasize the hermeneutical aspect of psychoanalysis, refusing the possibility of empirical generalizations. These theories build the self from meanings that are separated from natural and societal bonds.

Narrative psychology as psychology of meaning

Is it a matter of necessity for us to either renounce meanings or absolutize them in psychology? We argued in the Introduction that in a certain sense, our approach to narrative psychology is engaged in investigating the concept of meaning, but not in the way that cultural anthropology or psychoanalysis does. There is a difference between cultural anthropological thinking when, for example, it tries to reveal what a member of the Bororo tribe means under a statement that 'I am a parakeet', and psychoanalytical thinking when it interprets a patient's statement that 'I have conflicts with authoritarian persons'. In the interpretation of the former, Geertz (1975) demonstrates that the given meaning must have different interpretations in the religious and in the common sense contexts. Let us quote him in detail:

> In the religious, our Bororo is 'really' a 'parakeet,' and given the proper ritual context might well 'meta' with other 'parakeets' – with metaphysical ones like himself, not commonplace ones such as those which fly bodily about in ordinary trees. In the common-sensical perspective he is a parakeet in the sense – I assume – that he belongs to a clan whose members regard the parakeet as their totem, a membership from which, given the fundamental nature of reality as the religious perspective reveals it, certain moral and practical conversation, saying that, as myth and ritual demonstrate, he is shot through with parakeetness and that this religious fact has some crucial implications – we parakeets must stick together, not marry one another, not eat mundane parakeets, and so on, for to do otherwise is to act against the grain of the whole universe. It is this placing of proximate acts in ultimate contexts that makes religion, frequently at least, socially so powerful.
>
> (Geertz 1975: 113–114)

Thus, it can be seen that, when speaking about meanings, cultural anthropology focuses on their symbolic aspect, on their place in different realms of reality.

On the other hand, the usual psychoanalytical interpretation of statements like 'I have conflicts with authoritarian persons' refers not to 'societal or behavioural consequences', or to some actual internal conditions, such as frustration or anger, but to a particular phase of a hypothesized instinctual development, to the fact that the person has not solved his Oedipal conflict.

In narrative psychology, meaning is conceived as representation, as a psychological representation, but not in the sense of the information processing metaphor as in cognitive psychology, but in its intrapsychological and intersubjective relationships. When the events are formed into stories in narration, we will give sense to the acts at the same time. In Bruner's words this is a lesson of the great historians' debate in our era (J. Bruner 1986: 56): 'We embellish our hard-core *annales,* convert them into *chroniques* and finally into *history*' – since it is history that has sense. This is the meaning or sense which was referred to above as psychological reality. However, this meaning is only one plane of psychological reality; as Bruner terms it, it is the '*landscape of action*', which is organized by the actor, the intention, the goal, the situation, the means, that is by the arguments of action. However, in the story, in *all* stories, there is a '*landscape of consciousness*' as well: all what the actors know, think and feel, or all what they *do not know, do not think or do not feel* (italics added). In narrative psychology, both landscapes of narrative are 'in play'. On the one hand, at the level of action, it shows the rationality in which the actor lives, and on the other hand, inseparable from the former, it shows the 'irrationality' which forms a part of life, too. Interrelating these two aspects, narrative psychology tries to make both an object of rational, scientific reflection.

What is, then, the empirical material and the theoretical model with which narrative psychology works? The first half of the question is easier to answer. In both of its exploratory and hypothesis testing investigations, narrative psychology analyses the content and structural features of the narrative. However, the theoretical models are not so unambiguous. If we accept that the narrative is a basic principle of our construction of reality, then this principle, as an explanatory model, can be used for the interpretation of such 'traditional' psychological phenomena as memory distortions (Neisser 1976), or scheme formation in remembering (Bartlett 1932). But on the other hand, each narrative in vivo implies contents that refer to the emotional life of individuals and groups, to psychological development and conditions of people who live in their own families or groups – and these may be tested in the light of the hypotheses of either the existing or the newly formed psychological theories.

Summary

In this chapter we discussed various postmodern approaches to psychological meaning construction and contrasted them with the principles of the scientific narrative psychology. We called the reader's attention to the fact that narrative not only enables interpretation, but also brings constraints to it. We contrasted investigation of psychological meaning by scientific narrative psychological concepts and methods with psychoanalytic interpretation and compared these concepts and methods also with the analysis of symbolic meaning in cultural anthropology. The major contention of the chapter is that psychological meaning should be conceived and studied as representation in its intrapsychological and intersubjective relationships. The very problem of representation will be discussed in Chapter 5. But before turning to these issues, the cognitive psychological and experimental social psychological traditions of narrative psychology will be reviewed.

4 Narrative psychology's contribution to the second cognitive revolution

cognition – mental action or process of acquiring knowledge and understanding thru thought, experience and senses

Cognitive revolution, beginning in the 1950s, has made cognition the central topic in psychology. It succeeded with relative ease and as Gardner (1985: 174) remarked with somewhat militant metaphors, by the 1980s 'cognitive psychologists have won the battle on their chosen field within psychology. ... Nearly all researchers accept the need and the advisability of positing a level of mental representation.' In the year when Gardner's book was published, another revolution was already in progress. This more silent and more prolonged revolution has been initiated mainly by social psychologists, but some cognitive psychologists, for example Jerome Bruner, who had been active around the cradle of cognitive psychology itself, also participate in it. More radical representatives call this movement discursive revolution (Harré 1994), the driving force of which is the denial of mental representations, at least in the social psychology. Potter and Wetherell (1987) detach discourse analysis from the cognitive science in their programmatic book, and they place both analysis and explanation to a social psychological level, which is independent from cognitive representations.

> Discourse analysis has eschewed any form of cognitive reductionism, any explanation which treats linguistic behaviour as a product of mental entities or processes, whether it is based around social representations or some other cognitive furniture such as attitudes, beliefs, goals or wants. The concern is firmly with *language use*: the way accounts are constructed and different functions.
>
> (Potter and Wetherell 1987: 157)

Nevertheless, most directions in recent revolutionary movements, for example social representations theory or cultural psychology, do not rule out the idea of the individual mental representations. In Chapter 2 we also argued that scientific narrative psychology cannot renounce individuality and subjectivity. However, while in the cognitive psychology individual mental activity – information processing – is the object of study, and social and cultural factors play only the role of moderating variables as it is typical in cross-cultural research, new theories study socially and culturally determined meaning formation. Given that meaning is a relation to the world, meaning construction necessarily involves studying individual processes in relation to broader social and cultural phenomena. As Bruner (1990) writes, in cognitive psychology very early

> emphasis began shifting from 'meaning' to 'information', from the *construction* of meaning to the *processing* of information. These are profoundly different matters. The key factor of shift was the introduction of computing as the ruling metaphor and of computability as a necessary criterion of a good theoretical model. Information is different with respect to meaning. In computational terms, information comprises an already precoded message in the system. Meaning is preassigned to the message. It is not an outcome of computation, nor is it relevant to computation save in the arbitrary sense of assignment.
>
> (Bruner 1990: 4)

In contrast, Bruner highlights that humans are cultural beings, born, being raised, living in culture, and human mental capacities unfold through culture. These conditions make it impossible to build human psychology exclusively on individuals.

> Given that psychology is so immersed in culture, it must be organized around those meaning-making and meaning-using processes that connect man to culture. This does *not* commit us to more subjectivity in psychology [as opposed to objective methodology]; it is just the reverse. By virtue of participation in culture, meaning is rendered *public* and *shared*. Our culturally adapted way of life depends upon shared meanings and shared concepts and depends upon shared modes of discourse for negotiating differences in meaning and interpretation.
>
> (Bruner 1990: 12–13, italics in original)

Thus, in Bruner's conceptualization, the aim of the second cognitive revolution is embedding individual mental processes into complex social and cultural processes by studying meaning construction and meaning usage.

Forerunners of narrative psychology in experimental and social psychology

Narrative psychology is one of the directions of the second cognitive revolution, which is based on the fundamental role that the narrative function plays in constructing and communicating meaning. Scientific psychology has recognized the special role of narrative in organization of meaning from early on, for example Binet and Henri (1894) when searching for children's intelligence found an advantage of narrative in memory performance. Narrative, as meaning configuration, which is qualitatively different from elementaristic associative patterns (Janet 1928), or as a cognitive tool for assigning meaning to an action (Janet 1928) was introduced into psychological research. Nevertheless, the study of narrative in twentieth-century psychology is most closely related to the name of Sir Frederick Bartlett.

Bartlett and the psychology of meaning

Cognitive psychology respects Bartlett as one of its predecessors. Indeed, Bartlett's theory of memory schematization has allowed for developing information processing theories. That part of Bartlett's work, which is devoted to the meaning including the essence of the 'effort after meaning', has been sacrificed on the altar of the computation metaphor. Being particularly sensitive to cultural phenomena, even being experienced in doing field studies in African cultures, Bartlett showed that both content and structure of stories are results of social and cultural conventionalization. Storytelling

> cannot be treated solely as an individual response. Many of the complex influences that take part in shaping it, come directly from the social group ... I shall insist and again insist, that in certain perfectly definite respects the myth, the legend and the popular story, are immediately affected by influences arising from the social setting in which they take form and grow.
>
> (Bartlett 1923: 60)

In his classic book on remembering Bartlett (1932) connects experimental and social psychology already in the subtitle of the book. It is worthwhile to recall his thoughts in detail. In one of his experiments a line drawing of a wall and a gate with a board containing indecipherable characters was shown to the participants. The participants interpreted the text as 'Trespassers will be prosecuted'. The 'effort after meaning' goes beyond the visual context.

> The context, or situation, actually involved is the expression of a group of tendencies connected with an interest in country walks, or perhaps in social customs and prejudices. These active factors are a part of the meaning, and a part of the situation. They organise the sensorial material which is present. There is no psychological material without them, and they are an essential condition of the meaning which, once it is present, is referred to the material.
>
> (Bartlett 1932: 234)

Bartlett emphasizes that affect must be treated psychologically as a 'constituent of meaning', but he rules out also the conception that psychologically anything means the whole context or situation in which it is found. Meaning is limited by several active tendencies, as a result of which certain dominant or overweighted elements stand out in perception or recall. These tendencies may be individual, such as temperament, character or interest, others may be collective, for instance group interests, ideals or conventions.

Bartlett directs attention to the importance of the chronological arrangement from the point of view of meaning. 'In relatively simple cases, the meaning of part of a situation will be found in the reactions, material, and affect that most immediately follow them' (Bartlett 1932: 235). But in more complex cases, and most of the everyday life situations belong to this type, the simple chronological principle of meaning organization does not work. A lot of 'acquired material' or schematized experience cuts across the simple chronological principle of organization.

> An accomplished *raconteur* begins his story in such a manner as to express for himself and simulate in his listeners some group of interests. Then comes an interval. He holds the interests up, keeps them waiting, and in the end comes in with his 'fitting' material, and the interests are justified. The same thing happens in the case of the skilful orator, the musical composer, the accomplished writer. All difficult solutions of problems run much the same course. There are reactions, affects and psychological material which excellently 'fit' other reactions, affects and psychological material. This, perhaps, is simply an objective fact. But, like other facts, it may be reacted to, and, as in many other cases, the reaction may be witting or unwitting. The witting reactions of this type give us meaning on a high level. So we often find that the 'real' meaning of a situation, or of some part of a situation, is far removed in space or time from that of which it is taken to be the meaning.
>
> (Bartlett 1932: 235)

With the term 'fitting material', he points not only to the higher ordered temporal schemes, or more broadly to the narrative structure, but also to the close relationship between *meaning* and *coherence*.

> For 'real' meaning may be substituted 'conventional' meaning. Meaning arises out of the organisation of psychological material by reaction tendencies. Whenever any of these tendencies become conventionalised and established throughout a social group, they tend be expressed in every individual member of the group, provided he is reacting in a social manner. They thus uniformly determine situations and meaning throughout the group. 'Real' meanings, in this sense, vary from group to group, just as 'apparent' meanings may vary from individual to individual. Within the group the direction of reference of any situation dealt with by the group tendencies remains relatively constant. The 'real' meaning, for instance, of 'magic' may differ greatly as between a contemporary civilised European group and, say, a group of Australian aboriginals.
>
> (Bartlett 1932: 235)

Although Bartlett's contribution was extensively exploited later in several fields of cognitive psychology, eminently in memory research and in story grammars, his idea of merging cognitive and social psychology by studying psychological meaning as it evolves in social-cultural contexts had much less influence on the twentieth century psychology. Cultural psychology and narrative psychology partly draw back to the problem of psychological meaning in the sense that Bartlett originally put forward.

The problem of meaning in experimental social psychology

Mainstream social psychology of the twentieth century was just as reluctant to pursue Bartlett's 'efforts after meaning' as experimental psychology was. It was all in vain that outstanding figures in both fields – Mead, Vygotsky, Freud, Lewin, Piaget – clearly saw humans as meaning-constructing beings from early infancy. Experiments in social psychology were run with decontextualized stimuli and with subjects who were deprived from their social relations and culture. Ross and Nisbett (1991) characterize this scientific logic as follows:

> Social psychology has by now amassed a vast store of such empirical parables. The tradition here is simple. Pick a generic situation; then identify and manipulate a situational or contextual variable that intuition or past research leads you to believe will make a difference (ideally, a variable whose impact you think most laypeople, or even most of your peers, somehow fail to appreciate), and see what happens. Sometimes, of course, you will be wrong and your manipulation won't 'work.' But often the situational variable makes quite a bit of difference. Occasionally, in fact, it makes nearly all the difference, and information about traits and individual differences that other people thought all-important proves all but trivial. If so, you have contributed a situationist classic destined to become part of our field's intellectual legacy.
>
> (Ross and Nisbett 1991: 4)

The study of psychological meaning was still unavoidable in the field of social perception, and leading theoreticians of the Gestalt tradition, particularly Lewin and Heider, insisted on studying the meaning of the social situation. In Heider's theory of social perception, narrative plays a central role. It is the field of demonstration of the interpretive constructs by the help of which people assign meaning to an event. Heider (1958) using Aesop's tale *The Fox and the Raven* presented his 'perception devices', such as cause, try, aims at, that is the terms in which perceivers read out the meaning of the actions. The 'naive psychology', after multiple reduction, had continuation in causal attribution research (Jones and Davis 1965; Kelley 1967) and in theories of cognitive consistency (Abelson et al. 1968). In these streams of research, only the narrative patterns of knowledge organization, which is based on the logic of action remind of the original richness of the naive psychology (Schank and Abelson 1977, 1995; Wyer et al. 2002).

The fate of Lewin's ideas on the relationship between the cognitive structure and the meaning of an event had no more luck. Lewin insisted that psychological meaning of the environmental events should be derived from the psychological relation between events and actions:

Learning, as a change in cognitive structure, has to deal with practically every field of behavior. Whenever we speak of a change in meaning, a change of such cognitive structure has occurred. New connections or separations, differentiations or dedifferentations of psychological areas have taken place. The 'meaning' of an event in psychology may be said to be known if its psychological position and its psychological direction are determined. In Mark Twain's *Life on the Mississippi*, the passengers on the boat enjoy the 'scenery,' but for the pilot the V-shape of the two hills, which a passenger admires means a signal to turn sharply, and the beautiful weaves in the middle of the river mean dangerous rock. The psychological connection of these 'stimuli' with actions has changed, and therefore the meaning has changed.

(Lewin 1951: 364)

Writing about the general methodological problems of social psychology, Lewin recognized the primary importance of studying cognition. He stressed that instead of observing behaviour and assigning behavioural units to various psychological variables, social psychologists should grasp the social meaning of actions.

What is needed in social psychology today is to free its methodology from speculative limitations. We do well to start again with the simple facts of everyday life for which the possibility of an adequate social observation never could be in doubt because community life is unthinkable without it. Such an empirical basis should be one basis of the methodology of social psychology. The other should be a progressively deeper understanding of the laws of social perception.

(Lewin 1951: 368)

Thus, psychological meaning in social psychology arises from the relation between social events and actions. It is social meaning, which makes sense of the event and behaviour of the actors is related to this meaning, rather than to 'objective' stimuli.

The next example, which has its source also in Gestalt psychology, takes us even closer to narratives. In his classical conformity study, Solomon Asch (1952) asked his subjects to compare three lines with a standard line and to indicate which one of the three lines presented on the screen matched the standard line. They had to do this in the presence of a group of stooges, who, preceding the subject's answer, gave unanimously wrong answers. Many subjects conformed to the false judgement. Conventional views of conformity held that people are influenced by the view of their peers because they seek acceptance and fear rejection. Asch gave an additional explanation. The response of the peers defines the meaning of the stimuli; it is a strong suggestion how the stimuli should be interpreted. According to Asch, once one adopts the interpretation or definition offered by one's peers, one is likely to adopt their evaluations and behaviour as well. Subsequent studies (e.g. Ross et al. 1976) showed that whenever subjects had the chance to attribute rational motives to incorrect judgements of their peers, that is they were able to fill the situation with rational meaning, they had no problems with giving non-conformist correct responses.

If one looks for the major functions of narrative in human interaction, this aspect of making behaviour rational will certainly be salient. Narrative makes intentional actions coherent and meaningful.

Socio-cultural aspects of psychological meaning

Henri Tajfel's social identity theory offers an instructive lesson on the destiny of those strivings that set the object of cognitive social psychology in the study of social and cultural meanings. In his chapter 'Experiments in a vacuum', published in the classic textbook *The Context of Social Psychology* (Israel and Tajfel 1972), Tajfel outlined a theory on the experimental methodology in social psychology. As opposed to the most frequent and vehement critique on social psychology, which blamed its experimentalism for artificiality and low generalizability, Tajfel took a stand for the experimental methodology; however, he entirely reformulated the standards for designing and interpreting experiments. Tajfel saw the major problems with social psychological experiments that they pretend to be run in a social vacuum, in which only some universally human or biological essence manifests itself. According to him, it was a misunderstanding that values and social norms could be switched off from people's behaviour. Contrary to the ideals of experimental social psychology to purify experimental variables as much as possible, he reversed the aim of experimentation. Since norms and values that direct people's behaviour always contaminate experimental conditions, he suggested the study of the nature of this contamination as the central object of social psychology (Tajfel 1972: 76).

Nowadays it is virtually impossible to publish a social psychological reader without minimal group experiments (Tajfel 1970; Tajfel et al. 1971). In these experiments subjects are sorted into two groups on a minimal difference basis, such as according to the preference between two paintings or two musical composition. After being assigned to one of the two groups, subjects are asked to allocate money or other reward to the groups. The results of these studies converge to a marked in-group preference. As Tajfel (1972) stresses in his chapter, his aim with the minimal group paradigm was not to clean the experiments from the contamination of the social and cultural norms and to carry out hypothetico-deductive studies to test models for a universal human nature. Contrarily, he expected, and he interpreted his results accordingly, that social and cultural norms would manifest themselves in minimal group situations. He had, of course, assumptions concerning these norms, in other words he did not engage himself in open-ended exploration (cf. Denzin 1992), but he meant his studies to be discovery rather than verification enterprises and he interpreted his results accordingly:

> the most economical explanation of a complex set of results was the assumption that the subjects attempted to achieve a compromise between two norms and two values underlying these norms which, as far as they were concerned,

were pertinent to the experimental situation. The norms were those of 'group-ness' and 'fairness', and the values those of 'solidarity' and 'equity'.

(Tajfel 1972: 86)

Tajfel's experiments are not presented in contemporary readers and in the works of his followers as a social context fulfilling the role of a projective surface that obtains meaning by the process in which subjects project their norms and values feel relevant to the situation. The minimal group paradigm now appears as a situation, where inter-group discrimination can be attributed only to psychological processes. There is no indication that these experiments would carry information about the culture, and that this information could also be a matter of interest for other social scientists, for instance sociologists, anthropologists or historians, beyond the social psychological audience. The results of Tajfel's experiments are interpreted in terms of social categorization, social identity or uncertainty reduction that are reified psychological processes (see Condor 2003).

Communication and cognition

The natural field for the psychological study of meaning construction is com-munication, and language is the most important communicative tool for humans. Cognitivist study of the language focuses on the representational, information-processing and computational aspects. Pragmatic or behavioural aspects enjoy much less attention. Social cognition research as opposed to traditional cognitive social psychology, which practically ignored language, devotes due attention to linguistic communication. It is directed to adjusting the message to the social context of the language use, eminently to the social relations between the speaker and hearer. There are evidences for 'audience design', when speakers adapt their messages to specific listeners (Chiu et al. 1998), or for the dependence of choosing an accent on the cooperative or competitive relation between the com-munication partners (Giles and Coupland 1991). Interpersonal character of the communication is also traced in the representation of information. In the study of Higgins and Rholes (1978), interpersonal relation between the communication partners was manipulated either to promote speaker's positive self-presentation or intimacy to the listener. The results showed not only that the interdependence between communicator and recipient influenced the message subjects wrote but also that formulating the message in a given way also shaped their beliefs. It is obvious that this stream of research looks at formal and content characteristics of the communication as expressing interpersonal relations or reflecting changes in information processing, and overlooks the more general issues of how com-munication generates meaning in human society. Despite the lip-service to the social nature of communication, to the importance of constructing shared real-ity, or to the pragmatic rule systems, which often emerges in the literature, very little study contributed to these issues. Nevertheless, the fact that the language which is used in communication is pivotal in the representation of social reality as an 'implementational device' (Semin 2000) has attracted social psychological attention. The linguistic category model (Semin and Fiedler 1988, 1991) is based on meta-semantic or structural properties of language: the same event can be communicated on different levels of abstraction. A fight between two people can be reported with concrete descriptive action verbs, for example 'John punched Bill', with more general interpretive action verbs ('John hurt Bill'), with abstract state verbs ('John hates Bill') or, on the most abstract level, with adjectives ('John is aggressive'). Whereas descriptive action words retain the situational context of the event and thereby evoke in their listener the impression of a matter of fact report, the more abstract expressions are used, the more likely it is that the representation of the event will be influenced by interpretations based on conceptual generalizations and the listener will accept or decline this interpretation according to her relation to the speaker. The linguistic category model (LCM) deems the forms of linguistic representation, particularly the level of abstraction, as tools for structuring the world of the speaker and the listener. By choosing between the potential representational forms, the speaker influences the representations and actions of the listener. Experimental tests of the model come from the domain of inter-group behaviour. People describe the same socially desirable behaviour on a more abstract level, if this behaviour is linked with the in-group, as opposed to the out-group. The situation is reversed with the socially undesirable acts. So as to avoid a representation which depicts the negative behaviour as general and permanent characteristics, socially undesirable acts of the in-group members are described at a more concrete level (Maas et al. 1989, 1995, 1996).

Semin (2000) extended the LCM for comprehensive study of the linguistic procedures of matching the representational structures of the speaker and the listener. The new message modulation model (MM) is based on three principles.

1   Messages (speech acts) are *publicly accessible situated knowledge structures* that are mediated by the prepositional and structural properties of language.
2   The function of messages is the regulation (e.g. coordination and synchronization) of the cognitive, behavioural and motivational processes between speaker and audience.
3   The type of situated knowledge structure that a message constitutes is an emergent property resulting from the speaker–audience relationship.

(Semin 2000: 604)

It is important to note that the speaker–audience relationship is not an inherent quality of either of the two parties to the communication.

The speaker–audience relationship supplies the regulatory, motivational and affective processes that contribute to the shape of the message. Conversely, the message conveys information about the type of relationship between the speaker and audience and in fact reifies the relationship

(Semin 2000: 604)

If we are to analyse the relationship between cognitive and narrative psychology, it is hard to find a better starting point than social cognitive research in communication. In order to relate narrative psychology to social cognition, however, we should first summarize what we have said about narrative psychology so far and amend this where it seems to be necessary.

Narrative psychological approach

On the basic, ontological and epistemological level, narrative psychology is a metatheory, which renders general, anthropological character to the narrative function. In this sense, narrative already exists before the story or language as the natural mode of constructing and understanding reality in human consciousness (J. Bruner 1986; Ricoeur 1984–1989), therefore it is adequate to uncover human psychology from narratives, or as Sarbin (1986a) puts it, narrative can be a root metaphor for doing psychology. From an evolutionary perspective Donald (1991) looks at narrative as the major accomplishment and driving force of human evolution:

> The myth is the prototypal, fundamental, integrative mind tool. It tries to integrate a variety of events in a temporal and causal framework. It is inherently a modeling device, whose *primary* level of representation is thematic. The pre-eminence of myth in early human society is testimony that humans were using language for a totally new kind of integrative thought. Therefore, the possibility must be entertained that the primary human adaptation was not language *qua* language but rather integrative, initially mythical, thought.
>
> (Donald 1991: 215, italics in original)

The narrative metatheory is particularly influential in self and identity theory, where, based on the life story, it offers a non-essentialist solution for the unity and identity of the individual self (Bamberg and Andrews 2004; Brockmeier and Carbaugh 2001; Bruner 1990; Freeman 1993; Ricoeur 1991; Spence 1982). The conception of narrative as a mean of identity construction is summarized by Donald Polkinghorne (1988) as follows:

> The tools being used by the human disciplines to gain access to the self-concept are, in general, the traditional research implements designed for formal science to locate and measure objects and things. We achieve our personal identities and self-concept through the use of the narrative configuration, and make our existence into a whole by understanding it as an expression of a single unfolding and developing story. We are in the middle of our stories and cannot be sure how they will and; we are constantly having to revise the plot as new events are added to our lives. Self, then, is not a static thing or a substance, but a configuring of personal events into a historical

unity, which includes not only what one has been but also anticipations of what one will be.

(Polkinghorne 1988: 150)

Along the metatheoretical thread, some significant social psychological development also occurred. Reviewing Halbwachs' (1980) theory of collective memory, a new interpretation has been given to the collective. The narrative has provided a frame where interdependence of collective representations and group identity as well as dissemination and transmission of representations and identity became objects of study (Assmann 1992).

Nevertheless, narrative as a tool for organizing and communicating experiences has already been an object of psychological inquiry from the very beginning (Binet and Henri 1894), and it recurred sporadically in the literature in substantial contributions (e.g. Bartlett 1932; Blonsky 1935; Janet 1928) up until it became a central topic in the 1970s as key concept of the story grammars (Labov and Waletzky 1967; Rumelhart 1975; Thorndyke 1977) or episodic representations (Black and Bower 1980; Schank 1975; Schank and Abelson 1977, 1995; Wyer et al. 2002). The perspective of the narrative organization, however, has gradually been extended to other traditional psychological phenomena, such as thinking (J. Bruner 1986; Bruner and Lucariello 1989), emotions (Dyer 1983; Oatley 1992), memory (Nelson 1993; Rubin 1996), health psychology (Pennebaker 1993; Stephenson et al. 1997) or personality development (Stern 1995). Studies dealing with processing of literary narratives, that is with specific literary conditions of narrative comprehension (Halász 1987; László 1999) point into the same direction.

Most of these approaches can be accommodated within a more holistic frame of cognitive psychology, because they are directed to the study of the mental representations of individuals.

Last but not least, narrative also appears in narrative psychology as the 'carrier' of psychological states and relations. A recounted story, that is, the way people give sense and meaning to the events of their environment, expresses their inner states and their interrelationships. In the same way, canonized or representative stories of a group provide information about values and norms prevailing in the group, about the ways of coping accepted in it, about the properties of group identity, etc. In this third trend of narrative psychology narrative is viewed as the 'storehouse' (Ehmann 2000) or the 'indicator' (Pléh 2003a) of psychological phenomena. In some earlier work we have shown that in addition to thematic contents that can be unravelled with the help of quantitative analysis, the structural properties described by twentieth-century narratology can be related to the psychological states of the narrator, and on this basis we have elaborated the theory and method of narrative content analysis (László et al. 2002b, 2007). In our view it is possible to formulate hypotheses for the structural properties of narratives of life situations and events of life – such as temporal pattern, narrative perspective, evaluative pattern, narrative coherence, the complexity of plot, functions attributed to characters, etc. – and the relationships between psychological states and processes, and these hypotheses can be tested empirically by analyses at a textual level using relatively precisely identifiable structural constituents of texts. Although the results gained this way have only surface validity, by using control groups and other tools of psychological analysis it is possible to test their external validity too (see Chapter 9 and the Appendix).

Naturally, there is a deeper theoretical assumption behind positing a relationship between the structural properties of narrative and the psychological states of the narrator, which at the same time entails the unity of the three trends or levels of narrative psychology and the interrelationships between each of the levels. According to the so-called *correspondence hypothesis* (László et al. 2002b) there is a special kind of correspondence between the organization of manifest narratives and the organization of experience, the former being the natural manifestations of the latter. Building on this presumed relationship we can derive hypotheses concerning the structural properties of stories, while the theory and methodology of content analysis in narrative psychology also leave room for *inductive logic*; in other words, it offers an opportunity to recognize a relationship between a particular structural property and a given psychological state simply by analysing the text itself without any prior expectation or hypothesis. For the sake of a better understanding of this issue, here are some preliminary examples to illustrate the two types of logic. For the sake of simplicity the examples are taken from the area of correspondences between identity and narratives of life history. In the case of using deductive logic we start out from some sort of an existing psychological construct, for instance the theory of object relationships in borderline personality organization. The theory describes borderline personality development as a disorder in early object relationships which is supposed to lead to impairment in emotional self-acceptance and the emotive control of social relations. According to a hypothesis built on this theory the impairment is expressed in the life history of borderline patients, especially in stories about the caretaker or partner in the form of a relatively high number of instances of approaching and distancing that reflect emotional ambivalence. The hypothesis can thus be tested by using control groups. First, the hypothetical narrative variable or variables are identified, which in a given case may include emotive evaluation and position change (approaching or distancing). In the next step, linguistic variables that express the content of emotive evaluation and approaching–distancing need to be identified at the textual level, which is then followed by a frequency (quantitative) analysis of linguistic variables in the texts of life history produced by the groups in the study. Finally, the hypothesis is verified by statistical tests (see Pohárnok et al. 2007). Hypotheses may of course be built not only on theories worked out for patient groups but also on theories that use groups 'diagnosed' by means of personality questionnaires (see Hargitai et al. 2007; Pólya 2007). Inductive logic is used when a particular feature of narrative structure can be detected in a text which can be related to some psychological state. Ehmann and Erős (2002) for example 'seek' psychological states for the temporal patterns of narratives that describe the relationship between person and reality.

Social cognition and narrative psychology

Social cognition research, which has been the dominant paradigm in social psychology since the mid-1980s, embraces various fields of social information processing such as person perception, stereotypes, attitudes, decision-making, and so on. Comparing narrative psychology now to communication research, which is the closest domain to it within the broader area of social cognition, several substantial differences can be detected beyond the apparent similarities. Both LCM and MM as well as narrative psychology exploit the structural characteristics of the language. However, communication research treats language and cognition as separate phenomenal levels. It conceives language as a tool for implementing cognition (or psychological phenomena) in the communication. It is striving for a causal model, in which the choice of a linguistic form is determined by a mentally represented interpersonal or inter-group relationship, the goals pursued in the communication situation, or the content of the communication itself (Schaller and Conway 1999). Thus, the message structure is an emergent characteristic of the communication situation, which is co-determined by the mental representations of several factors. So as to infer the speaker's attitudes and motivations, a listener should implicitly know the relation between the linguistic form and the attitudes. It is necessary, but not sufficient. To make proper inferences, the listener should also share situational knowledge with the speaker, which interprets a given occurrence of a particular linguistic form.

Theoretical models and experimental methodology of the social cognition research dealing with communicative acts are directed to individual mental processes as they are influenced by the linguistic structure. These models construct more complex units of psychological representation (e.g. attitude, stereotype) from elements of basic psychological processes (emotion, thinking, motivation). They deconstruct the situation and try to capture the mental representation of the elementary situational information, or of some combination of such elementary information on one hand and mental representation of the assumedly enduring interpersonal or inter-group relations on the other in a unitary model. Linguistic behaviour is conceived as a result and indicator of these internal representational processes. In other variants, these models disregard the mental representation of the social situation and treat society or culture as external factors or moderator variables (Giles and Coupland 1991)

The branch of narrative psychology as we understand it deals also with linguistic structures, but it does it in a different theoretical framework. It considers narrative to be a natural form of organizing experiences, which shapes internal world of humans and, in the same time, links them to their society and culture. Narrative exists before the actual story, and stories generated either spontaneously or elicited in interviews carry the psychological meaning of people's internal world, as well as these stories reflect their relation to the world. Elementary linguistic forms are analysed in terms of the holistic narrative structure, which is held to be the carrier of the psychologically relevant material. Thus, linguistic structure is *not* an implementation of mental functioning, in other words, mental functioning is *not* a causal factor in the emergent linguistic structure. It is rather an expression of complex psychological states and processes in terms of which people organize the meanings of their world and of their own selves.

Based on these assumptions, narrative psychology has the capacity to leave the reductive situation of the laboratory experimentation and to go out to study *in vivo* material. It also follows from the above assumptions that, in contrast with scientific causation, or in addition to it, narrative psychology prefers looser forms of causality based on interpretation. It extends empirical assessment and measurement to meaning, but, accepting the uncertainties in the construction of meaning, it is content with explaining and predicting tendencies rather than strict universal rules.

To illustrate the narrative psychological approach we have developed for studying psychological phenomena through narrative structure (László 1997; László et al. 2002b), we present some results of one of our recent studies, which concerns the relation between narrative perspective and identity states (Pólya et al. 2005).

The narrative structure of self-narrations has four possible variations in terms of the perspective and the temporal position adopted by a narrator. In the first case, the narrator may adopt the perspective of an *observer*, when the narrator is located in the 'here and now' and the narrated event is located in the 'there and then'. In the second case, in what we may term the *re-experiencing* perspective, both the narrator and the narrated event are located in the 'there and then'. In the third case, which we may term the *experiencing* narrative perspective, both the narrating person and the narrative event are located in the 'here and now'. (The fourth case, when the narrator is located in the 'there and then' and the narrated event is in the 'here and now' is extremely rare, therefore we did not deal with it.)

The three narrative perspectives of interest can be linguistically operationalized; even they are amenable to automatic coding (Pólya et al. 2007). Intuitively it may be inferred that the use of different perspectivization reflects different identity states. When the narrator's position is clearly differentiated from the narrated events (the observer perspective), the narrator's identity-state is settled and coherent, the narrator is well adjusted. When the narrator uses a re-experiencing narrative perspective (as if participating in the event), it reflects a more intense identity-state, and suggests conflicts concerning the identity. Finally, when the narrator uses the 'experience' perspective, in a sense reporting the identity event as if was occurring in the here and now, the identity state is even more intense and suggests unresolved identity-conflicts.

In a study (Pólya 2007) three groups of subjects were interviewed about a traumatic life events. Young Jewish people reported the event when they first came to know their Jewish origin (after the Holocaust many Jewish families kept secret their background in Hungary), young homosexuals told of their coming out episode, and women participating in IVF therapy spoke about when they learned of their infertility. They also filled out identity-state questionnaires: Profile of Mood States (McNair et al. 1981), the State Self-esteem Scale (Heatherton and Polivy 1991) and Self-coherence Scale (Antonovsky 1987). Results with each scale showed good correlation with the narrative perspective used in the life stories. Subjects reporting their traumatic life-episode from an observer perspective turned out to have more stable mood state, higher self-esteem and higher sense of coherence of the self, than subjects using the other two perspectives. In some cases the scales also differentiated between the *re-experiencing* and *experiencing* subjects.

An experimental study was carried out to validate the above results (Pólya et al. 2005). If there is a relation between narrative perspectives and identity states, then lay people, as naive perceivers, should have a sense of this relation based on their everyday experiences. In the experiment, lay subjects were presented with three standardized life stories about the three traumatic life events used in the previous study. Each story had three variants according to the *retrospective*, *re-experiencing* and *experiencing* perspective. When reading a set of stories, subjects had to judge on the narrator's social value, impulsivity and anxiety after each story. The results were fairly consistent with the hypotheses. The target person received a significantly higher evaluation, and was perceived to be less impulsive and having less anxiety, in the cases when retrospective narrative perspective was applied.

Summary

This chapter outlined the differences between studying information processing and studies of psychological meaning construction, and reviewed the work of Bartlett, Lewin and Tajfel, who were pioneers in the empirical study of psychological meaning. We took communication as prototypical example of social cognition research and contrasted it with narrative psychology. Social cognition research treats language as a tool for implementing cognition in the communication. In this approach, the choice of a linguistic form is determined by a mentally represented interpersonal or inter-group relationship or by other situational factors. In contrast, narrative psychology conceives narrative-linguistic forms as expressions or carriers of complex psychological states and processes in terms of which people organize the meanings of their world and of their own selves.

5　On representation

From previous chapters it is obvious that the mental representation of reality is a key problem in psychology. This question was raised by Descartes when he divided the world into physical things and the cognitive subject. The basic thesis of dualism sets the subjectivity of the mind in opposition with the mechanical, physical nature of the body, and excludes any causal interaction between the two in a physical sense. The dualist view and the attempts to overcome it have had a constant influence on the history of science and the history of psychology too (Bolton 2003). The review presented in Table 5.1 sorts theories of knowledge and experience in terms of assumptions about representation and its nature, and about the relationship between the individual and reality or subject-object. The table clearly shows that essentially six theoretical positions can be distinguished. Radical representatives of cognitive neuroscience (Churchland 1995; Pinker 1997; Stich 1983) question not only the social standpoint but also psychology itself, viewing it as a sort of 'folk' science operating with somewhat obscure notions.

In their view mental or representational notions like thinking or memory are typical products of everyday consciousness which cannot be used in a scientific causal explanation of human behaviour. The golden age of cognitive science will come when – in a way that is reminiscent of the behaviourist doctrine – the objective information of the external world can be mapped onto the neural states of the organism.

In contrast, the central category of cognitive psychology and cognitive social psychology is mental representation. This is a true Cartesian psychology in which the subject faces information coming from the outer world and processes this information in a species-specific way through its individual nervous system. To avoid dualism, most cognitive psychologists advocate a so-called 'token physicalism', which holds that each token of mental states and processes can be mapped onto corresponding tokens of neural states and processes, but individual mental types do not necessarily map onto types of neural processes. In other words, neural processes cannot be directly mapped onto mental representations. However, mental types should be described in a way that the description contains how tokens belonging to a type are materialized. For instance, it is quite common in cognitive psychology to describe mental states in a way that the description can be materialized in computer models (Block 1980).

Table 5.1 Views on representation

Theoretical domain	Assumption about mental representation	Locus of representation	Subject–object relationship
Cognitive neuroscience (Churchland; Pinker; Stich)	No mental representation	Reduction to neuronal processes	Organism–object interaction
Cognitive psychology, cognitive social psychology (Neisser; Forgas)	There is mental representation	Independent mental level	Subject–object interaction
Standard social sciences (Durkheim)	No mental representation	Collective representation	Social facts are independent of individual minds
Social constructivism, discourse analysis (Gergen; Harré)	No mental representation	Socially construed meaning instead of individual minds	There is no subject, only a socially construed meaning
Social representation (SR) (Moscovici)	There is mental representation but only in relation to SR	The social is expressed in individual minds	Mediation between the individual and the social
Scientific narrative psychology (Bruner; László; Ehmann; Péley; Pólya)	There is mental representation but only in relation to narrative structures; representation at the level of experience; patterns of social knowledge and emotions	Culturally valid meanings are represented in individual minds at the level of experience; correspondence between narrative and mental representation	Mediation between the individual and the social

Cognitive social psychologists also postulate separate individual minds that the stimuli of the social world are mapped onto and are in opposition to. In the history of twentieth-century social psychology the importance of distinguishing between objective, 'cultural' reality and subjective representation, and the priority of subjective reality from the point of view of decision-making and action were represented most decisively by social psychologists like Lewin, Asch and Heider, who were committed to the tradition of *Gestalt psychology*. Lewin (1951) describes the *living space* that determines action in terms of the current subjective reality of the individual. Asch (1952) maintains that the evaluation of an object and the

behaviour towards it are preceded by interpretation, the establishment of the subjective meaning of the object.

In sociology a radical step towards separating individual and social forms of
knowledge or representations was taken by Durkheim (1947 [1893]). However
mentalistic the category of *collective representation* may sound, it is the sort of
thing that stands in opposition to individual minds in an objective way from the
outside as an object, and theoretically and methodologically it is aimed at describing and explaining social processes, independent of the working of individual
minds.

The endeavours to explain the control of social behaviour and behaviour based
on knowledge by eliminating the representational assumption and by relying on
the analysis of public and private meaning relations can be interpreted as an answer
partly to Durkheim-like sociological objectivism and partly to psychological individualism and mentalism. Although these trends, often labelled as constructivist,
have several versions, at this point we have to be content with briefly summarizing the views of one of their distinguished representatives, Kenneth Gergen. The
starting point of the social constructivist movement is to question the notion of
knowledge as mental representation. This notion – which, in Gergen's view, gives
rise to several insoluble problems – may be replaced by language use. Language
use is part of social practice. In this view knowledge is not something that people
have in their heads but it is what they do together (Gergen 1985: 122).

According to Gergen the sensory experience of the world in itself does not
define the notions in terms of which we understand the world. The notions of
understanding the world are social products that are created as a result of historically embedded interactions among people. The question as to how long a given
form of understanding prevails or survives depends on social processes and not on
the empirical validity of the given perspective. 'Negotiated-consensual' forms of
understanding have an outstanding importance in social life, as they are crucially
related to nearly all other human activities. The world, especially the social world,
is construed through these negotiated-consensual forms. This construct is realized in language use, in discourse, and therefore the explanation of human action,
or rather, the locus of its explanation – instead of the mind or identified with the
mind – is transferred from the inner regions of the mind to human interactions.

The theory of social representations that is linked to the name of Moscovici
(1976 [1961], 1984) intends to overcome both the passive information-processing view and the unified, closed individuum concept of cognitive psychology,
the rigid separation of individual and social levels and the construction of social
and individual reality that lacks subjects and minds. It is Durkheimian in the
sense that it adopts the relative autonomy of social reality and the guiding force
of human thinking and action. However, it obviously runs counter to Durkheim
when – in accord with Freud, Mead, Piaget or Vygotsky – it assumes that the
construction of reality cannot be made independent of psychological processes.
The ambivalence is nicely reflected by the name of the theory itself, as well as
by placing the theory in the conceptual framework of representation, and even by
replacing the collective attribute by the term social.

At first glance social representations theory is inconsistent with the individual, mental, intersubjective, social objective view of representation. It is social constructivist in that it views representation as the elaboration of a social object rather than as the mental representation of some external reality independent of the subject. At the same time, in its language, and occasionally in its methodology, or even in the questions that it raises, it implies that collective meaning is meaningfully connected to individual mental processes, though it cannot be fully reduced to them. As was put by Pléh (2003b):

> For Durkheimian thinking there is a special interaction between individual and social representations. Individual representations, the thoughts of John Smith, select from and get filled by social representations, but the individual also exists. ... In similar trains of thought, or in other words, for the purpose of explaining the mediated, remotely controlled determination of individual behavior, the theory of social representations came to the foreground again in the seventies, mostly in the works of Serge Moscovici.
>
> (Pléh 2003b: 52–53)

Jovchelovitch (1996: 122) describes this as follows: social representations 'appear in the space of intersubjective reality, although they are expressed in individual minds.' A separate chapter (see Chapter 6) is devoted to social representations theory, since its message comes very close to the view of narrative psychology advocated in this book. The conceptual space of social psychology is articulated by Castro (2003) along the dimensions of individual and social meaning construction and representation as shown in Figure 5.1

Finally, the view of representation in scientific narrative psychology, as has been seen in preceding chapters, starts out by analysing the experience-like nature of mental representations, the function of culturally sharable narratives in organizing experiences and the correspondence between public, sharable narratives and mental representations. *According to this view, narratives and narrative forms are linguistic representations that involve patterns of the individuals' mental constructs of reality (hence patterns of concurrently cognitive and dynamic guiding principles).*

Experience as a representational form

When we run through the psychological literature of the past few decades, we can hardly find the category of experience mentioned in the pages of either bulky volumes of books or in thin journals. It is rather symptomatic that Mérei's only paper that has up to the present day had a resounding international success, 'Collective experience', was published in the journal *Human Relations* and later in by now classical social psychology readers under a title – 'Group leadership and institutionalization' – that evades the notion of experience (Mérei 1949). However, if we go back a little further in history to the turn of the century, we can see that experience as a mental process studied introspectively was a central subject of psychol-

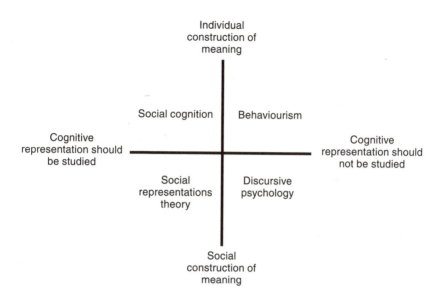

Figure 5.1 The conceptual space of social psychology (following Castro 2003)

ogy, including not only conceptual experience (Wundt and Bühler) but emotional experience too (here reference should be made first of all to William James). Then the ruling psychology of the first half of the twentieth century, behaviourism eliminated experience together with all other mental processes from the list of legitimate psychological phenomena. If for the behaviourists memory and imagination, as Neisser (1976: 14) writes, appeared to be 'too mentalistic, too inessential, and too intangible', it was obvious that they could not do much with a complex and plastic concept like direct experience. The study of experience, especially the description of various types of experience, was left to the representatives of speculative psychology in the framework of moral sciences also cultivated in Hungary between the two world wars (Mátrai 1973; Prohászka 1936).

However, there were a few areas and trends in psychology in which the study of experience-like mental content was not suspended, even though the term *experience* itself – not being a *comme il faut* – was generally replaced by some other words. First of all, it was psychoanalysis that traced the transformation of direct sensory experience governed by the dynamics of instincts in dreams and fantasy images intertwined with intense emotions, etc. In the same way, developmental psychology could not evade the problem of experience either, which is inherently concerned with the transformation of mental content, though from its own developmental perspective. When analysing intellectual development, developmental psychology – whether the works of Piaget, Wallon or Vygotsky are considered – finds itself faced with the problem of duplicating reality and the representation of experience, and proceeds in describing the milestones of development from primary, unstructured, experience-like impression towards increasingly more complex and abstract schemas. Finally, Gestalt psychology and within it the field theory of Lewin also introduce phenomena that can be related to direct experience, when it speaks about a psychological field existing at a given moment. This field may be interpreted as the representation of the entire situation in which the really interesting thing is not perceptual mapping but rather the appearance of the totality of emotional-motivational relations within the situation.

Cognitive psychology, which studies the cognitive processes of adults, did not know how to handle the experience-like nature of human knowledge, despite the fact that the theory of memory proposed by Bartlett (1932), who may be regarded as the forerunner of cognitive psychology, offered a possibility to study experience-like representations. According to Bartlett (1932: 197–198) 'the outstanding characteristics of remembering all follow from a change of attitude towards those masses of organised past experiences and reactions which function in all high-level mental processes', then he describes attitudes as follows:

> The construction that is effected is the sort of construction that would justify the observer's 'attitude'. Attitude names a complex psychological state or process which it is very hard to describe in more elementary psychological terms. It is, however, as I have often indicated, very largely a matter of feeling, or affect. We say that it is characterised by doubt, hesitation, surprise, astonishment, confidence, dislike, repulsion and so on. Here is the significance of the fact, often reported in the preceding pages, that when a subject is being asked to remember, very often the first thing that emerges is something of the nature of attitude. The recall is then a construction, made largely on the basis of this attitude, and its general effect is that of a justification of the attitude.
>
> (Bartlett 1932: 206–207)

Since experiences loaded with emotions did not fit into the study of information structures, the paradigm of information processing, with a few attempts as exceptions (e.g. Brewer and Nakamura 1984) excluded the possibility of studying them. The social and experiential aspects of Bartlett's ideas have been reviewed in a collective memory (Middleton and Brown 2005) or social representational (Jovchelovitch 2006) framework only recently.

An interlude: one more time on literature

It is hardly an accident that it was scholars interested in literary text analysis that were the first to return to the category of experience in cognitive psychology. When reading literature, recipients do not read because they want to get some information, but in the strict sense of the word they want to obtain some experience that may at best have some long-term indirect cognitive functions but even these functions serve the purpose of self-knowledge. Our own studies in the psychology of literature have presented several pieces of empirical evidence that when people read a literary text with the intention to understand (which they are pressed to do by the text itself, in addition to contextual signals: László 1987), experience-like elements emerge in the course of processing the text. They form a mental image of literary heroes and situations (László 1990). They mobilize their own personal experiences, and the phenomenal quality, the vividness and intensity of these experiences are closely related to the narrative perspective (Larsen and László 1990). Interestingly enough, the distinction between emotions ensuring *fast* evaluation connected to actions and *slow* emotional processes connected in their function to self-knowledge that create a personal relationship with the events also appeared in literary analyses in the cognitive research on emotions (Cupchik 2004). Our own investigations show that the reception of action-oriented and experience-oriented narratives can be characterized by different emotional patterns, and accordingly, by different temporal patterns. While the former are characterized by excitement, curiosity or surprise, the latter are typically characterized by emotions that concern empathy or identification. The reading pace of the two types is also different: people read action-oriented stories much faster (Cupchik and László 1994; László and Cupchik 1995). All in all, the experiments supported the hypothesis that conceptual automatisms get decomposed during reading literature. The processing of literary texts is subjectivized processing in which readers relate to the text in the most personal way possible and in an experience-like fashion.

Returning to the forms of representing experience

For the study of duplicating reality and representation as psychological meaning we have to go beyond cognitive psychology, that is, theories which study cognitive processes in and by themselves independent of emotional experiences and social relations and analyse, at best, the interaction of cognition and emotions or cognition and social relations. In this enterprise we will be assisted by Ferenc Mérei's *theory of allusion* (1984). Without questioning the importance of the establishment of conceptual schemas, Mérei clearly sees that the semantic relationship between the signifier and the signified, event and representation is not a simple duplication, but a *state of equilibrium* created through a long intra-mental process; it is the experience of an event, a situation that is articulated, compressed, simplified and at the same time enriched, coloured, added to, subtracted from and shaped in many ways. A lot of things get lost and a lot of things are retained through the chain of transformations and replacements.

> The intra-mental units are duplications because another unit is created as the duplication of the experience unit (from a situation or action a view is created, from a view an inner image of the view, etc.), and they are transmissions because the components of the original unit (tension, substantive or formal aspects) are transmitted to the new unit created through duplication. The essence of transmission is that duplication is at the same time real replacement: the intra-mental process is not interrupted.
>
> (Mérei 1989: 264)

The new unit is the replacement or representation of what it has duplicated. In the representation of behavioural situations there is still a chance to re-experience the emotions and social tensions connected to the event even after conceptual thinking emerges. Later, in Chapter 7, when analysing Stern's (1989) theory of self-development, we will see that the early experiences of infants concerning interactions with the mother or the caretaker, which lay the foundations of its self, although they get lost for conscious reflection after language appears, continue to live as early forms of organization 'under' the control of a verbally expressible and narratively organized self. What is more, they even exert their influence in the representation of newly experienced situations, thus in narratives about the self. From another aspect, narrative is a way of re-experiencing, or at least an opportunity to do so, as has been suggested by Bruner and Lucariello (1989); situational action, thinking and emotions appear in unity in narrative, but this form also offers a possibility to reflect on each of them with a different emphasis in the narrative framework. It is precisely these two aspects that make it possible to analyse narratives about the self from the point of view of the organization of experience and identity, but the same aspects are the sources of difficulties that we have to face when analysing narratives about the self in a scientific way.

Allusion

By allusion Mérei (1984) introduced a form of representing experience that serves, as it were, as an example for the study of psychological meanings or patterns of experience. This is why it is worth taking a closer look at it. A special way of re-experiencing is the creation of tradition in a group. Tradition is created through repetitions. Original, spontaneous events, or better to say, their fragments are repeated by their experiencers and moulded into a permanent shape. However, the psychological background of repetitions is different in each case. In contrast to later repetitions, which signal a ritualized sense of belonging together, the first repetitions of the fragments of spontaneous events recall the full content of the original experience together with its emotional tensions in those who experience it. Tradition expresses the sense of belonging together and the accumulation of collective experience in a ritualized form, but any concrete detail representing the entire experience signals a concrete collective experience. Thus, collective experience is a special form of sign emerging in the group; it is a *secondary meaning* that recalls the entire experience in its full emotional richness. This special representational form was named *allusion* by Mérei (1984) and was rightly considered by him to be the mother tongue of social figures.

In allusion as a communicative form and in the underlying representational mechanism Mérei (1984) not only discovered a special developmental milestone of organizing experience and the mental duplication of reality but also demonstrated the different versions of allusion in intimate communities of shared experience and in the arts.

The processing of experience through allusion is based on the fate of a special group of experienced events. Some of the experiences that are driven to the edge of the mind, as has been explored by Freud, fall prey to defence and sink into the unconscious through suppression. Others gradually become void of excitement, get sketchy and emotionally dry as new experiences begin to shine. This is the process of schematization so finely described by Piaget and Walton. However, there is a third possibility, which is quite common in nursery-school age when the mechanisms of defence do not yet work perfectly. An experience captured close to the mind may be able to keep the lively totality of reality and its emotional tension for a while. If a concrete fragment gets separated from this 'heated' experience 'still pulsing with a sense of reality' and springs back to mind, it can represent the full emotional tension of the original experience. This fragment returning to the mind is what Mérei (1984) calls allusion. The concept of allusion bears witness to a productive encounter of Freudian and Wallonian ideas. Topology (mind, unconscious, edge of the mind) comes from Freud. However, the dynamics is not the consequence of an intensive process whereby the experience unit conquers the libido, as assumed by Freud concerning part for whole relationships, but rather, it is fundamentally of a social origin, in the sense of Wallon, and feeds on the emotional tensions experienced together with partners. The conceptual germs of the presumed mechanism, allusion as a signal process, also spring from Wallonian ideas. Allusion represents a special branch in the series of five meaning relations (signal, proof, simulacrum, symbol and conventional sign) that replace a real experience or action increasingly more indirectly and economically in that the recalling fragment working as a signal not only replaces the recalled situation in a cognitive sense but also retrieves its almost full emotional spectrum. In fact, it contains additional emotional meaning for all those who have experienced the situation collectively.

The most frequent version of allusion is the spontaneous substitution of direct experience. The spontaneous repetition of one fragment of a social event of the previous day, or any other harmonizing situational moment, as a signal retrieves the emotions and moods associated with the original experience for the person who repeats it and for all the partners. Later the allusion becomes an intentional triggering signal whereby the collective experience may unfold again and again. Finally, after several repetitions the experience action becomes simplified, and the emotional content of the original experience unites with the joy of repeating. At this point allusion becomes a tradition signal. As an example for this process, let us now take a look at what Mérei observed in a nursery.

Several children are playing under a large table in a nursery. They are packing things here and there and fiddling with them. One boy is sitting on the table pushing a watering can about. Another boy passing by asks him for the can. 'I won't give it to you' – the boy says – 'I need it. I am playing firefighter.' At this point three small boys come out from under the table and one of them says, 'I am also a firefighter', and they immediately begin to push the table. This is the fire-engine. A bigger boy, who has till now been playing with some cubes, jumps up on the table and says he is the driver. At his request the fire-engine is pushed to the toy shelf and they begin putting out the fire in the burning house.

The game lasts for a relatively long time (some ten minutes). Several children participate in it; they jump around, make a lot of noise and are very passionate.

Two days later, during the half hour reserved for free play one girl stops by the toy shelf and cries out: 'My God! I am getting burned!' According to the reconstruction of the events, this is what was said in the game but not exactly in the same form. A bigger girl has just put her dolls to sleep next to the burning house of the firefighter game and now she cries out: 'My God! These kids are going to get burned!' This is the element that another girl revived 48 hours later, and as soon as she had uttered it, all the other children started shouting: 'Fire!' and they did not waste any time in pushing the fire-engine there, the watering can was found in no time too, and in a matter of a few moments the firefighter game was in full progress again with a lot of enthusiasm.

Later it was observed several times again that the fragment 'My God, I am going to get burned' or the fragment 'getting burned' triggered the entire game together with all of its excitement, richness and whirling. The duration of the game revived this way changed from time to time, sometimes it lasted only for four or five minutes, but occasionally it served as a one-minute insert in another game.

The frightened versions of the exclamation 'getting burned' played the role of a *triggering signal* for the nursery group that started the collective play of the game. The game repeated this way had become a habitual game and emerged independently or as a fragment of another game in the activity of the group as a *tradition signal*.

In adulthood allusion emerges in intimate communities and between partners who are accomplices. Communication apparently takes place with the help of conventional signs that are understandable for everybody, but these signs carry fragments of experience as underlying content for those in the know, whose essence is the ability to recall the entire collective experience. Phenomena of allusion may appear in the unconscious too; it can be demonstrated, for example, that in the case of certain slips of the tongue the problem is not directly caused by an unconscious desire; but rather, there is a similar experience close to the mind whose concrete fragment of full value is pulled out and mistakenly inserted in the statement by the speaker.

The formulation and return of experience in narratives

We have seen that in situations involving actions the narrative mode is the mental tool of creating sense, constructing meaning in the sense that it creates the conditions of a rational world and rational adaptation. However, narrative has another ability plentifully utilized in literature; namely, the ability to carry, shape and rewrite the experience content of significant interpersonal interactions – and here early interactions that determine the development of personality are also included – as well as of collective events. It is in the experience-like representational forms of these one-time or repeated events involving actions that the layer of the self, which is narratively organized in a natural way, comes into being and fills up rational action plans with emotions and motivations in the relationship of the self with the world. The extent to which an event evokes anxiety, drives somebody to despair, raises responsibility, paralyses, frees or fills a person with enthusiasm, or urges somebody to intervene depends on how organized the self is and what experience representation of collective experiences is involved in it, and conversely, we take action in an event to the extent that we are anxious about it, it fills us with despair, we feel responsible for it, it paralyses us, it fills us with enthusiasm, it liberates us, it urges us to intervene, it prompts us to show solidarity, etc. These qualities of the self are carried by narrative. They can be unfolded from self-narratives, especially from self-narratives about significant or traumatic events of life, just like the qualities of group identity can be unravelled by telling significant events of group history. In Chapter 9 we will see that the goal of narrative analysis is not to achieve a total mapping between an event and an experience but rather to unfold event representation as a form of experience representation for individual and group identity and for the behavioural tendencies that result from them.

Dissemination of representations

Experiential character of narrative representations certainly delimits validity of one of the most popular contemporary theories of cultural evolution. Sperber (1985, 1990) seeks answer in his epidemiological theory to the questions how social and individual can be integrated in representation. In his discussion of representations, Sperber (1990, 1996) takes a strong materialist stance. He acknowledges mental representations of the world as material objects, because they are carried by the nervous system. He also accepts public representations as material objects, because these representations are embodied in sound and light waves. However, he refuses to accept entities such as cultural representations as material, although it is claimed to be a material object in the Standard Social Sciences Model. Instead of resigning himself to ontological pluralism, Sperber (1990) offers the following solution:

> The materialist alternative is to assume that both mental and public representations are strictly material objects and to take the implications of this assumption seriously. Cognitive systems such as brains construct internal representations of their environment partly on the basis of law-governed physical interactions with that environment. Because of these interactions, mental representations are, to some extent, regularly connected to what they represent, and, as a result, they have semantic properties or 'meaning' of their own. ... Public representations, on the other hand, are connected to what they represent only through the meaning attributed to them by their producers or their users; they have no semantic properties of their own. In other terms, public representations have meaning only through being associated with mental representations.
>
> (Sperber 1990: 27)

Sperber does not exclude interpretation from possible explanations of cultural and social phenomena. He insists, however, that theoretical hypotheses can only be built on causal explanations. This is why he abandons cultural holism, and focuses on the spreading of material representations in an epidemiological framework.

When we talk of cultural representations – beliefs in witches, rules for the service of wines, the common law, or Marxist ideology – we refer to representations, which are widely shared in a human group. To explain cultural representations, then, is to explain why some representations are widely shared. Since representations are more or less widely shared, there is no neat boundary between cultural and individual representations. An explanation of cultural representations, therefore, should come as part of a general explanation of the distribution of representations among humans, as part, that is, of an *epidemiology of representations*.

(Sperber 1990: 29, italics in original)

In the elaboration of the epidemiology of representations, Sperber drew a lot from the results he had achieved in cognitive pragmatics. Sperber and Wilson (1986) broke away from a code-like concept of language and worked out a model that placed emphasis on reasoning processes. This model treats the Wittgensteinian family resemblance problem at the level of representations, that is the fact that there is generally a larger or smaller degree of similarity in human communication between the thoughts of the communicator and the addressees, and full correspondence is the exception rather than the norm. As compared to earlier epidemiological approaches (e.g. Cavalli-Sforza and Feldman 1981; Dawkins 1976, 1982; Tarde 1895), which took the basic process of cultural transmission to be one of replication (i.e., mutation is an accident and replication is the norm), Sperber points to the pivotal role of communication, and the regular transformation of representation in communication. Given that representations are necessarily transformed in communication between sender and recipient, Sperber (1985, 1990) claims that only those representations will end up belonging to the culture, which *are repeatedly communicated* and *minimally transformed* in the process of communication.

It is easy to see that these ideas can be fertile effects from the point of view of narrative psychology. On the one hand, with respect to the a priori nature of cultural or social meanings for everybody and their subjective construction, they formulate as a sensible question the process in which despite individual differences valid cultural representations are established, survive and decline in a given group. On the other hand, it directs attention to psychological and socio-cultural factors that are in a causal relationship with the evolution of representational patterns.

Sperber represents the view that it is impossible to calculate in advance what factors will play a role in the explanation of a particular representational pattern. He classifies the potential factors into psychological and environmental (ecological) types. The former include, among others, the memorizablility of representations, the amount of background knowledge from the point of view of which the representation is relevant, or the motivation to communicate the content of the representation. The ecological factors include the frequency of occurrence of situations in which the appearance of a representation evokes corresponding actions, or the accessibility of external memory stores, such as the accessibility of writing, or the existence of institutions specialized for the transmission of representations.

The epidemiological metaphor defines the relationship between the nature and patterns of representations and their processes of evolution and gaining ground in a relatively precise fashion. In classical epidemiology the recognition of an epidemiological phenomenon is assisted by the study of individual pathology. The same is also true in the contrary direction: epidemiology often contributes to the recognition of particular diseases. Similarly, if particular types or patterns of mental representations are recognized at the psychological level, it helps understand how they are spread, and conversely; once representational patterns are identified epidemiologically, it may contribute to the understanding of their psychological nature. Just like the relationship between pathology and epidemiology, psychology and the epidemiology of representations are mutually relevant for each other.

Whereas Moscovici focuses on the typology of relations between dissemination and communicative processes, Sperber treats communication as implicit, and concentrates rather on the particular forms of representation, on the driving forces that motivate spreading, and on cognitive and ecological factors, as Table 5.2 suggests.

So as to remain a widespread representation in a non-literate community, a myth needs to be easy to memorize, that is well organized and attractive (cognitive factors). It should be believed as true, and the authority of the elders should make the rest of people accept this truth. The recurrence of the occasions where the myth is being told belongs to ecological factors.

An ideological belief, such as 'all men are born equal', is simple and easy to remember. Its fate depends not so much on cognitive factors, but on its relevance to people and on the institutional environment (ecological factors). A complex scientific theory poses a heavy cognitive load even on experts. It is accepted and disseminated in the scientific community, if it proves to be true.

However, the extent to which such views can gain ground depends on ecological factors. The truth of views is guaranteed by the authority of the scientific community and transmission by the institutions of communication. Thus, scientific views

Table 5.2 Strength of cognitive and ecological factors affecting dissemination of knowledge

Type of knowledge	Driving force of spreading	Cognitive factors	Ecological factors
Religious myth	Authority of the elders	Strong	Weak
Political ideology	Relevance in people's lives	Weak	Strong
Scientific theory	Credibility of the scientific community	Strong	Strong

are accepted by players of the scientific community and everyday people on an entirely different basis and due to transmission scientific knowledge is transformed and simplified to a significant extent in everyday knowledge. This is exactly what Moscovici's research on the reception of psychoanalysis in everyday thinking in France sheds light on, as we will see in Chapter 6.

While social representations theory intends to articulate both cognitive factors (the content and structure of representational patterns) and ecological factors (the media of transmission, social institutions), the epidemiological theory of the spreading of representations focuses on the motivation for or explanation of the spreading of representational patterns by means of cognitive and ecological factors. One important strong point of the epidemiological theory with respect to social representations theory is that by capturing the problem of causing in terms of how representations spread and survive it essentially resolves the relationship between representation and intentional action that is unsolved in social representations theory. However, social representations theory can say a lot more as to how representations are constructed and transmitted. Pléh (2003b) is right in saying that what we have here are theoretical possibilities that complement rather then exclude each other.

Narrative spreading

What is involved here is that while Sperber relates the spreading of representations to a biologically grounded rationality, to increasing an individual's chance to survive, he derives the rationality of the cultural diversity of reflexive beliefs from the authentication of the given beliefs by the source. However, at this point we immediately have to face inevitable questions concerning the relationship between individual and group identity and representational patterns.

Sperber's hypothesis is most likely true for intuitive, that is, directly experienced or simply deduced beliefs, but it does not seem to be a satisfactory explanation for taking over reflexive beliefs, that is, beliefs with large cultural or across-group differences that are communicated by others, so Sperber refines it with respect to reflexive beliefs:

> when social subjects construct and organise their representational fields, they do so in order to make sense of reality, to appropriate and interpret it. In doing so, they state *who* they are, how they understand both themselves and others, where they locate themselves and others, and which are the cognitive and affective resources that are available to them in a given historical time. Social representations, therefore, tell us about *who* is doing the representational work. This can be fully appreciated if we consider the trade-offs between representational work and identificatory work. The complex interactions between self and other are the basis of both phenomena. There is no possibility of identity without the work of representation, just as there is no work of representation without an identificatory boundary between the me and the not-me. It is in the overlapping space of the me and the not-me that both representations and identities emerge. Furthermore, social representa-

tions are a network of mediating social meanings which lends texture and material to the construction of identities.

(Jovchelovitch 1996: 125)

From the above quotation it appears as if Sperber placed the spreading of reflexive beliefs in the framework of a social learning theory inspired by behaviourism. This is so because Sperber disregards the condition that representations, or at least all reflexive beliefs have, in addition to an aspect that refers to the world, an aspect that is related to group affiliation or group identity. This aspect roughly means that I cope with the world together with people who are important for me, or that I gain my own group identity partly from this group by the very fact that we have common representations. This problem is excellently illuminated by Assmann's (1992) work on cultural memory. As in the preceding paragraphs we have demonstrated the same connection with respect to the representation of experience. At the same time there is nothing wrong with considering identity as part of rationality, even though we often run into views or actions concerning the maintenance of identity that appear to be spectacularly irrational; moreover, we sometimes describe even the self – as is done by modern theories of self-development – in a concrete case in terms of the representation of experience. In any case, *it is practicable to consider identity functions as an independent group* among the factors that have an impact on the spreading of representations. These factors, though related to both cognitive and ecological factors, can have a relatively independent influence on the spreading of representations. In this area, that is, in the exploration of the relationship between the spreading of representational patterns and identity, representatives of social representations theory and researchers of cultural memory have already produced some significant results.

If identity is regarded partly as personal self-identity, continuity and detachment from others and partly as a sense and awareness of identity with social partners – with significant other selves and groups – and these two aspects of identity, *personal identity and social identity*, are given ample emphasis, then it is easy to see that the representational processes of the group are also significant for group identity, and as a result, for the personal identity of group members. The social representations created in the group and maintained collectively by group members contribute to the establishment of group identity. Sharing the representations of a group becomes, as it were, the symbol of group membership and provides the basis for understanding why group members should follow the group's goals. This idea has been formulated in the most general way by Moscovici and Hewstone (1983), who believe that the social representations established and maintained by a particular group contribute to group identity even by the fact that the common 'world view' manifest in collective representations reinforces the experience of collective identity.

Social representations have another function in connection with group identity, and thus with the individual's social identity; namely, the function they fulfil in identifying the symbolic boundaries of a group. The boundaries of a particular group are drawn where the boundaries of collectively organized representational fields lie. (For more on this see Chapter 6.) Similar arguments are used by Assmann (1992) when he sheds light on the role of cultural memory in ethnogenesis.

Thus, the rationality of the spreading of reflexive beliefs bound to the authority of partners must be embedded in the rationality of the elaboration and maintenance of personal and group identity, which means that the social-psychological aspects of identity functions should also be considered in the study of the relationship between representational patterns and patterns and conditions of spreading. For example, Assmann (1992) derives the birth of the state in Egypt, of religion in Israel and science in Greece from this aspect of cultural memory. This view still does not question the materialism and methodological individualism proposed by Sperber, since Assmann (1992: 130) also accepts the view that in the last analysis 'Collective self-identity is a matter of individual knowledge and consciousness.'

From this point of view too, and not only from the aspect of economic efficiency insisted on by Sperber, narrative has a distinguished role. On the one hand it is indeed true that narrative organizes knowledge in an economic way. When discussing myth, Sperber's analysis also draws attention to the significance of narrative as a strong representational form maintaining knowledge, and scholars of memory research like Binet (Binet and Henri 1894) or Bartlett (1932) came to the same conclusion too. The maintenance and transmission of narrative representations is assisted by variation, first studied by Bartlett (1932), which is typical in the transmission of narrative. More recent research (Rubin 1995) confirms Sperber's hypothesis that the spreading of representations follows the principle of selection rather than of replication, and multiple variations functions as a factor of increasing stability. On the other hand, as is demonstrated precisely by genesis myths, it is narrative that carries the cultural memories loaded with emotions which are necessary for maintaining group identity.

Representatives of social representations theory generally envision the cognitive organization of representation as a 'conglomerate' of heterogeneous cognitive elements – images, beliefs, naive theories, attitudes, etc. – making up some sort of categorial knowledge. Jovchelovitch (1996), Flick (1995), László (1997) and others have shown that knowledge concerning social life is organized by the logic of narrative and communicated in stories. If this is so, then in addition to cognitive figures these stories also involve emotive-impulsive contents, that is, experience-like representations which are related to the dynamics of a group and the maintenance of group identity.

Summary

This chapter discussed relations of major psychological theoretical schools with the notion of representation. It introduced the concept of narrative representation, which is organized according to narrative principles, holistic, and has the capacity to include the richness of contextual and experiential elements. It was shown that the narrative mode not only is the mental tool for creating sense, constructing meaning in the sense that it creates the conditions of a rational world and rational adaptation, but also has the ability to carry, shape and rewrite the experiential content of significant interpersonal interactions. We claimed that narratively organized and represented life episodes make up the self of individuals, just as narratives of significant group episodes form group identity. We argued that the goal of narrative analysis is not to achieve a total mapping between an event and an experience but rather to unfold event representation as a form of experience representation for individual and group identity and for the behavioural tendencies that result from them.

6 Theory of social representations

Serge Moscovici first published his monograph *La Psychoanalyse, son image et son public* in 1961, in which he outlined the conceptual framework of social representations theory in relation to the analysis of the reception of French psychoanalysis. The large-scale empirical study intended to capture the process in which *the scientific theory of psychoanalysis* had become part of *everyday thinking and knowledge*. The study consisted of two parts. In the first part a survey using a questionnaire was conducted with 200 subjects. The survey covered a representative sample of Parisians but special sub-samples for age, social status or lifestyle were analysed separately. The groups were compared according to their knowledge about psychoanalysis and their attitude towards psychoanalysis. The analysis revealed that middle-class subjects had significantly more information about psychoanalysis than working-class people, and there were considerable differences among the groups in terms of the age variable too. In the case of most groups a positive or negative attitude towards psychoanalysis was correlated with the amount of knowledge about psychoanalysis.

The analysis also revealed that by the 1950s psychoanalysis had penetrated the mind of the French society to a considerable extent, but the results also showed that reception had not covered the entire theory but only particular aspects of it. Certain notions, like the unconscious, suppression or complexes, had become part of public thinking and parlance, while other, equally important concepts of the theory, like libido or sexuality, were largely neglected. Moscovici (1976: 116) used the term *figurative core* for the mutually related basic notions around which knowledge about the subject was crystallized. In the case of psychoanalysis the figurative core was constituted by the suppressive mechanism that connected two layers of consciousness, the unconscious and the mind. Moscovici attributed a dual function to the figurative core. On the one hand, it constitutes the centre of the cognitive organization of representation and discourse about the subject. On the other hand, it symbolically concretizes the abstract notions of thinking and discourse. In the case of psychoanalysis the layers of the conscious and the unconscious, the hydraulic principle of suppression associates concrete concepts with abstract notions like mind or soul.

In the second part of the study 1,600 articles from 210 newspapers published between 1952 and 1956, half of them published in the capital and the other half in the country, were analysed using the method of content analysis to describe special types of mediation in the mass media. Popular papers with a wide circulation are characterized by a communication feature called *diffusion*. These papers adapt to the interest of readers and aspire to pass on knowledge gained from specialists and create some sort of collective knowledge. *Propagation*, which has been found to be characteristic of religious press, places new knowledge in an established system of a well-organized world view. It tries to match the notions and procedures of psychoanalytic knowledge with those of religion, thus analysis itself is interpreted as a metaphor of confession. In contrast to the former, Marxist press is characterized by *propaganda*. Here communication is embedded in advance in social relations of conflict and reflects an antagonistic viewpoint. The goal is to separate true and false views and to stress the incompatibility between the views of the source and mystified analytic views.

Moscovici demonstrated that each communicative feature was characterized by a typical cognitive organization of the messages. *Diffusion* is characterized by alternating a weak integration of topics, the representation of conflicting positions, seriousness, reservation and irony. *Propagation* stresses the conformity of the theory with religion, for example the need to get a comprehensive understanding of humans, symbolism or spiritualism, but rejects libido as a general explanatory principle. *Propaganda* rejects psychoanalysis as a rival ideology. The adaptation of global ideological schemas, such as the American–Soviet Cold War opposition, loads the exposition with factual mistakes, for example the view that psychoanalysis is Americanized.

Thus, social representations theory originally intended to study the process in which *a scientific theory – Freudian psychoanalysis – becomes part of common sense*; through various channels of social communication abstract notions of experts largely unknown to the public become meaningful tools for the interpretation of everyday behaviour and for creating behavioural plans. The category of social representation itself fits well into the Durkheimian system, being, as it were, an intermediate representational form between *collective* and *individual* representations. Durkheim (1947 [1893]) saw collective representations embodied in language, institutions and habits. He regarded these objectivations, described by him as independent of individual consciousness, as the essence of social operation and the subject matter of sociology. He saw an explanatory principle in collective representations which itself is sufficient to shed light on the operation of society; that is – similarly to the atom notion of classical physics or the gene notion of genetics – it cannot be subjected to further analysis. At the same time Durkheim designated an independent domain for social psychology in the system of social sciences, and it happened to be the study of the structure and dynamics of representations. Moscovici (1984) justifies the introduction of the category of social representations in addition to the study of formal-structural and substantive features of communicative mediation by arguing that in modern, articulated societies the collective representations described by Durkheim, like science or religion, no longer covered the life of the entire community. Each social subgroup establishes special representational forms in relation to various cultural objects, and the study of these forms is the task of social representations research. Social representations are sets of concepts originating from everyday life and explanations emerging from communication among individuals. In modern society they are equivalent to the myths or belief systems of traditional societies; they might as well be seen as the modern versions of common sense. In modern information society the direction of communication between common sense and the sciences has changed. While in previous centuries science was based on common sense, though isolated from everyday knowledge, nowadays we witness not only an explosion-like expansion of sciences but also the reflow of scientific information and knowledge to everyday knowledge. The representations of the world created in common sense, however, provide knowledge that can be accessed and used more directly than scientific knowledge. Social communication and everyday thinking transforms scientific knowledge into naive theories that can be used by common sense. This kind of social communication rewrites not only scientific theories and knowledge but also all the new phenomena of the world, or phenomena that have again become timely, creating social representations of these phenomena that can then be used by the community.

The psychoanalysis study distinguished three types of communication system or mode, and each of them was characterized by a special cognitive organization. It is not mere analogy when Moscovici (1976) draws a parallel between diffusion and opinion, propagation and attitude, and propaganda and stereotype. The parallel shows that when it comes to thinking and/or communication, there are always two cognitive systems at work. One of them works with associations, discriminations, inferences, etc., while the other uses symbolic rules to select, verify and certify as to whether the former are rational and logical or not. The rules of the social metasystem are related to well-defined positions of social relations, and the organizational rules of these metasystems change with the positions. For instance, in the psychoanalysis study the rule system related to the position of the Catholic press operated a representational mode characterized by propagation. Using another example, the rule system governing cognition prescribes a different mode of thinking and communication, that is, a different mode of representation in the case of scientific research – the strict use of logical principles – as in other cases, when for example the cohesion of a group loaded with conflict should be maintained. In the latter case the operations of thinking and communication are governed by special normative rules which result in stereotyping the own group positively and the other group negatively through the selection and distortion of information (Table 6.1).

Table 6.1 Types of mediating and representing psychoanalysis

Medium	Mode	Cognitive organization
Educational paper	Diffusion	Opinion, knowledge
Religious paper	Propagation	Attitude
Marxist paper	Propaganda	Stereotype

Source: following Moscovici 1976 [1961]

The distinction between opinions, attitudes and stereotypes thus has significant consequences for the nature of social representation. First and foremost, it expresses that social representation is not a tacitly agreed belief of a smaller or larger group of people – at best stereotypes can be regarded as such – and the description of pure cognitive content and its organizational forms do not exhaust the research of social representations. The content and structure of phenomena identified as opinion, attitude or stereotype in individual cognitive systems and their governing principles, validity and rationality are given by symbolic rules – a sort of socio-cognitive metasystem – and the organizing principles of this socio-cognitive metasystem are differentiated along different social positions. Thus, research into social representations is aimed at *the relationship between the dynamics of symbolic relations and individual cognitive organization* (Doise et al. 1992).

The functions of social representations

Social representations theory is a markedly constructivist theory, as *for cultures, groups and individuals, social reality is represented by social representations.* Thus, the construction of social reality is the key function of social representations. This construction takes place in processes of communication and social interaction: previously unknown, meaningless actions, objects, events or concepts turn into meaningful representations for the group in the communication among group members and become part of the social reality of the group (for a comprehensive review see Wagner and Hayes 2005).

The psychoanalysis analysed in Moscovici's study (1976 [1961]) contradicted several aspects of the social representation of contemporary medical science and medical treatment. A psychoanalyst physician does not do any physical examination and does not prescribe any medication, but he simply talks with the patient, who has to take an active part in the treatment, etc. Therefore, psychoanalysis was an unknown and in many ways troublesome activity for the different groups of society. Moscovici's analyses showed how different groups of society 'made' this 'troublesome' activity 'familiar' for themselves.

This sort of analysis is reminiscent of Piaget's ideas concerning assimilation to schemas or accommodation to schemas or Bartlett's (1932) explanation for the function of schemas in constructing meaning, but it also points out several differences. One such difference is why social representation cannot be regarded as a social schema in the sense of cognitive psychology. While in cognitive psychology schema as a representational form, together with its autonomous organizing principles, is the most important category of individual cognitive operation, social representation transfers emphasis from individual cognitive schemas to a form of representation that is realized in social communication and connected to symbolic relations of society. However, this does not necessarily mean that a 'group mind' floating above individuals should be posited. However consensual and conventional social representations are and however regularly they can function for a given group, social representations theory takes them to be the achievement of individual minds realized in communication. At the same time, research on social representations does not intend to explore universal individual cognitive modes and individual behavioural patterns based on them. Quite the contrary, it attempts to explain the behaviour of individuals on the basis of social representations maintained in their groups.

Social representations theory is also interested in the conditions which trigger a representational process in a group, and sheds light on the possibility of the evolution of competing representations within a group.

The process in which representation is formed is called *thematization* by Moscovici and Vignaux (2000). Thematization is underlain by the routines of common sense, which represents the world in terms of dichotomic categories or antinomies. Such antinomies include, for instance, 'us and them', 'edible and uneatable', 'free and oppressed' or 'human and animal'. These antinomies and the cultural consensus in categories organize common sense and social life without having to make any special effort to clarify them. However, there are events regularly taking place in a group and in the environment that impacts the group, which raise doubts about the routinely accepted and used categories. The threat by an unknown, novel phenomenon triggers thematization, as has been seen in the case of talk about safe and unsafe sex when AIDS appeared, or about edible and uneatable things when gene-manipulated food products appeared.

Each antinomy may be thematized again in a given group. There is no rule as to what general antinomies can be thematized. Markova (2003: 187) uses the Scottish national banner (blue background and white St Andrew cross) as an example to show how hot a debate can emerge about the categories of 'blue and not blue' once the colour has some symbolic significance within a group. For centuries now Scottish law has not stipulated what shade of blue the national banner should have. Any shade of blue has been acceptable. It had never been a problem until a group of nationalist Scottish MPs submitted a motion to the Scottish parliament to define the shade of blue of the national banner; after all, it is a disgrace that any shade of blue, from the colour of a duck's egg to navy-blue, is allowed. Although a good majority of members stuck to tradition and refused to stipulate a particular shade of blue, the example illustrates well that minimal categorial differences may give rise to a new theme if group dynamics triggers thematization.

The example also demonstrates that the content and scope of antinomic categories are not necessarily identical for every member of a given group. Moscovici (1988) distinguishes *polemic* (competing social representations of different social groups), *emancipated* (social representations that fit on the basis of a few criteria) and *hegemonic representations* (unified social representations widely accepted in a society). The coexistence of different forms of representation and the tolerance towards the representations of minorities may be a good indicator of the state of a social group and its ability to develop.

The processes of social representations 1: anchoring

The two basic processes of social representations, *anchoring* and *objectification* (objectified mapping) have a typically 'dual character' and refer both to individual minds and to the culture of a group. According to Moscovici (1984: 29) the process *and* mechanism of anchoring (the double nature of the terminology indicates that it refers to events taking place both in the communication of social groups and in the minds of group members) ensure that we can fit unknown, troublesome concepts into the context of familiar categories and concepts. Anchoring reduces fear caused by unknown phenomena by offering familiar categorizations and names to cope with them. It is anchoring that makes it possible to integrate a represented object into an already existing system of ideas (Jodelet 1984: 371). The process of anchoring consists of two inseparable procedures, *classification* and *naming*. In the course of classification an unknown thing is compared to the prototypes of a given category. This can be done in two different ways. In case we want to emphasize the similarity of the thing to be represented to a given category, we disregard the differences from the prototype of the category and reduce these differences; in other words, we *generalize*. However, when we wish to stress the peculiarity, the abnormality of the thing, we highlight its difference from the existing prototypes: we *particularize*. Whether we use one or the other procedure depends not only on the actual similarity between the thing and the prototypes of an existing category but also on the goals of the group and its values associated with the thing in question and its social representation (Purkhardt 1993).

Classification necessarily entails *naming*. A name is not a pure label that is used to identify a named object; it defines the relationship of a represented thing to other things and events by means of its place in the system of linguistic categories. A named thing can be described by and equipped with properties that conform to the relationship between the name and other words. The named thing becomes separated from other things through the properties that are captured by naming. Finally, naming ensures that the representation can be communicated in a given linguistic group, for the thing becomes conventional for all those who use the same name or convention (Moscovici 1984).

The processes of social representations 2: objectification

The process of objectification turns abstract concepts into familiar, concrete experiences and 'materializes' them, as it were. The way this transformation takes place is that some sort of a vague concept or the iconic symbol of an object is associated with the concept, which then turns into an image. Next, the concepts turned into images, symbols and concrete experiences are integrated into a figurative core, in other words, into a complex of images that symbolizes a certain complex of ideas (Moscovici 1984: 28–43). This is how something thought of becomes perceived, 'the invisible becomes visible' (Farr 1984: 386).

Contrary to anchoring, the process of objectification does not cover every concept. Objectification appears only in the case of concepts that can be used to create a figurative core. The process of objectification is well illustrated by Moscovici's psychoanalysis study. On the way from an abstract scientific concept to common sense, the abstract concept of the conscious and the unconscious gets filled with the physical images of the body: through objectification, mental processes turn into mental 'organs', layers under and over one another that are connected by well-known processes of hydraulics, such as suppression. This way the abstract concepts of consciousness or the mind gain a fairly concrete form.

Objectification may take place not only through images but also by means of object symbols, as shown by the process in which the condom has become the figurative core of the social representation of AIDS: all the procedures that can ensure protection for the individual or are meant to introduce social control over the propagation of AIDS are related to the condom.

The figurative core plays an important role both in a cognitive (storage) and a discursive (use in communication) sense. It is constantly thematized in talk about the given phenomenon and can always be referred to. Last but not least, the images and object symbols, etc. condensed in the figurative core represent the reality of everyday life. They offer concrete ideas for the interpretation of abstract, verbal concepts and for dealing with the phenomena they represent.

The relationship of social representations theory with traditional theories of social psychology

From the very beginning researchers interested in social representations have put special emphasis on separating this trend from the tradition of cognitive social psychology. Obviously, social representational research could not be distinguished from research in cognitive social psychology by saying that the former, in contrast to the latter, views the mental representation of objective social reality as the decisive factor of social behaviour, since social psychology 'always considered the subjective properties of social stimuli and inspiration more important than their physical and objective counterparts in the study of social behaviour' (Zajonc 1969: 320). The idea of cognitive organization or cognitive structure is also common to both trends. As for the functional approach, no significant difference can be found in this respect either. Moscovici (1973) attributes a dual function to social representation. On the one hand, social representations create the order that enables individuals to find their way in their material and social world. On the other, they make communication possible among members of a community by providing a code for social interaction and the code that is used for clearly classifying and labelling different aspects of their own world, their own personal and group history. However, these functions do not substantially differ from the hypotheses of Anglo-Saxon social psychology concerning the functions of cognitive representations, whether we consider the theory of personal constructs (Kelly 1955) or the categorization theory of social cognition (Hamilton 1981).

What social representation seems to produce as a genuine novelty is the attention directed at the *social origin of the principles of organization*, in short, *the process of social construction*.

But is the emphasis on cognitive contents and social origin a truly radical approach to the description of cognitive structures in social psychology? The excellent analysis of Jaspars and Fraser (1984) demonstrates in several ways all those social psychological traditions in which the orientation to content and the social origin of cognitive representation play a distinguished role.

First, the category of *attitude*, as it is interpreted nowadays in social psychology, refers to individual cognitive representations, cognitive-evaluative responses, that is, individual intra-mental entities. In the framework of social psychological theorizing the question why different individuals give different responses to the same stimulus object becomes explainable through the concept of attitudes. In this view, for example, the question why person A chooses party X that is not chosen by person B can be explained in the last analysis by their different attitudes towards parties. However, the category of attitude has become a decisive category of *individual mind* only from the 1930s, following Gordon Allport's (1935) study, in which social origin appears only in acquiring predisposition socially and the coverage of reality only in the content of evaluative answers, that is, in the abstraction of evaluation. This is a significant modification with respect to how the concept of attitude was introduced into social psychology by Thomas and Znaniecki (1918–1920: 1, 1–86), who rejected Durkheim's famous thesis that the explanation for a social phenomenon, like suicide, should be sought in another social phenomenon rather than in the individual. In their view the explanation for a phenomenon, be it individual or social, always lies in some sort of a combination of social and individual phenomena. Social theory should include the cultural elements of social life and the objective features of the members of a social group jointly, correlating one with the other. Thomas and Znaniecki (1918–1920) called the former *values* and the latter, the cultural knowledge with value content objectively characteristic of group members, *attitudes*. In their work entitled *The Polish Peasant* in Europe and America, in which they sought an explanation as to why the life of Polish peasants immigrating to the United States fell apart, objective cultural features, that is, 'values' were represented by American culture, while the immigrant group was characterized by an 'attitude' that they had brought with themselves from home. Thomas and Znaniecki derived the 'anomic' phenomena arising in the life of the immigrant Polish peasants from the collision of the two. Thus, for Thomas and Znaniecki (1918–1920) attitudes were still somewhat close to the concept of collective representations. In any case, one of their important properties was that members of a community collectively possessed them. The individualization of the concept of attitude after Allport (1935) obscured the collective nature of attitudes. While the classical procedures of measuring attitude were based on the presupposition of collective representations about attitude objects, the common stimulus representation, since the 1930s measuring attitude has become the measure of evaluative, individual response dispositions. And with the advance of cognitive psychology attitude was used not only for the description of response dispositions but also for that of individual differences even from a cognitive aspect.

Second, in the history of twentieth-century social psychology the importance of distinguishing between objective, 'cultural' reality and subjective representation and the priority of subjective reality from the point of view of decision-making and action was represented most decisively by social psychologists like Lewin, Asch and Heider who were committed to the *Gestalt psychology* tradition. Lewin (1948) describes the *life space* that determines action in terms of the current subjective reality of the individual. Asch (1952) maintains that the evaluation of an object and the behaviour towards it are preceded by interpretation, the establishment of the subjective meaning of the object. Even in the interpretation of the famous conformity experiments – besides the need for recognition by partners and the evasion of refusal – he stressed the role of partners in providing information as to how the object (the line offered for matching) should be interpreted. Asch believes that the acceptance of *judgements* provided by social partners is preceded by the acceptance of the *interpretation* offered by partners. While the social origin of personal interpretation is obvious in the above interpretation of conformity experiments, the regularities of social perception as subjective construction of meaning were sought by Gestalt psychologists not in the procession of social transmittal but first of all in the individual mind. They wanted to explore universal dynamic, Gestalt organizational principles that become active in the case of any arbitrary cultural content and create a subjective representation of objective social stimuli.

This is also valid for the work of Heider (1958), who has, without doubt, created the most comprehensive theory of the naive psychology of social perception among Gestalt social psychologists. Although the Heiderian naive social psychology places principles of creating cognitive structures, such as the principle of equilibrium or the principle of attributing cause in the centre, this theory cannot fully disregard the content of social stimuli at least in two respects. On the one hand, the research on creating perceptual unity in the social world called attention to the fact that the operation of the consistency principle is not independent of the content of a given unit (e.g. Jordan 1953) demonstrated that perceived emotional relationships produce unity in a different way from ownership relationships. On the other hand, the universal mental categories postulated by Heider such as ability, causing or trial, as was demonstrated by Abelson (1968) in the analysis of psychological implications, always create implicational molecules on the basis of common sense and reality.

Finally, we have to briefly touch upon a methodologically elegantly supported theory that assigns central importance to cognitive content and the act of construction. The hypothesis of *personal constructs* developed by George Kelly (1955) and the repertoire-network test related to it, as is suggested by the name of the theory, assumes that people perceive and anticipate the world in cognitive constructs that are characteristic of their personality, that is, they differ from one another in how they construe events. As Bannister (1966) writes,

> If somebody has a 'construct' of a Greek vase, then he will find one somewhere. If he does not have such a construct, he will only find a vase; if he does not have a construct of a vase either, he will find an object. In other words, there is an attempt in the centre of the theory (as there is one in the centre of any theory) to explain a fundamental phenomenon, namely that two people can react in a totally different way in the same situation. The explanation is simple: in fact they are not in the same situation.
>
> (Bannister 1966: 367)

Thus, the hypothesis of personal constructs, similarly to traditional theories of social psychology, start out from the assumption that there is a social world 'out there' (e.g. a Greek vase) that is individually mapped in accordance with the subjective cognitive organization of the individual and characterizes individuals, or even empirically distinguishable groups of individuals, by means of formal and substantive properties of organization.

By comparison, social representations theory does not accept the existence of such an 'external' world but starts out from the assumption that – although it can never be taken for granted by common sense – social reality is created by people, so it is interested in the processes and conditions of social construction. As was put by Moscovici (1988):

> All this leads us to believe that 'creating' a reality means that we generally experience and think in terms of 'potential' worlds which are set in 'real' worlds. What I mean is that our worlds, such as they are or such as we think they are, are partly constituted by recollections of what they used to be, mixed in with anticipations, calculations, and alternatives that bring us together and make us act. The greater the extent to which a representation of this world is shared with other people, the more this world which is of our making, 'in here', seems to be autonomous, existing on its own 'out there'.
>
> Moscovici (1988: 231)

If external, objective reality does not exist, the study of the correctness or truth of representations does not make sense. And indeed, social representations theory does not raise questions of this type. However, it does not share the view of certain postmodern theories either, which put an equal mark between science and common sense by relativizing possible worlds; that is, they deny the special nature of science. By using special tools of scientific methods and rationality, social representations theory studies the deterministic conditions of everyday reality and the 'emergence' and operation of common sense. The advantage of social representations theory over postmodern theories relying on spontaneous common sense is nicely expressed by Moscovici's (1988) claim:

> social representations, to rephrase a common expression, are ways of world making. There is nothing arbitrary in this process, since the regularities of thought, language and life in society all act together to delimit the possibilities. That is why the concept of construction, once it is trivialized, loses its exact, emancipating character, if it is envisaged as a simple product of talking and of consensus among individuals. It anything goes, then the act of constructing is less a creative liberty of reality than an illusion about the conditions of this liberty.
>
> (Moscovici 1988: 231)

Jovchelovitch is hardly mistaken when she considers the social-psychological reinterpretation of representation to be the key element of social representations theory. As she writes:

> A representation ... is the activity *of* someone, who constructs a psychic sub-
> stitution of something which is *alter*, other, to oneself. The subject and the
> object, therefore, do not coincide. There is a difference between them, and in
> order to bridge this difference, a representation emerges. This process does
> not involve a mirroring between the subject and the object; rather, it involves
> at one and the same time a work of constructing links and preserving dif-
> ferentiation between self and alterity. A representation links self and other
> and yet, by the same token, it differentiates self and other, for a representa-
> tion is something that stands *in place of* something else. Representation thus
> is both a *mediation* that links presence and absence and a *boundary* that, in
> separating what is present from what is absent, allows for differentiation and
> meaning to emerge.
>
> (Jovchelovitch 1996: 132, italics in original)

Thus, representation involves mediations between subjects and objects (other
people and things), and is active only between attaching to them and separating
from them. It is through these representations that psychological processes construe 'external' social reality, while from another aspect this reality construes the
psychological processes themselves. According to social representations theory,
representation is neither internal (mental) nor external (public, like a sentence
or any other material sign is), but is a special relationship between the two. The
term 'social' is not the attribute of some mentally represented object (king as
opposed to the asocial throne) but that of a relationship between a person and the
objects and events that constitute his or her world. In this framework, representation is complex social psychological process, 'a practice, which implies relation
and communication' (Jovchelovitch 2006: 102). The study of social representations embraces not only the content of knowledge, but also the symbolic aspect
and dynamic context of knowing: Who are the people doing the representational
work? How do they do this? Why and for what do they do representations? When
seeking answers to these questions, social representations research reformulates
classic social psychological problems of identity, communication, attribution or
justification (see Jovchelovitch 2006: 102). The traditional dichotomy of individual and society is resolved in this view, while the theory also offers an alternative
to some postmodern endeavours which, by denying representations, maintain that
the individual and the social can be reduced to each other, or view them as if they
did not have to do anything with each other.

The large-scale framework of social representations theory leaves several problems open. While it considers the relationship between people and the world to be
its subject matter, and stresses that a 'socially valid world' (Wagner 1998: 304) cannot be independent from the people who live in it, it is less specific as to whether
the theory can be made to cover every phenomenon of social reality, every form of
social knowledge, or whether it includes only those phenomena, facts and institutions that play an important but hitherto unspecified role in the world view or world
construction of social groups.

The empirical study of social representations

Social representations theory has inspired a large number of empirical studies, and they can hardly be accused of methodological orthodoxy. In addition to quantitative methods (Doise 1993), or even experiments and quasi-experiments, qualitative anthropological procedures have a long-standing tradition in interviews and focus-group research (see Breakwell and Canter 1993b). Following the ideas of Geertz (1975) based on *thick description*, Duveen and Lloyd (1993) rely on observations and data collected in conversations in their research and address the issue of the social representation of sexual roles on the basis of these data. More recently, qualitative and quantitative methods are used jointly too: the content analysis categories of verbal, visual or audiovisual material that are derived from preliminary interpretation are quantified, and the various groups or individuals are inserted in the qualitatively category matrix with the help of quantitative analysis procedures (see Flick 2005); another possibility is that patterns gained through a quantitative procedure are used in the interpretation. In addition to verbal and behavioural analysis techniques, social representations research, in view of the role objectification into images and metaphors plays in the theory, has a liking for using visual procedures, such as selecting among pictures (de Rosa et al. 2002) or film analysis (Wagner et al. 1999).

Thus, nearly every possible method of the social sciences has been used in the empirical study of social representation (Breakwell and Canter 1993a). Fundamentally, these methods can be divided into two groups, one is experimental, and the other is not in its character. What might appear to be surprising in the study of social representations on the basis of what has already been said about the theory and of the demonstrations that have been presented, is the relatively large number of experiments using variable conditions (Abric 2001; Codol 1984; Moliner 1995). In psychology, and thus in social psychology too, an experimental method is used to verify or falsify a hypothesis. An experimental or quasi-experimental plan or field work is based on whether the factors manipulated by the investigator or – in the case of field work – the naturally changing causal factors and the subsequent effects can be identified or measured in the right way. Although it is indeed difficult to set up a linear relationship between either social or mental variables and cognitive and behavioural manifestations in the framework of social representations theory, the experimental method has been proved successful in the study of the figurative core of representation and the identification of central and peripheral components. Occasionally, the experimental method is combined with a questionnaire. In their experiment Wagner et al. (1995) studied the representation of fertilization. Since most people are unable to observe the interaction of an egg and a sperm directly, they are dependent on scientific education and concepts formed in everyday communication. Researchers assumed that sperms would take on the properties of sexual stereotypes that are compatible with sex in the representation. Experiments have verified the prediction. Subjects attributed a significantly larger number of masculine stereotypical features (hard, active, fast, dominant) to sperms than to women, while in the case of eggs stereotypical feminine features were more dominant (soft, passive, slow, self-subordinating). The researchers also studied whether the subjects preferred descriptions of a social or a natural character when they were asked to choose from alternative metaphoric descriptions. Here, a clear preference for social metaphors was found. The experiment was complemented by a questionnaire that measured the subjects' stereotypes concerning sexual roles. The results of this experiment showed that the above-mentioned two effects were significantly stronger in the case of subjects with conservative stereotypes than in the case of subjects with more liberal stereotypes concerning sexual roles. Often quasi-experimental plans were used in investigations in which the natural change of conditions resulted in a change in the content and form of social representations (Di Giacomo 1980; Galli and Nigro 1987). However, it is obvious that it is not experimental methods that are decisive in the study of social representations. The generation of data using non-experimental methods, such as individual or group interviews, questionnaires, sorting cards, associations and natural texts, is different from experiments not only in that in this case – contrary to experimental methods – the control of the researcher over the phenomenon under study goes only as far as determining the range of data to be collected, the ways of data collection and the identification of samples, but also in that these methods are not meant to verify a preliminary hypothesis. (This does not, of course, mean that in the case of non-experimental methods the researcher necessarily has less influence on the phenomenon under study, for the data can be distorted even during the selection and collection process.) These studies are of an 'exploratory' nature, attempting to capture the complex organizational forms and the dynamics of social representations, while they handle causal relationships between different phenomena in a much looser way in terms of a remote effect as a schema-like relationship mentioned in Chapter 2 in connection with Hayek, and typically provide posterior interpretations.

This research strategy again does not mean the non-experimental research of social representations is confined to descriptive-interpretative data collection used in anthropology. The use of quantitative data collection and analysis methods has a wide scope in the non-experimental research paradigm on social representations too. This is made possible, last but not least, by the rapid development of multivariable statistical methods and information technology.

Although these investigations target various aspects of social representations, they all unanimously share the view that in the sense of the world view embodied in social representations theory the system of meanings in which individual thinking is anchored is by its nature *categorial*. They often take people to be naive scholars who attempt to find their way in the world in this naive capacity using their naive theories that are created by naively anchored and objectified categories. However, in the *consensual world* of common sense – in contrast to the *objectified world* of sciences (Moscovici 1994) – *communication gets the upper hand:* that is, a mode of operation in which relations with other people rather than merely with themselves are much more important for people. The former world makes science possible which uses the formal logic as instrument. In the second world the rules are different, the formal logic replaced by the *natural logic* (Grize 1989). In this world decisions are taken through dynamic processes of convergence and adjustment, as identified by now classic research in social psychology. The distinction between these two schools of thought, one based on 'scientific logic' and the other on 'natural logic', was already described by Moscovici (1976) when he contrasted scientific argumentation based on the rules of formal logic with communication used to maintain group cohesion. This fact, however, appears to have escaped the attention of researchers studying social representations, although the narrative principle has gained an increasingly stronger emphasis in the social representations research of the past few decades.

The use of the narrative train of ideas in social representations research

Narrative ideas and methods are by no means foreign to the intellectual tradition of social representations. One of Durkheim's students, Maurice Halbwachs, provided powerful arguments as to how important a role narratives played in the formulation and organization of social experience. He too was consistent in claiming that people create stories because they want to understand their world, and they also share these stories with others. The sense of community and social identity are both rooted in narratives; furthermore, even the social anchoring of our seemingly most individualistic memories takes place with the help of narratives.

The representative of the school of structuralist anthropology, Lévi-Strauss (1992) uses the label *myth* for stories that provide a narrative form for ideas which concern a given society. He sees these myths as 'constitutive units' or 'classificatory units', ensuring that a society understands itself and the world around it. Like Bettelheim's (1975) tales at an individual level, myths ensure integrity and continuity at the level of society by integrating otherwise broken beliefs and values and making them part of collective understanding.

MacIntyre (1981) writes about the socializing function of tales:

> It is through hearing stories about wicked stepmothers, lost children, good but misguided kings, wolves that suckle twin boys, youngest sons who receive no inheritance but must make their own way in the world and eldest sons who waste their inheritance on riotous living and go into exile to live with the swine, that children learn or mislearn both what a child and what a parent is, what the cast of characters may be in the drama into which they have been born and what the ways of the world are. Deprive children of stories and you leave them unscripted, anxious stutterers in their actions as in their words. Hence there is no way to give us an understanding of any society, including our own, except through the stock of stories which constitute its initial dramatic resources. Mythology, in its original sense, is at the heart of things.
>
> (MacIntyre 1981: 201)

Bakhtin (1981) stressed the intersubjectivity, the public discourse function of narrative. According to Bakhtin narrative is not only and not in the first place an individual ability to tell stories but rather the *public carrier* of human experience.

Narratives exist like discourse taking place in the public spaces of cities and villages, social groups, generations and eras witnessed in tragedies, dramas, comedies, dance and painting (Bakhtin 1981: 259).

Bartlett (1923) stressed the relationship between storytelling and human communities; that is, he also considered storytelling to be a social act rather than an individual manifestation. Several of the complex forces shaping storytelling originate in social groups. Bartlett (1923: 60) emphasized that in a certain respect myth, legend, popular story and oral tradition were directly influenced by the social setting in which it is formulated and spread.

This omnipresence and all-pervasive nature of narrative offers a good basis for the interpretation of Sperber's (1996) theory on the epidemiology of representations (see Chapter 5). According to Sperber, the way in which communities 'catch' representations and the way representations are shared among different populations and spread from one population to the other are directly related to the form of representations. The process whereby populations transmit and mediate their representations sheds some light on the nature of these representations, as epidemiology can shed light on pathology. Narratives thus conceived are cultural mediators which feed the social representation into the communities in which they circulate and continue to shape these communities.

The idea of narratives as cultural mediators was discovered as early as at the beginning of the last century. Interestingly enough, this discovery happens to be related to the concept of attitude. Thomas and Znaniecki (1918–1920) – partly arguing with a Durkheimian objectivist approach to social facts – conceived of attitudes in a way similar to later social representations theory; that is, as socially acquired and shared representations governing human thought and behaviour. Phenomena of attitudes contrasted with *values* appearing as objective for individuals in the Durkheimian sense were derived from personal narratives realized in letters and biographies.

The later individualization of the interpretation and use of personal documents, just like the individualization of the concept of attitude (Allport 1935, 1955), cannot conceal the fact that social psychology first analysed narratives in terms of their social meaning. A more obvious phenomenon concerning the nature of this relationship, what is also closer to present-day social representations research, is the use of narratives in ethnographic investigations based on interviews (Herzlich 1973; Jodelet 1991). In many respects, interviews are pseudo-narratives in which the thread of the plot is weaved partly by the interviewer – the goal is to produce some sort of a fabric whose patterns can be used by the investigator to unravel a system of meanings or the interpreting context of the phenomenon under investigation. However, what is really strange, and reflects theoretical and methodological orthodoxy, is that Herzlich (1973) and Jodelet (1991) deliberately ignored the narrative qualities of the material gained through interviews, and instead of considering the narrative character of the explanations they devoted their attention exclusively to the conceptual anchoring and objectification of health and mental illness. In turn, Jovchelovitch (1995) regarded interview as a true narrative genre. After the fall of the Brazilian president, who was relieved of his office in 1993 due to some corruption scandals, he held narrative interviews with the members of congress who sat on the congressional committee investigating the instances of presidential corruption. By analysing the stories using narrative techniques – among others by analysing the themes raised in the stories and their qualification, the main characters and their characterization, the sequence of events and their cause–effect relations and the metaphors running through the stories – she managed to explore several important aspects of the social representation of Brazilian public life. Of her many discoveries perhaps the most interesting one was the recognition that one of the main functions of narratives is to shut down the possible field of representation, to exclude any possible new meaning from the representation of a never-occurred event, namely, the replacement of the president. According to the analysis two representational fields are connected to the replacement. One representational field includes narrative elements that justify the (previously) unimaginable and inconceivable nature of the replacement. These elements include the shortcomings of politicians and the Brazilian people, the emphasis on the gap between politicians and the society as well as an overt or covert reference to the relationship and the complementary nature of the two. The other representational field includes meanings related to the new era that began in the Brazilian society, the new relationship between parliament and society and the conclusion of the historic period in which corruption could be exercised routinely without the danger of punishment. Although at the beginning of the narratives the two representational fields are weighted equally, as the stories progress, the 'unimaginable' and 'inconceivable' representational field becomes increasingly more dominant. This is further reinforced by a sense of frustration; a sense of 'nothing has changed' appearing in the characterization of the events after the replacement of the president. Jovchelovitch (2006: 165–166) concludes that narratives are powerful instruments for studying local representational systems. 'They are particularly apt in situations where knowledge about specific events is being investigated and the focus is on the different perspectives that combine to produce the overall account about the situation in questions.'

Beyond content analysis narratives also lend themselves to structural analysis, drawing conclusions about the features of representational content on the basis of structural properties. One interesting and in many ways pioneering example of this is Rose (1997), who analysed the positions of the camera when shooting television soap opera scenes and drew conclusions on this basis about the representation of mental illness in the media. On the basis of such observations as mental patients appearing significantly more often in close-ups, that is, visually isolated from their partners, than other characters, or the narrative conclusion quite common in soap operas is missing in the scenes involving mentally ill characters, Rose demonstrated that the media represents mental illness as a dangerous and unpredictable phenomenon. On the one hand, this sort of representation is at variance with statistical data (mental patients perform significantly fewer aggressive acts than normal people), and on the other, it undermines several modern aspirations that try to bring the treatment of mental patients back to local communities and the family from psychiatric hospitals (Wagner et al. 1999).

No doubt social representations theory, as formulated by Moscovici and his followers, shows a strong inclination to describe the world in terms of categories or concepts, values, stereotypes and images as cognates of these notions (see Moscovici 1973: xiv). However, in addition to these, the claim is there all along that social representations work as 'theories' or 'domains of knowledge', and in this capacity they serve the discovery and organization of reality (Moscovici 1973). The status of a theory, be it scientific, naive or some sort of a transition between the two, is always shaky. Theories proved to be stories even in abstract fields like physics, not to speak of disciplines concerned with human things like historical science or, mutatis mutandis, psychology (see Haraway 1984, 1989; Mulkay 1985). Theories – in the generally accepted sense – are always causal and explanatory in their nature. In the case of several phenomena of the world causality can be deduced from the influence cause exercised on effect. This is exactly what is done by traditional attribution theory (Jones and Davis 1965; Kelley 1967). Moscovici (1984: 46) – often just like several American scholars heavily criticized by him (e.g. Kruglanski 1975) – directs attention to another type of causality, the one that is more at home in the world of social relations and is related to *intentionality*, or as is called by Moscovici, *'finality.'* Let us quote him at some more length here:

Since most of our relationships are with live human beings we are confronted with the intentions and purposes of others which, for practical reasons, we cannot understand. Even when our car breaks down or the apparatus we are using in the laboratory doesn't work we can't help thinking that the car 'refuses' to go, the hostile apparatus 'refuses to collaborate' and so prevents us from pursuing our experiment. Everything people do or say, every natural disturbance, seems to have a hidden significance, intention or purpose which we try to discover. Likewise, we tend to interpret intellectual polemics or controversies as personal conflicts and to wonder what reason there can be for the protagonists' animosity, what private motives are at the bottom of such antagonisms.

Instead of saying: 'For what reason does he behave like that?' we say: 'For what *purpose* does he behave like that?' and the quest for a cause becomes a quest for motives and intentions. In other words we interpret, look for *hidden animosities* and *obscure motives* such as hatred, envy or ambition. We are always convinced that people don't act by chance, that everything they do corresponds to a *plan*.

(Moscovici 1984: 46, italics are added)

According to Moscovici, we all aspire to personify motives and intentions (which means objectifying them) so that we can represent some cause in the form of an image (e.g. we use the Oedipus complex for one particular type of human behaviour). In addition to the idea of objectification in images, this argumentation clearly refers to the narrative nature of everyday explanations, and in this quality it does not differ radically from what narrativists claim, namely, that narrative is the 'organizing principle' of how people give sense to the world (Sarbin 1986b: 2). The study of the attribution of unemployment (Breakwell 1986) and of responsibility (Markus and Kitayama 1991; Miller 1984) makes it clear that the alternative quest for causes and intentions is largely dependent on the intentionality captured in a given social representation.

The fact is that social representations theory is mostly concerned with the issue of objectifying anchored categories, and apparently – at least for empirical study – pushes the intentional character of social thinking into the background. Although the materialization of abstract knowledge indeed appears as one of the basic processes of social representation, it is still true that abstract, conceptual knowledge and its equivalents objectified in the thinking of social groups are related to the stories circulating in these groups through thousands of threads. This is why narrative methods are also necessary for the study of how meanings are objectified by social groups.

Nonetheless, narrative methodology is also remarkably suitable for the study of the anchoring process. Flick (1995: 85) notes that every so often there are insurmountable difficulties when we want to examine how the social representation of novel, unknown experiences develops. It appears that we have to know all the cognitive and/or social systems of categories that had existed before the new experience arose. This is needed so we can learn what category the new phenomenon is integrated into or anchored in, and whether any new category has been generated in the course of anchoring the phenomenon. In the same way it is important to know exactly when unknown phenomena are likely to emerge. However, social representations research typically discovers these phenomena for itself only when they have already penetrated into public thinking. This is what happened in the case of AIDS (Joffe 1995) and nuclear disasters (Galli and Nigro 1987); in both cases life itself offered natural experimental situations. Even the study of events that take place as a stroke of lightning and have an influence on the entire world, like the terrorist action of 11 September 2001 and the representation of terrorism following this event, could obviously work only with retrospective, narrative material, although research began practically immediately afterwards (de Rosa et al. 2002).

To overcome these difficulties Flick (1995: 85–86) introduced the notion of *retrospective anchoring*. This type of anchoring makes it possible to get close to the subjective and at the same time social construction of phenomena and fragments of reality related to them. Flick (1995) believes that narratives created and recounted by people imply the ability to retrospectively outline the effects of a theory or a cultural object, and the circumstances under which they appeared, and they do so by creating a 'dense description' of the phenomenon (Geertz 1975). More will be said about the relationship between social representations 'elaborated' in narrative and group identity in Chapter 10 in connection with the social representation of history.

As a summary of the above we can say that the narrative approach to processes of social representations offers a model of social knowledge in which the objectification and anchoring of new, unknown phenomena are closely related to the aspect of categories whereby they appear as part of some coherent, culturally acceptable narrative. In fact, the place of individuals or groups in the system of common, socially shared meanings can also be understood the best if we learn how people place these categories in a narrative context. Finally, individual and collective stories jointly create a 'dense narration' of phenomena that can then be treated analytically.

How narrative approach contributes to the explanatory potential of social representations

When deriving social representations from collective representations, Moscovici (1984: 19) makes the following distinction between the two: 'collective representations are an *explanatory device*, and refer to a general class of ideas and beliefs' whereas social representations are phenomena that are related to a particular mode of understanding and communicating 'which need to be described and *need to be explained*' (italics are added). But what do social representations themselves explain?

In cognitive psychology, representation is conceived as mediating variable between stimuli and responses. Moscovici (1984) refers to Fodor (1975), who codified this position as follows:

> It has been a main argument of this book that if you want to know what response a given stimulus is going to elicit you must find out what internal representation the organism assigns to the stimulus. Patently, the character of such assignments must in turn depend on what kind of representational system is available for mediating the cognitive processes of the organism.
>
> (Fodor 1975: 198)

In contrast, Moscovici (1984) conceives social representations as independent (i.e., not mediating) variables or explanatory stimuli. He writes:

> Each stimulus is selected from a vast variety of possible stimuli and can produce infinite variety of reactions. It is the pre-established images and paradigms that both determine the choice and restrict the range of reactions. ... In other words, social representations determine both the character of the stimulus and the response it elicits, just as in a particular situation they determine which is which.
>
> (Moscovici 1984: 61)

Moscovici claims that if we want to understand group processes, we should learn about the relevant social representations in the group, and the meaning of these representations. However, conceived in this way as rational knowledge systems in the group, social representations cannot be causal explanations of the behaviour (Wagner 1993, 1995). If a group forms a social representation about madness and an element of this representation is the belief that madness is contagious, then washing mad people's clothes separately from other people's clothes, that is the behaviour, is not the consequence of the social representation or locally constructed naive theory. Rather it is a behavioural description or illustration of a further belief belonging to the same representation, that is separate washing of mad people's clothes prevents infection. According to Wagner (1993, 1995), social representations, because of their consensual and rational character, can rather be approached analytically, than synthetically in a deductive-nomological framework. They cannot be brought into an 'if–then' type causal relation with the behaviour.

Wagner (1995) following Bourdieu (1980) and Doise (1976) points out that research of social representations may be directed to uncovering structural homologies between social and mental structures. In this case, social representation is the *explanandum* and socio-genetic conditions of its emergence are the *explanans*. On the other hand, social representations may enter the explanation as *explanans* of the phenomena following them. In this case, study of social representation proceeds on the level of individual social knowledge and social interaction, but the explanation is not directed to the individual action, instead to social objects or facts. As Wagner (1995: 172) claims, these social objects or social facts are action consequences, which are not logically connected to representational beliefs, as actions themselves are. For example, Di Giacomo (1980) studied a students' protest movement at a Belgian university, where protesters split into two distinct groups having more militant versus more lenient representations about the issue. These discrepant representations led to serious difficulties in communication between the groups and finally resulted in failure of the protest movement. According to Wagner (1995), it is not the individual or group behaviour that is explained in this study by social representation or discrepancies between the two sets of social representations. Behaviour is only one of the possible expressions of mental representations. The same can be told verbally in an interview or can be given in writing when answering a questionnaire. What is explained is a social fact: the failure of the protest movement.

This interpretation has several problems. The most apparent one is that it neglects the fact that the failure itself enters immediately the process of social representation. Social representations are evolving about the failure of the protest movement whose consequences are much less ready to identify. Another problematic element of the above interpretation is that the failure as social fact is a behavioural event in itself. It is a decay and a cease in protest activity. Social representation of the protest movement involved goals, means serving these goals, and activities corresponding to the goals and means. The discrepancies in goals and beliefs in the two groups led to abandoning the protest in both groups. As the example of the two student groups in the protest movement shows, there are more possible social rationalities within a single culture. Different groups may represent the same social object differently, that, in turn, may lead to misunderstandings and aborted actions. This latter aspect may better enlighten the status that is attributed by the narrative approach to the social representations in the explanation of social behaviour. In relations with the goals, representations also imply (and predict) behavioural outputs and reactions to the results of actions. This implicational relationship provides grounds for a modal (Kutschera 1982) or scheme-like (Hayek 1969) explanation in which social representation does not cause social behaviour, but it implies behavioural and mental consequences (see also Wagner 1995: 172). On the other hand, representations of each group, as far as the goals, means, conditions and expected results are concerned, seemed to be coherent in itself. In our view, this coherence within the possible rationality domain is provided by the narrative organization of the representation. Behavioural and mental consequences of the failure do not belong to the protest-narrative, however, they may form the elements of a subsequent narrative which is in implicational relationship with the former one.

The power of the coherence can be illustrated by a study by Rowett and Breakwell (1992), in which the researchers dealt with the situation of social workers who are attacked by their clients. They uncovered a strong social representation or naive theory among social work professionals of why and how a social worker gets attacked. Parts of this representation are lack of skill, low experience and authoritarian behaviour of the social worker, and dangerous environment. There is also a theory about the nature of the interactions which generate violence. The researches also pointed out that this theory is wrong in literally all respects. Nevertheless, despite considerable attempts to dislodge it, the social representation which offers a coherent explanation of violence is still pervasive. Social workers who became victims of such assaults, both mentally and behaviourally react by decreasing their self-evaluation and by forming assumptions about their inadequacy and inefficacy.

The above examples illustrate that the analysis based on the narrative organization of the social representation relates representation to social interaction by implication. The narrative approach to the social representation includes behavioural goals and results of actions, as well as anticipations and evaluations concerning the results. The examples also show that logical analysis is not sufficient to generate implicational explanations: empirical studies are needed.

Identity and social representation

As for identity, we can distinguish two concepts of identity in social psychology. One group of theories, which is inspired by psychoanalysis and marked primarily by the name of Erikson, is aimed at exploring the developmental regularities of a so-called *personal identity*. What is stressed in these theories is continuity, organization, and the internal and external balance of the self. The other major concept, inspired by group psychology and linked to Anglo-Saxon authors, especially to names like Tajfel, Turner and Breakwell, the so-called theory of *social identity*, takes as a starting point individuals identifying themselves with groups and examines processes whereby the independence and the worth of individuals and their capacity to act are maintained. The category of identity is also used by symbolic interactionist role theory which captures identity as a *role identity* (Turner 1968). The fruitfulness of this latter approach largely depends on the current state of role theory. It would be a valid theory only if all the components of identity could be interpreted in the categories of role theory. However, the recent history of role theory in the past few decades has not shown any signs of development in this direction.

Personal identity

Erikson's (1959) theory of psychosocial development divides the human life cycle into eight stages. In each stage changes take place both in the individual and in the individual's social environment. Internal changes and changes in the relationship to the external world jointly result in a natural developmental conflict that determines the particular stage of life. In normal development of personality the conflicts corresponding to a particular stage of life cannot be evaded. The mental and the social proceed in close unity with each other in the course of development, and with the resolution of conflicts in each stage of life both are restructured at a new level. For Erikson (1959) identity involves the restructuring pattern of 'the early' which links the individual's past with the present and the pre-empted future. In this sense real development of identity begins in the fifth stage proposed by Erikson, when the benefits of childhood identifications can no longer be exploited. Identity

> arises from the selective reproduction and mutual assimilation of childhood identifications, and their absorption in a new configuration, which in turn, is dependent on the process by which a *society* (often through subsocieties) *identifies the young individual,* recognizing him as somebody who had to become the way he is, and who, being the way he is, is taken for granted.
> (Erikson 1959: 113, italics in original)

The inclusion of the social element makes it obvious that the identity crisis that takes place in adolescence is culturally and socially rather instable. For instance, in archaic societies the problem of establishing adult identity is resolved by initiatory rituals: in the form of a single, unrepeatable ceremony their youngsters leave behind their adolescent (childhood) state of being and step into an adult state that is characterized by very different internal states and external system of relationships (Leach 1976; Péley 2002). In modern societies adolescence is stretched in time; in Erikson's words the adolescent is given a psychosocial moratorium in which he has the chance to break away from his values rooted in the past, from his roles, relations and self-image. Furthermore, he also has the possibility to actively experiment with new values, roles, relations and self-images. Initiation, the adoption of adult identity is replaced by commitments urged both by internal and by external forces and by making long-term decisions like choosing a career or an ideology. At the same time elements of normativity are also present here: if the commitment to adult roles takes place too early without proper preliminary experimentation and weighing, a so-called identity state of early closure is created, which may lead to adaptation disorders of personality in later stages of life.

By taking into consideration the rules of mental and social development and their social-cultural embedding, the psychosocial theory of personal identity can provide a rational explanation for patterns of behaviour appearing in crises, in the storms of adolescent age, which are difficult to handle for common sense by relating them to the fulfilment of an actual identity task the adolescent has to face.

Social identity

The other identity theory of social psychology mentioned in the Introduction, the theory of social identity is entirely different in its nature, and was primarily developed to explain relationships between groups. Briefly summarized, the theory assumes that people have a basic need for social identity and this need, that is, their positive self-assessment and self-esteem can be satisfied by belonging to a group. They identify with a group as a social category, and this identification becomes part of their self-concept. The existence of other, 'strange' groups is indispensable for the creation of identity, for identity itself is established in the course of making comparisons among groups. Therefore, competition and conflicts among groups emerge not only in the case of limited resources but also in the case of symbolic 'goods' that are available without limits or are by themselves useless. What are involved here are irrational phenomena related to identity, like when one dollar is sold for three at an auction.

Group identity and the representation of the social world

If the group they belong to plays such an important role in shaping and maintaining the social identity of individuals, then there is good reason to believe that – as has been argued by Breakwell in several of her studies (Breakwell 1993; Breakwell and Lyons 1996) – the system of views, the construction of reality in a broader sense, which they work out and maintain together with their group will be important for them. One of the most important developments of social psychology since the mid-1990s is that social representations theory, which explores representational forms of the interpretation and explanation of the world taking shape in the communication of groups, has gained a significant ground. What Breakwell proposes is essentially to combine social identity theory and social representations theory. The difficulty of realizing this proposal is that we are dealing with two radically different paradigms of social psychology. While the theory of social identity, combining the dynamics of individual identity and that of inter-group relations, works out explanatory models for the interpretation of inter-group conflicts and differentiation, that is, it is positioned within the paradigm of social psychology focusing on individual cognitive processes, social representations theory is typically a constructionist theory that lays emphasis on the description of representational processes and the analysis of representational functions. Even versions of social representations theory that explicitly try to link empirically explored representational forms to well-definable groups (see e.g. the theory of Doise et al. 1992) do not intend to explore principles and rules whereby particular representational contents and/or processes should be derived from specific relations within or across groups. Thus, the integration of the two theories is indeed an enterprise whose goal is to 'take' models of social psychology, which concern individual social behaviour and the cognitive processes underlying them, and which, in the words of Breakwell (1993: 199) involve a narrow spectrum of behaviour in a specific environment, 'out' into real social space. By analysing the processes of identity creation and social construction (that is, what has a meaning in a group, what is accepted as reality) in correlation, the integrated model makes it possible to raise questions as to why and how a given social representation takes the specific shape that can be observed in a group. In other words, the question is how group dynamics influences processes of anchoring and objectification at the level of the individual and the group. For example, it is obvious that prestige and power relations among groups play a decisive role when social representations are adopted, as it is also easy to see that the tendency in the representation of AIDS to view the disease as a divine punishment inflicted by God on homosexuals serves to promote prejudices among groups. Tajfel's characterization of the functions of stereotypes – groups use stereotypes, for example scapegoats to establish social causality, justify themselves and distance themselves from other groups – appears to be valid for social representations too. However, the study of social representations in the case of group contexts of stereotypes taken in the sense of Tajfel – which usually means a so-called minimal group taken out of the historical and social context in laboratory studies – can be realized only in a significantly broader context both from a historical and from a social aspect. The exploration of the correlations between power relations and the adoption of representations for example require a temporal (historical) analysis of inter-group relations and the use of representations. Group history in itself may have an important role in the development of group identity (Bruner and Fleischer-Feldman 1996). This issue will be discussed in more detail in Chapter 10 in connection with the relationship of the representation of history and national identity.

The study of Lyons and Sotirakopoulou (1991) also sheds light on the role of temporality, demonstrating that 'traditional' social representations of a group restrict the dimensions along which a particular group can achieve positive, advantageous discrimination as compared to other groups. In the study mentioned above even the most unflinching British nationalist preferred France to England as far as fashion or cuisine was concerned, simply because the opposite would not have had much credibility within the reality of traditional social representations.

In addition to functions serving the interest of a group in inter-group comparison outlined above, social representations have another important function in creating and maintaining group identity. Social representations collectively maintained by all group members contribute to the development of group consciousness; as Breakwell (1993: 203) puts it, sharing the group's representations becomes, as it were, the symbol of group membership and helps group members understand why they have to follow the goals of the group. These functions of constructing group identity are thus no longer related to the system of group interests that ensure positive identity in comparisons among groups but rather to processes which shape group identity within the group. This idea has been formulated in the most general way by Moscovici and Hewstone (1983), who believe that the social representations established and maintained by a particular group contribute to group identity even by the fact that the common 'world view' manifest in collective representations reinforces the experience of collective identity.

Group identity as the demarcation of group boundaries

Finally, from the point of view of group identity, and as a result, of the social identity of individuals, social representations have yet another function that cannot be related to either within-group processes or processes of comparison among groups, namely, the function fulfilled by social representations in drawing the symbolic borders of groups. The borders of a particular group are drawn where the borders of collectively organized representational fields lie.

Certain authors (e.g. Jovchelovitch 1996) consider these latter two functions to be one single function. As she writes:

> when social subjects construct and organize their representational fields, they do so in order to make sense of reality, to appropriate and interpret it. In doing so, they state *who* they are, how they understand both themselves and others, where they locate themselves and others, and which are the cognitive and affective resources that are available to them in a given historical time. Social representations therefore, tell us about *who* is doing the representational work. This can be fully appreciated if we consider the trade-offs between representational work and identificatory work. The complex interactions between self and other are the basis of both phenomena. There is no possibility of identity without the work of representation, just as there is no work of representation without an identificatory boundary between the me and the not-me. It is in the overlapping space of the me and the not-me that both representations and identities emerge. Furthermore, social representations are a network of mediating social meanings which lends texture and material to the construction of identities.
>
> (Jovchelovitch 1996: 125)

This view is different from Breakwell's (1993) idea of integrating social representations theory and identity theory in that Jovchelovitch does not use Tajfel's (1978, 1981) social identity theory to combine social representations theory with identity theory. Therefore, she does not devote any special attention to the function that social representations are assumed to fulfil in processes of inter-group comparisons for the 'benefit' of the group. At the same time Breakwell (1986, 1993) herself is not content with Tajfel's theory, which derives the dynamics of identity exclusively from the need for positive social identity and its goal is practically to explain the dynamics of inter-group behaviour. In addition to the need for positive social identity, there are several other needs of identity dynamics that play a role in motivating behaviours and beliefs relevant for group dynamics in the identity process theory developed by Breakwell (1986, 1993): the need for *positive self-assessment*, the need for *continuity* in the sense of Erikson in identity conceived of as self-identity, the need for the *individuality* of the self, of *being different*, and the need for the *efficiency* of the self. According to Breakwell, these needs not only motivate the choice of an individual as to which group he or she selects for membership, in other words, which social category the individual adopts as part of his or her social identity, but also determine the construction or adoption of social representations that the individual will be sensitive to. Thus, as compared to Tajfel's (1978, 1981) theory, in which the social identity related to groups or social categories represents a relatively independent subsystem of the self, in Breakwell's (1986, 1993) identity process theory social identity is not independent of the rest of the self (of personal identity characterized by self-assessment, individuality, continuity and efficiency) and of its own dynamics of identity construction governed by the four needs outlined above. Nevertheless Breakwell assumes that the dynamic effects of personal identity also manifest themselves through group identity, thereby having an influence on the relationship to the social representations maintained by the individual's own group and by 'foreign' groups.

The integration of identity dynamics and group dynamics in this way, complemented later by a causal and predictive model of social representation, has two apparently inevitable consequences. On the one hand, using the terminology of social representation, traditional topics of social psychology, such as the credibility of the communicator or the issue of conformity, are revived. This is well illustrated by the following analysis that concerns the acceptance or refusal of social representation.

> Memberships will affect acceptance (or rejection) of the social representation. They do this sometimes by establishing the extent of the credibility of the source of the social representation. They do it at other times by explicit commentaries on the representation. Failure to accept the group's verdict on a social representation can put the individual at risk of censure or even rejection. The consequences of rejecting the group's preferred representation of an object clearly vary with the importance that it has for the group. The consequences will also depend upon the individual's power within the group.
>
> (Breakwell 1993: 206)

In Coyle's (1991) study, in which it was shown that young men who had adopted a homosexual identity consistently looked for the company of other homosexual men during the establishment of the new identity and were especially responsive to acquiring the established patterns of homosexual social representations prevalent among these people, the reduction phenomena of cognitive dissonance clearly manifest themselves. On the other hand, now using a more modern overtone and focusing on identity, several notions of the social cognitive paradigm that was dominant in the social psychology of the 1980s and issues of individual information processing emerge in the study of social representations. The issues raised in this context include the relationship between being exposed to information and acquiring information (Augustinos 1990) or the consequences originating from the problem whether social identity has a central or a peripheral place from the point of view of self-concept or self-schema. The latter problem is illustrated by Gurin and Markus (1988), who demonstrated that women for whom the non-traditional female role was a central factor of identity constructed much sharper and more explicit social representations about social inequalities between the sexes than those who preferred to place a more traditional female role in the centre of identity or for whom gender role was not of central importance in their own identity. There are several studies belonging here too that investigated the different effects of context. These studies are in harmony with research in which it has been demonstrated that different elements of identity become dominant in different situations (e.g. McGuire and McGuire 1988). In the following quotation social representation might as well be substituted for nearly any cognitive structure, from stereotype to opinion, that is common in cognitive social psychology or the research on social cognition: 'The same social representation will vary in actual importance to the group over time and across situations. The relative importance of different social representations will similarly vary with circumstances' (Breakwell 1993: 204).

It seems then that although social representations theory as an interpretative framework allows for taking into consideration individual mental processes and group-level processes (be they within-group or inter-group processes), when it comes to exploring the representational field of a particular social structure (social group, subculture), any attempt to find predictive causal relationships between the processes of group dynamics and social construction is inevitably compelled to reduce the social aspects of representation (which, after all, is in the centre of social representations theory) and as a result, we are practically back to cognitive representations.

Enterprises that try to find a direct relationship between individual identity dynamics and processes of social representations appear to be more promising from the point of view of the integration of social representations theory and identity theory. Even without the somewhat artificial argument that people who define themselves as shy not only belong to the category of shy people but also will look for the company of shy people, whereby they become members of the group of shy people not only virtually but practically too (Breakwell 1993: 193), it is easy to see that shyness as a personality trait may be an essential part of identity, and as such, it has an impact on the establishment, acquisition and use of representations concerning shy behaviour. From the point of view of clarifying the relationship between identity and social representation, it is more important that members of a real social structure should really have the given personality trait as an element of identity, be it shyness or anything else, and the representational field handled by the group should affect this element.

If these conditions hold, as shown in several studies of Breakwell and her group, identity dynamics may prove to be useful in understanding and interpreting the processes of social representations. If, for instance, the place where they live is an important aspect of identity for members of a residential community, since it provides a sense of uniqueness or extraordinariness for them, any view 'coming' from the social environment that is meant to convince them, even supported by scientific arguments, that there is strong pollution of the environment in their residential quarters, is flatly rejected (Bonaiuto et al. 1996). The above example also demonstrates why scientific arguments generally play a much smaller than expected role in disputes connected with environmental risks, such as when new power plants are installed or waste disposal facilities are established. In the same way, if in a group of adolescents the identity element of being faithful has great significance, members of the group will have trouble accepting representations of sexual behaviour that stress the risks involved in it (Stephenson et al. 1993). In a study carried out in a secondary school in Budapest, Csabai et al. (1998) demonstrated that the representations of these young people concerning health-conscious behaviour are in sharp contrast with what could be expected on the basis of scientific views – among other things, they form a somewhat ironic and unfavourable picture of people who actively live a healthy life – and the reason for it may be that the representations supported by scientific research contradict a property that is crucial for their own identity, namely sociability.

Breakwell et al. (1993a) call attention to another interesting aspect of the relationship between identity and social representations. In this study they investigate the relationship between *political identity* and the *system of political views*. The study was conducted over three years, taking data in every year. Political identity was 'measured' by the consistency of party preference (for the British Labour Party and Conservative Party). Perhaps their most interesting result was that only an insignificant minority of young people had any unified, consistent pattern of political attitude and political views. Most of them advocated fragmented, inconsistent views concerning political issues that often changed with time. The same majority changed their party preference at least once during the three years of the investigation. However, the minority that had a very consistent and logically coherent view of a wide range of issues, from taxation to social networks and immigration, showed preference either for the Labour Party or the Conservative Party during the entire three-year period. Thus, those young people who identified themselves with a political party; that is, political identity became an important element of their own self, had also acquired a coherent system of political ideology and were not driven to try to match fragments of political views taken from various sources when they were confronted with such questions.

Joffe (1996) made an explicit attempt to fit processes of social identity and self-development into the theoretical framework of social representations. As compared to what has been discussed before – although identity continues to be in the focus – this attempt represents a significant theoretical transition, as Joffe uses a psychodynamic model of the theory of psychoanalytic object relationships for the characterization of representational processes. Joffe (1996) lays emphasis on an aspect of social representations theory which says that social representations serve the function of making newly emerging, unknown social phenomena familiar and mitigating the shock brought about by novelty. At the same time, from the point of view of ontogeny any phenomenon is new when it is first encountered. In this capacity novelty means threat, since it questions the ability of individuals to control their environment. This is further compounded by the fact that novel events are by themselves scary, as they endanger individuals either physically or symbolically. After intensively studying the social representational processes of several threatening social phenomena in various cultures, for example mental illness, environmental disasters and AIDS, Joffe (1996) calls attention to some interesting, apparently universal substantive patterns of representation. These sorts of representations typically exhibit some 'cocktail of sins' in which strange or perverse procedures are involved that are often overgeneralized and assigned to specific subgroups of society or to strange groups (Joffe 1996: 202). This unconscious process of defence against anxiety was called 'splitting' by Melanie Klein and was characterized by her as an inevitable mechanism of early self-development, the separation of the self and non-self (the 'object': see Klein 1946). Joffe (1996) transfers the dynamics of self-development handled at an intra-individual and interpersonal level to the analysis of social representations taking place under specific historical and social circumstances as a reaction of social groups to danger. In this kind of defence it is the projection of anxiety-generating fantasies to strange groups that plays the central role. The question as to which groups become the embodiment of 'the bad other one' is decided by already existing representations that have been created historically in the group (Gilman 1985).

Although phenomena corresponding to individual psychodynamic processes of defence have also been found – for example Bion's (1952, 1961) studies showed that early splitting also appeared in the interaction of therapeutic groups – the methods of the social sciences (questionnaires, attitude scales, or even interviews) are not sensitive enough to be able to access the defensive processes observed in social groups that provide the dynamics for the representation of threatening novel phenomena arising in these groups, the defensive processes that are reconstructed by psychodynamic theories at an individual level in a series of therapeutic sessions taking place in a special atmosphere by means of transference and counter-transference. As a possible solution, Joffe (1996) proposes the analysis of texts and pictures in the media, as for example the cultural anthropologist Gilman (1985) demonstrated the operation of splitting in media materials. However, this method has the disadvantage that it is overly static and cannot follow the occasionally fine changes of the position of the person who created the representation. Analysing interviews of life history made with second generation Jews, Erős and Ehmann (1997) demonstrated the appearance of splitting and the corresponding identical features of representation in processing the trauma of the Holocaust. In autobiographical interviews looking back to the political transition of 1989 Erős, Ehmann and László (1998) showed a correlation between the security of self-definition (the more or less resolute placement of the self in events) and value-driven representations of the political transition. These studies already lead us to the relationship between the dynamic processes of identity and narrative, to be discussed in Chapter 7.

Summary

This chapter had a comprehensive look at social representation theory. We devoted detailed attention to this theory, because its approach resembles narrative psychology in several respects. Not only is it engaged in studying meaning construction, but also it strives to achieve its goals by developing empirical methodologies. Social representations theory has deep insight into the relation between representations and identity. However, this theory is more interested in categorical representations than in narratives. The chapter included several suggestions as to how narrative principles could be used to map the social representation process and to strengthen the connections between social representations theory and narrative identity theories.

7 Identity and narrative

The idea that identity has a narrative organization goes back to Erikson's psycho-social theory of identity (Erikson 1959, 1968). According to Erikson, the past should be continuously reconstructed in the light of the present and the future. Even independently of the allure of postmodern narrative metatheories, this theory almost automatically entails the metaphor of narrative: essentially, identity is nothing else but a *continuously reconstructed biography* (Ricoeur 1991). Thus, a story that individuals construct about themselves will have a distinguished role from the point of view of the continuity, integrity and unity of their own self and from the aspect of other qualities of their identity. The intensive use of the narrative metaphor in self-psychology that began in the 1980s (Gergen and Gergen 1988; Mancuso and Sarbin 1983) raises several issues that have already been discussed in part in Chapter 3. These problems include, for example, the author-ship of narrative, that is, the real identity of narrative substance and life story, the social construct of life story, the relationship between historical and psycho-logical truth, the status of narrative structures in the autobiographical construct, the problem of who is the biography addressed to, the issue of monologicity and dialogicity in narrative, or the problem of how the story-like formulation of iden-tity is related to other possible, for instance categorical formulations. Several of these questions have been discussed in Chapter 1 on the foundations of narra-tive psychology. Of course, the theory that self can be conceived of as a biogra-phy, a narrative is in accord with social constructionist metatheories which deny that self, or the things of the world are stable, secure starting points, so-called 'essences' (Bruner 1991). Ricoeur's (1965) interpretation of psychoanalysis is a classic example of the psychological use of postmodern narrative theories, which sees the patient's various manifestations not as symptoms of a biologically deter-mined instinct dynamics but rather as a text that the analyst should interpret to-gether with the patient. Joint text construction – therapy – results in a new, more coherent story.

Nevertheless, the narrative concept of identity as a psychological construct cannot be exhausted by mechanically translating the notions of narrative meta-theories. Philosophy seeks an answer to the question as to how narrative creates the identity of the narrator (and the recipient of narrative). However, in psychol-ogy the main questions we need to answer are what conditions life stories originate from, what are the main functions and qualities of life stories and how they are related to various identity states, or how identity states manifested in life stories are related to problems of social adaptation. Philosophers, like Ricoeur (1991) or Dennett (1991), propose different solutions for the concept of self that is not based on essence. The former derives the identity of self that changes in space and time from the identical nature of autobiographical narrative, while the latter views self in a somewhat metaphorical sense as the narrative gravitational point of life stories that change in space and time (Pléh 2003a). However, in psychology we also need to answer questions that concern the relationship of life stories to other mental mechanisms and their function in social adaptation.

Research on life stories began in anthropology in the nineteenth century by using inductive generalizations for typical walks of life. The study of life stories in psychology also began by using inductive procedures in Vienna in the 1930s. Charlotte Bühler published her work, *Der menschliche Lebenslauf als psychologisches Problem* in 1933, and similar research was pursued by Else Frenkel-Brunswick (1936), who later published excellent research on authoritative personality. It was also in the 1930s that Henry Murray (1938) and then later Gordon Allport (1955) turned their attention to biographies. These works made it obvious that these scholars went beyond descriptive generalizations that can serve only as posterior explanations and made an effort to explore predictive regularities in psychological processes that make the formulation of hypotheses possible. In other words, they attributed a *symptomatic value* to autobiographical narratives from the point of view of the development and integrity of personality. They believed that an internally consistent, balanced life story is an important sign of mental health; as Butler (1963) suggested, a well-integrated life story is the desired outcome of psychological ageing. Csíkszentmihályi and Beattie (1979) extended the biographical approach not only to the past but also to the present and the future of the individual, pointing out the importance of the evolution of coherent life themes in lifelong personality development. Hunt and Hunt (1977) showed that the coherent biographical reconstruction of marriage and divorce was an indispensable precondition of enduring the emotional strains of getting a divorce. Rainer (1978) and Progoff (1975) analysed personal diaries and demonstrated the function of narratives in creating coherence and reducing emotional tension.

McAdams' model for analysing autobiographies

McAdams' (1985, 1993, 2001) theory of narrative identity, which combines Erikson's psychosocial theory of development with his own analysis based on the narrative typology of biographical narratives by Frye (1957) and Elsbree (1982), proposes several verifiable hypotheses concerning the normal and abnormal development of identity. This model does not wish to capture the complex personality but instead puts the emphasis on identity by treating it as identical with biographical narrative. It investigates constituents, variables and formal features on the basis of which conclusions can be drawn concerning the state, maturity and integrity of identity.

The identity (life story) of an individual consists of four main constituents: nuclear episodes, imagos, world view and generativity scripts. These four constituents are complemented by thematic lines and narrative complexity. Thematic lines are recurrent content units of a life story. According to McAdams (1985), the recurrent, crucial elements are related to motives of power and intimacy (see Figure 7.1).

McAdams views narrative complexity as the index of self-maturity. Emphasis is placed on story structure; stories are different from one another not only in content but in complexity as well. In relatively simple stories there are very few characters, the plot is linear and includes a small number of subplots. In contrast, complex stories are subtle and include many elements and distinctions. The narrator establishes several different relationships among the various elements and integrates all of them into a hierarchical pattern of structure. The degree of complexity can be regarded as a 'development index' because it shows to what extent and in what way personal experience is related to the integrative framework of meaning. At a 'more mature' level of development the individual framework of meaning is relatively simple and uses a holistic, all or none approach to the understanding of self and society. In the case of a 'mature' level the individual framework of meaning is subtle and hierarchically integrated in which paradoxes and contradictions can be tolerated and the individuality of others can be recognized and respected.

It is obvious that in McAdams' narrative model analysis targets psychological contents that can be captured at the semantic plane of narrative, whether it is the constituents of a life story or the thematic lines mentioned above that are taken into consideration. This sort of content analysis can be implemented with the categories (imagos, nuclear episodes, thematic lines, etc.) of an identity model that is constructed in advance. Although McAdams should no doubt be given credit for including biographical narrative as an empirically manageable source of data in the study of identity and for taking pains to test the hypotheses – that is, the validity – that follow from the model by using a projective test of personality, the identification of the model's categories and the content analysis using these categories – due to their abstract nature – involve several elements of uncertainty.

Barclay's model for analysing the coherence of autobiographical narrative

Barclay (1996) worked out a system of categories for the analysis of coherent biographical narratives (Figure 7.2) which can be identified much better at the level of the text. In this model analysis is carried out along an information structure and a narrative organization. The information structure is made up of elements like leading and supporting characters, scenes and activities that constitute the plot and their main features. The amount of information has a significant influence on the liveliness of a narrative, or conversely, the coherence of a narrative lacking sufficient information or crammed with information deteriorates significantly. The analysis of narrative structure takes place in accordance with three

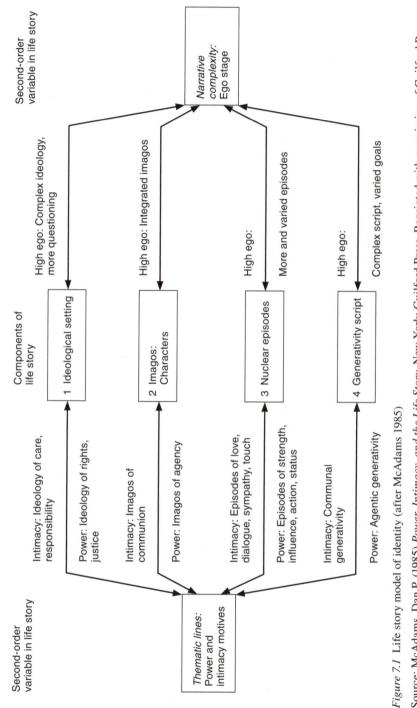

Figure 7.1 Life story model of identity (after McAdams 1985)

Source: McAdams, Dan P. (1985) *Power, Intimacy, and the Life Story.* New York: Guilford Press. Reprinted with permission of Guilford Press.

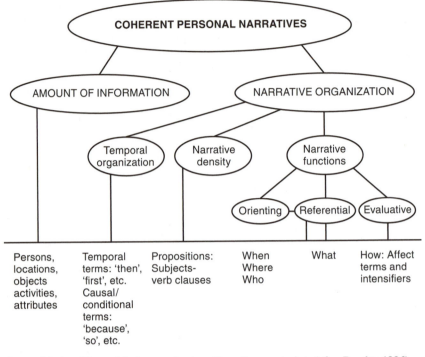

Figure 7.2 Autobiographical remembering: Narrative constraints (after Barclay 1996)

Source: Barclay, Craig R. (1996) 'Autobiographical remembering: narrative constraints on objectified selves', in David C. Rubin (ed.) *Remembering our Past*. Reprinted with permisson of Cambridge University Press.

criteria: temporal structure, narrative density and narrative function. Temporal structure is generated by two constituents: on the one hand by linguistic forms that refer to spatial and temporal relations (tenses, time and place adverbials) and on the other by expressions that carry causal-conditional relations (adverbs of cause, explanatory conjunctions, etc.)

Narrative density refers to the number of elementary utterances contained in the text. This index is relevant for coherence in the sense that an overly low or an overly high number of elements should destroy the coherence of the story (however, here Barclay fails to provide a reference number!). In the case of narrative functions Barclay (1996) practically investigates the extent that the three functions defined by Labov and Waletzky (1967), orientation, referring and evaluation, are fulfilled. For instance, in the case of the orientation function what he considers is whether information concerning the place, time and circumstances of the action are present in the text and what the individual, social, cultural and historical context is in which these pieces of information appear. Evaluation involves the subjective experience of the narrator concerning the emotional value of the narrated event along a positive–negative continuum. Attributes that refer to emotions (e.g. 'I was happy') and verbs expressing a change of emotional state

('I felt relieved') carry the largest amount of evaluative information. Evaluation often follows canonical forms in autobiographical narratives. There are three basic narrative forms. A progressive narrative begins with some negative emotion (negative emotional evaluation of the events), and as the events proceed, evaluation gets more and more positive. A regressive narrative form also evolves in time; however, the direction of the changes in evaluation is just the opposite: the starting event is seen as positive, and this evaluation changes into a more negative view over time as the events unfold. Finally, the evaluation of stable narratives, whether positive or negative, does not change over time. Evaluative patterns are closely related to the schemas of genres. For instance, tragedy follows a regressive schema of evaluation, while in comedy or romance a progressive schema can be observed. According to Barclay (1996):

> through an analysis of a coherent personal history, it is possible to construct a theory of a person and the deep motivations that give him or her a sense of meaningful being and a sense of groundedness in the present time and space.
>
> (Barclay 1996: 109–110)

Empirical studies targeting the analysis of biographies were made extremely difficult before by the fact that there were no procedures for content analysis available that could be used relatively easily and securely for the analysis of relevant psychological contents. It was largely due to this fact that extremely time-consuming research on the content analysis of life stories had been relegated to the background for many decades. The rapid propagation of the narrative-autobiographical approach to individual identity in the past few years has largely been facilitated – in addition to a change in the rigid positivist climate and a boost in research on narrative, that is, narratology, mostly in literary theory but also in other disciplines – by the speedy development of information technology, which made it possible to conduct computer-assisted content analysis research. Chapter 9 will present a so-called *narrative psychological content analysis* model that aspires to explore the psychological meanings of narrative not only at the level of words or themes but also at the level of narrative, along the lines of narrative qualities like structure, organization, perspective, temporal relations and coherence.

The roots of knowledge about the self

Integrity, internal consistence, complexity and coherence are traits of life stories that make it possible to draw conclusions about the state and maturity of an individual's actual identity. However, these are obviously *cognitive* variables that do not reveal much about the emotional qualities of the identity of adults who have verbal memory and a mature self, about a healthy confidence in reality, or the lack thereof, about a readiness to change reality and about the complex process of self-development. When commenting on autobiographical memory, Barclay and Smith (1992) argue that the memories that we accumulate during our lives are deeply rooted in our early relationship with objects. Infants learn about their own subjectivity in their relation to their caretaker. This is where infants experience their relation to their mother, their physical and emotional dependence on her. The self is created through detachment from the mother. One essential element of this process of separation is a potential space between mother and infant in which several symbols of unity with the mother might emerge and gradually escape from the almighty control of the infant. The infant can tolerate separation if the caretaker is a trustworthy mother who cares about the needs of her infant. In such cases, for instance, infants may safely shut their eyes, because they can be sure that their mother will be there when they open their eyes again. This is how confidence is created. If infants can trust the external reality, they have no reason to maintain the illusion that things are under their own control. Giving up the illusion of control may be facilitated by so-called transitory objects – like plush teddy bears or nappies for sleeping – that remind the infant of those properties of the caretaker over which the infant is believed to have almighty control. Plush teddy bears and nappies are later replaced by fantasies and stories; in fact Barclay and Smith (1992) suggest that autobiographical memories are such 'transitory objects' too:

> Memories, and autobiographical memories especially, are precisely such transitional phenomena – symbols of the deep templates of caregiving we come to rely upon, again and again, to serve our needs for emotional support and responsiveness. We release such constructions into the space between ourselves and significant others as a way of recapitulating and 'structure-building' that occurred in our pasts. No less than a child will change its story to suit its feelings, we also adapt our memories as our needs change or as the needs of our partners change. Indeed, reconstructed memories in this sense become a kind of currency of social life, especially for the purchase of intimacy. It is only in the presence of trusted others that we really surrender our illusions, and indeed bring them under another's control. Serving a significant other's needs, likewise, we adapt our memories in natural responsiveness to their emotional states.
>
> (Barclay and Smith 1992: 89)

Narrative ideas in the research on self-development

How does autobiographical narrative enter into self-development? According to Stern (1989) several different forms of a sense of self evolve during the first years of life. *Core self* emerges in the second or third month, which includes the sense of agency, coherence, continuity and affectivity. This self is not reflexive and not conscious.

Subjective sense of self begins to develop at around the ninth month. Subjective sense of self is not reflexive or conscious either. Infants become aware through experience that they have subjective states of consciousness which can be shared with others, with other people who also have their own subjective states. This new subjective self makes it possible to experience intersubjectivity and engage in interaction. Contents of consciousness like the focus of attention, intentions and emotional states become shareable.

Verbal sense of self begins to evolve at around the fifteenth to eighteenth months. This sense of self is already self-reflexive and makes it possible to objectify the self, as shown by the use of personal pronouns or by behaviour in front of a mirror.

The different senses of self all organize subjective perspectives that refer to the self. During the time of developmental leaps, when new cognitive, affective, motivational and motor abilities appear as a result of maturation, infants have to create a new subjective perspective of themselves that can organize the new abilities. It is in this sense that the various senses of the self can be regarded as the organizers of subjective perspective. Every new sense of the self opens up a new dimension of experiences without fully absorbing or eliminating the old ones. Different senses of the self live side by side. At around 2 years of age narrative sense of the self begins to emerge. This is also partly the outcome of new abilities like language or concept-formation. These new capacities enable and at the same time force children to reorganize their subjective perspective into a new form. The senses of agency, coherence, continuity, affectivity, intersubjectivity and self-reflection are now reorganized in a narrative form. The monologues that can be observed in the cot at around age 2 fulfil this function, the stabilization of narrative self. This is the self that children will build on in the rest of their lives when giving an account of their lives to others or to themselves.

With the evolution of narrative self the child crosses the border between the reconstructable and the unreconstructable past. However, the assertion of the subjective perspective, giving meaning to events of life, is not eliminated by narrative; quite the contrary, meaning is provided precisely by narrative. What happens to us becomes one of our own by the fact that it has some meaning for us. It makes a contribution to the organization of the self, our knowledge about ourselves. Bringing back the memory of some events of life and their narration in a particular situation show how an individual attributes significance to events, and what organizing principles and processes of meaning creation participate in the reconstruction of the events. The story of a slap in the face by a parent may be put in several different ways. It may involve something like 'Parents occasionally beat their children.' Or: 'I will never be able to forget or forgive that slap in the face. I felt myself humiliated to the dust.' Or in yet another way: 'I had never been hit before, and that slap in the face made me think. I would never have thought that I could make my parents so angry.' The first case is characterized by generalization, an impersonal way of putting the event into words, as if it did not involve any emotions, or as if it was not possible to remember what had happened. The second case may be thought of as a story that is organized along the lines of vulnerability, defencelessness and humiliation. The third one can be viewed as the story of dependence, responsibility, a strong relationship and realization. Note that the subjective perspective, meaning based on experience and the ability to reflect on it consciously are expressed by specific linguistic patterns in stories about the self. In Chapter 9 we will attempt to identify exactly these linguistic patterns (see also the Appendix).

Two more things need to be emphasized at this point. One of them is the effect of early experiences and early self-development on the evolution of adult personality, including the emergence of pathological forms as well. Early senses of the self, as Stern (1989) writes, do not get lost; however, access to them is possible, if at all, only indirectly. In her research on deviant and normal youngsters for example, Péley (2002) shows that the accounts of several events of their lives given by deviant youngsters include stories in which there are many threatening, frustrating and pressing psychological aspects and several instances of neglect on the part of the main characters, especially the parents, which – in regard to what was said concerning meaning creation in the actual situation – indicates some serious problems in early self-development in the case of these young people.

On the other hand, most of the experiences that emerge after the self is established do not necessarily become conscious and accessible to self-reflection. However, these experiences – and here we mean experiences with a traumatic effect in the first place – can disrupt the coherence and continuity of the self through their emotional content and shake the foundations of a sense of security, value, confidence in others, that is, everything that is needed for the integrated operation of an adult self.

Trauma and narrative

The life stories of people who have gone through a traumatic event show what sort of defence techniques and methods are used to elaborate the traumatic situation as well as what the state of the self is during the process of elaborating the traumatic event. Auerhan and Laub (1998) describe the characteristic forms of remembering a crucial trauma of the twentieth century, the Holocaust. There are several primitive defence mechanisms, processes of denial, splitting, de-realization and so on at work in *not knowing* or not remembering. In *tattered, fragmentary memory*, experiences are isolated from one another; they have no context and the narration of events lack coherence. Kaposi (2003), referring to the strange structure of Imre Kertész's novel, *Fateless* (1975) written about the Holocaust, that evokes a sense of present time, recognizes Kertész's greatness in venturing the impossible. What should be told is a story for which the survivor of the events does not have a tale, a narrative. There are some *cover-up memories* that often appear in connection with traumas. These are stories with fictitious or partly true elements, for example jolly, anecdotal details that cover up the experiences that are associated with the real events. When remembering traumatic events, we can observe the phenomenon of *reliving*, when the narrator switches off the reflexive self and recalls behaviours and emotions relating to the traumatic situation. There is an interesting observation concerning the trauma of the Holocaust which shows that similarly to early relationships with objects, this trauma that is suffered at a relatively early age can play a crucial role in the perception of interpersonal relations and meaning creation in interpersonal events in the future life of an individual. When going through a trauma, the individual *transfers*, as it were, his or her own experiences to actual life situations. The difficulties of coping with a trauma are shown by *overgrowing narratives*. This type of memory is characterized by con-scious self-reflection that controls the narration; memories break loose and are recalled with the intensity of the original experience, overflowing consciousness. Four further forms of recollection indicate the restoration of self-identity, or we might say, a more advanced state of mental health. An individual may make the traumatic experience *the topic of life* or *the topic of identity*; in a positive case for example, an individual may make sympathy and giving assistance to others the guiding principle of his or her life story. An individual may also take the position of *a person giving evidence*; from this position the narratives that recall details may lose their strongly emotional content. *Trauma as a metaphor* as a type of memory indicates that the traumatic experiences have been elaborated in a creative fashion. In this case an individual can use the experiences relating to traumatic events in a creative way in resolving the developmental, emotional and intellectual conflicts of his or her life and use certain aspects of the trauma as a metaphoric tool. Finally, the resolution of traumatic events may lead to *knowledge of action*, a state of identity in which the individual not only knows facts but also knows what to do with these facts. This means the restoration of the agency, the disposing capacity of the self.

These types of memory tied to traumatic events, which can be related to differ-ent states of identity, show again that the organization of events that create iden-tity can be tracked in the linguistic expression of narrative. The question again is whether these linguistic forms are accessible only to a hermeneutic interpretation or whether they exhibit patterns whose identification can lead to information of diagnostic value.

Therapeutic narratives

It was Pennebaker (1993) who pursued pioneering research on the therapeutic function of narrative and the possibility of drawing conclusions and predictions concerning the state of mental health on the basis of the qualities of a narrative. He requested his subjects, suffering from different physical and mental problems, to periodically rewrite the story of a 'traumatic event' that meant a huge emo-tional burden to them. He analysed the narratives in terms of the categories of the words and the qualities of the story (coherence, organization, structure). His most interesting findings concerned temporal changes in the narratives. The positive emotional charge of the original story at the level of words and the completeness of it at the story level could predict the resolution of the emotional state much less than the change that occurred, in a positive direction in regard to positive emo-tional content and coherence, between the original story and the one that was the product of several attempts of rewriting. Similar results are reported by Stephen-son et al. (1997), who analysed the therapeutic diaries of alcoholic patients and found that therapy was successful with those patients who had a negative relation both to themselves and to the therapeutic process at the outset, and this relation turned more positive as therapy or the writing of the diary progressed.

Life story as a social construct

While scientists involved in research on narrative identity take life story and its occasional reconstruction to be a natural means of maintaining identity in which individual modes of adjusting to the world are formulated, according to Gergen and Gergen (1988: 87) 'narratives of the self are not fundamentally possessions of the self'. They view life stories as social constructs, linguistic tools that are worked out and used by people in their interrelationships to maintain, intensify or prevent various actions. The personal past is constructed in conversations (Harré 1983b; Pasupathi 2001), and the methodology suggested to study life stories is *collaborative narration* instead of mere recollection of one's autobiography (McLean and Pasupathi 2006; McLean and Pratt 2006). The task, the objective or the subject matter of psychology in their view is not to explore the process in which individuals attain some sort of an understanding or behavioural response as a result of some consultation with an inner narrative. Narrative about the self works much like history in societies. It is a symbolic system which can be used for social purposes like verification, judgement or the consolidation of society. It can also be used to predict future events, but in itself it does not constitute the basis for any such action.

The analyses of life stories discussed before that seek universal symptomatic values characteristic of individuals in the text do not exclude the possibility to tie the genesis of these texts to social groups or cultural processes outside the individuals, as shown in several studies (e.g., Erős and Ehmann 1997; Erős et al. 1998; Joffe 1996; Jovchelovitch 1996; Péley 2002). In fact, the social representational concept of identity represented through life stories can make a significant contribution to providing more precise predictions concerning individuals and groups of individuals.

Life stories or stories from life: significant life events

The social conventions of constructing life stories on the other hand may even make it more difficult to reach deep layers of identity that are organized in terms of meanings based on experience. In Eco's witty words (1994: 117–118) 'life is certainly more like Ulysses than like The Three Musketeers – yet we are all the more inclined to think of it in terms of The Three Musketeers than in terms of Ulysses'.

According to Barthes' (1977) typology discussed before, life stories are closed 'readable' text with a limited repertoire. It is a basic condition, accidents, mistakes and misunderstandings notwithstanding, that a story in the conventional sense should be rational, uniform and intentional (Baumeister 1987; McAdams 2001). The closed inventory of genres provides assistance in making conventional sense. As far as the construction of the plot in the autobiographical narratives of non-professional authors is concerned, we still live in the world of romantic stories, comic books and soap operas, despite the many innovations of modern and postmodern novels. We have a well-defined narrative repertoire at our disposal, and we select from an inventory of biographical patterns.

Brockmeier (2001) draws attention to the fact that a retrospective teleology manifests itself in biographies. A life story, similarly to biological life, sets out from somewhere, from birth, and is headed for somewhere, for death. The need for a meaningful and good life presses us for straightening out our wrinkles, and we can do it at the level of interpretation, conscious reflection. This is true even if, as has been seen before, we cannot always perform this interpreting-rationalizing job perfectly in the case of serious traumas. Because of its 'roundedness', conventionality and conscious reflexivity, a complete life story is thus not suitable under any circumstances for an analysis that is meant to draw conclusions for the development of the self, the organization of identity and a particular state of identity. Integration and coherence are only one aspect of identity that appear, if you like, at the *plane of the plot*. The development, the states and the qualities of identity, however, can in the first place be studied at the *plane of experience*. This plane of experience emerges with much more probability in the narration of events that relate to strongly positive or strongly negative emotions. The technique of narrating significant events of life was introduced by Fitzgerald (1988, 1996) to the study of autobiographical memory. Fitzgerald gave the following instructions to his subjects when he requested them to tell a story:

> Tell us three stories from your own life. We'd like you to select events that are important to you. Often these are vivid memories but they don't have to be. Think of these as three stories that belong in a book about your life.
>
> (Fitzgerald 1988: 263)

The results of an empirical, descriptive study using another technique similar to the above show that significant events of life can be grouped into four categories (Pataki 2001). The most frequent events were those related to some sort of an achievement, followed by stories related to archetypal experiences (birth, death, etc.), stories of personal relations (friendship, love) and stories of failure. Pataki (2001) analysed the material from the point of view of accepting or rejecting categories of identity. However, these types of stories also have a message for the creation of identity concerning the organization of personal meanings on the basis of experiences. This is because these stories obviously imply emotions, indeed, very strong ones. Through the identification of the emotions and feelings involved in them we can get to much deeper layers of self-organization.

Some authors working in the life narrative area ask for *self-defining memories*. They define this type of memories as vivid, highly memorable, personally important, at least one year old, and convey powerfully how one has become the person one currently is (McLean and Pasupathi 2006; Singer and Salovey 1993). A similar technique is to elicit *turning point* narratives when subjects are asked to write about an important transition or change with respect to their understanding of themselves (McAdams 1993; McLean and Pratt 2006).

A further advantage to an episode of life story – as compared to a complete life story – is that although it appears in a story format, it can take into account the fragmented nature of the self and emphasize particular aspects of the self.

It is less reflexive than lifelike in its nature; it is less tied to conventions, and is governed, at best, by narrative conventions. Any deviation from these conventions can be interpreted in terms of the emotional meaning of the event. Thus a complete life story is not necessary for self-development and for drawing meaningful conclusions about identity states and qualities. The qualities of self-representation and intra-psychic states are expressed in the narration of significant autobiographical episodes. However, it requires the narration of potentially significant events of life that affect some fundamental dimensions of emotional meaning creation. In Péley's (2002) research on normal and deviant young people, the self-representational qualities of *defence* and *security* were 'triggered' by recalling a successfully resolved threatening situation and another one that the subject could not overcome. The need for *separation* and *detachedness* and the experiences related to them were expressed in the episode relating the events of straying away for the first time, and *self-evaluation* and the internal efforts and representations of support related to it were mobilized by an achievement story that the individual was proud of.

Stories about the self are analysed by sophisticated coding schemes (McAdams et al. 1996) or by ratings (Pennebaker 1993), if not qualitatively. These stories, however, all have *composition*, which, in turn, can be analysed at a linguistic level. If we can uncover correspondences between the compositional characteristics of life stories and the identity of the narrating person, we make a significant step ahead towards transforming narrative psychology to real science.

Summary

This chapter outlined psychological approaches to the relation between various forms of life narratives and various forms of self and identity. Theories which have also developed empirical methodologies in order to infer to different qualities of identity from narratives or to trace the process of identity construction through narratives are presented more extensively. The overall characteristic of these approaches is that they deal exclusively with narrative content. When they draw inferences to identity, they consider only content configurations, at most. The chapter also discussed the social constraints on life narratives and the role of narrative in psychotherapy, particularly in trauma elaboration.

8 Language and soul

The title of this chapter refers to the fact that language is in intimate contact not only with cognition and consciousness, as has been analysed in Chapter 2 when discussing the epistemology of psychology, but also with the entirety of human mental life. The categories of the relationship to reality are formulated in language and through language, but in the same way it is language that mediates emotions and motivations that produce the patterns of these relations characteristic of individuals and groups of individuals.

Language and world view

The recognition that reality is mediated to people by language and their world view is determined by language goes back to Wilhelm von Humboldt. According to Humboldt, people live in a world that their language defines for them. The first book of Wundt's ten-volume *Elements of Folk Psychology* (1916) also deals with language, and when dissecting the above idea, it draws conclusions concerning the mentality of different peoples with language as well as their mental frame on the basis of linguistic features, vocabulary and grammatical structure. This trend takes language to be a cultural object form which psychology can be unfolded through interpretation, and there is no way to empirically verify the relationship between linguistic data and psychological phenomena. Similarly, there is no way to explore relationships between collective identity and the mental processes of individual people that constitute collective identity. The theory of linguistic determinisms (discussed in Chapter 2), which was motivated not by the preliminaries of folk psychology but rather by the linguistic observations of cultural anthropology initiated by Franz Boas, also tries to capture the relationship between language and culture.

The fallibility of the folk psychological approach is clearly illustrated by Sándor Karácsony's (1976) analyses of the relationship between the Hungarian language and the Hungarian frame of mind. From the observation that 'Hungarians do in fact prefer to use coordinative sentence structures using "and", "but", "or", "thus" and "therefore" to using so-called clauses; therefore it is a coordinative language', Karácsony (1976: 26) derives traits of the Hungarians such as a special conception of authority relations or a disposition to passive resistance. In Karácsony's opinion these dispositions are in some sense the essential properties of Hungarians that they had brought along from the Asian wasteland.

> So, if a Hungarian crumples the top of his high cap when the storm is coming, he is not lagging behind and to perish; quite the contrary, he survives. This is the only way for him to survive (even ice rebounds from his cap). It would be a mixed metaphor to suggest to him that he should seek shelter, or else he will get beaten to death by the heavenly sling-stones. In that part of the world where this sort of world view prevails there is no shelter that can be reached within such a short period of time. What is needed in a place like that is to struggle, not to act (for there is no way to act). This view obviously eliminates any possibility for linguistic and cultural change, taking them to be instances of deterioration as compared to a perhaps never existing golden age. There is only one way to have the Asian soul waste time for no use; by making it accept a form that is foreign to its essence and requiring it to be 'active', to 'pick the flower of every hour' and to 'measure out its course'. In such a case the Asian soul trifles about and fiddles around, fritters away all the dear hours and years, blackmails the 'soil' or leaves it uncultivated, gets absorbed in its tasks and remains to be unsuccessful. If it were to be possible to replace the golden pillars of the soul, we could even ensure that the Hungarian soul should get ruined, perish and die. Our only hope is that nothing like this could be possible. The Hungarian soul can be bound hand a foot, crippled, killed but it can never be made Indo-Germanic.
>
> (Karácsony 1976: 24–25)

Disregarding for a time the romantic features of Karácsony's national characterization, what we would like to highlight is the fact that he draws conclusions from the surface grammatical properties of language about the system of conditions for linguistic evolution on the one hand, and about the social-psychological dispositions of a nation on the other. In both cases there is absolutely no analysis of the processes that mediate between the presumed relationships, thereby eliminating even the theoretical possibility to provide any sort of scientific verification for the hypotheses.

Linguistic forms and forms of thinking

Iván Fónagy (1989) formulated an empirically testable hypothesis of the relationship between linguistic forms and forms of thinking. He starts out by analysing the emotional value of sounds. In some of his earlier works for example, he assumed that hard, tense sounds, like *k*, *g* and *r* were associated with aggression, while *m*, *l* and *j* were rather related to tender emotions. Then he compared the frequency of occurrence of sounds in love poems and in some other poems about fighting by the great nineteenth-century Hungarian poet Petőfi, and found that the hard consonants were much more frequent in more aggressive poems while the soft ones were more common in love poems.

Based on the above approach he also analysed the mental content of figures of speech (Fónagy 1990). Pulling apart closely related speech components, the use of deviation from normal, logical word order by interpolating elements in sentences (known as *hyperbaton* in rhetoric) for example are interpreted as an active and aggressive intervention by him, for these interrupted statements are quite frequent in hot debates and passionate speech. The comparison of Verlaine's two poetic cycles shows that hyperbaton and overlap (*enjambement*) were in fact much more frequent in aggressive poems than in idyllic ones. At the same time, the analysis of Proust's prose raised the possibility of another kind of psychological meaning due to hyperbaton. In Proust's works, who liked to use lengthy texts interpolated in passages, hyperbaton in Fónagy's view represents the dynamics of meeting–departing. In this concept the figure of speech is a tool for suggesting a content that is hidden at a deep mental level.

Content analysis

The actual use of language, verbal or written (pictorial) communication can be analysed from a psychological point of view as well, so content analysis as a procedure has been used in psychology for a long time (see Ehmann 2000; Holsti 1968). Psychological content analysis seeks content in texts that can be assigned to some mental process (disposition, motivation, evaluation, intention, etc.) and whose frequency of occurrence can be used to infer the mental processes of speakers or their effect on some general *behaviour* of the speaker. One classic example of psychological content analysis is the research conducted by McClelland et al. (1953) on achievement motivation. In this study, which involved more than twenty different countries, the frequency of topics related to achievement, among other things, were analysed in different media. The most striking result of the research is related to content analysis. Economic boost in a country had the strongest correlation with the number of topics related to achievement in children's literature published in the previous twenty-five to thirty years.

Language and personality

In the 1950s Gottschalk and his research group (Gottschalk and Gleser 1969; Gottschalk and Hambridge 1955; Gottschalk et al. 1958) began content analysis research on different aspects of linguistic behaviour and the stable and transitory states of personality. This research had a diagnostic objective. Scientists wished to use their findings for the identification of personality disorders and mental illnesses. They made efforts to establish scales that could measure the features of the speaker's states on the basis of a weighted evaluation of content categories taken from speech samples. Weighting was calculated according to the degree of self-involvement and the directness of emotional expression. For example, the largest scores on the anxiety scale were given to contents in which anxiety over death, mutilation (castration), separation, guilty conscience and shame was expressed directly and closely related to the self. Lower scores were given for mentioning anxiety experienced by others or for mentioning symbolic forms of anxiety. Finally, the lowest scores were given for denying anxiety. The speech samples were gained under controlled conditions using standard procedures. One instruction in a procedure that was used for several different scales was as follows:

> While you are here in the hospital, and getting treatment, there are certain examinations that I will be doing every week. I'd like to explain one of these. I would like you to pick up this 'telephone' and talk into it for three minutes. It doesn't matter what you say; anything that comes into your mind. The important thing is to say everything that comes into your mind. I will tell you when three minutes are up. You probably wonder where this 'phone' goes to. It goes to a dictating machine so that one of our secretaries can type up what you say. In this way we will have a weekly record which will be kept confidential in your hospital chart. Do you have any questions?
> (Gottschalk and Gleser 1969: 187)

Gottschalk and his collaborators tested and refined the validity of the verbal scales by personality questionnaires and projective personality tests. The scoring system worked out for the content analysis of the different forms of anxiety and aggression were finally used mostly in pharmaceutical tests in which the effect of drugs on emotional state had to be measured repeatedly and the repeated use of personality tests was limited by habituation and the possibility of adaptation.

Beyond establishing the fact that the flow of imagination is expressed in spontaneous speech Gottschalk and his collaborators did not formulate any hypotheses concerning the relationship between language use and the stable or actual state of personality, and as for language, they considered only the direct or symbolic contents of speech. Although they made great efforts to make coding clear, due to the abstract nature of the categories of content the task of coding remained to be a very complicated task, requiring special expertise. This was the main reason why the procedure did not become generally accepted.

Weintraub (1981, 1989) inferred preventive mechanisms of subjects from spontaneous speech samples taken in mildly stressed situations and from the frequency of particular words in these speech samples. The investigated words represented fifteen different linguistic dimensions. Among other things, he studied the singular and plural forms of first person personal pronouns, negations, expressions of emotions, comparison of adjectives and adverbial forms. In accord with data in the literature he found, among other things, negative correlation between depression and the frequency of use of first person plural pronouns, which reflects the withdrawal of the depressed individual from the world.

Language and situation

When discussing the linguistic category model (Semin and Fiedler 1988, 1991) and the message modulation model (Semin 2000) in Chapter 4, we have already mentioned that the surface linguistic form of a message expresses interpersonal and between-group relations. The changes related to social and situational relations in language use are stressed by symbolic interactionists, especially by Goffman's (1959) theory of self-representation. Sociolinguistics as a research trend was created for describing the rules of language use dependent on social situations. In their classic study Brown and Gilman (1960) for example demonstrate how power and solidarity relations between partners are expressed in addressing people. In the same way, the formality–informality or the honesty–dishonesty dimension can be described in terms of a special register.

The automation of content analysis

The analysis of word frequency

The analysis of word frequency became possible in the 1960s, at a time when computers used punched cards. The essence of this method is that researchers select a word category and make up a list of all the words that belong to this category in their view. There are numerous such categories; practically anything can belong to categories like these. The emotion dictionary of the Harvard General Inquirer (Stone et al. 1966) for instance identifies expressions of emotion in a text. There are dictionaries that have been compiled for the identification of contents corresponding to primary (dreamlike) and secondary (logical, discursive) thinking described by Freud (Regressive Imagery Dictionary: Martindale 1975) and there are others that measure the 'fundamental tone' of political texts in the dimensions of optimism, certainty, realism and banality. These dictionaries can be used in content analysis to test a large variety of hypotheses. For example, using the Regressive Imagery Dictionary, Martindale confirmed the hypothesis that periodic changes in the arts are predicted by contradictory movements of formal and semantic complexity that balance each other (cf. narrative canons: pp. 19–22). Given that content analytic programs are able to grasp several aspects of meaning in narratives, Martindale even suggests the use of the term *quantitative hermeneutics* for this type of content analysis (Martindale and West 2002).

Traditional word frequency content analysis programs contain a word category list, a so-called 'dictionary file' and an 'exe' file. The latter matches each word of the word lists with the words of the analysed text and produces a number for each category that shows the percentage of that category in the analysed text. Whereas in classic forms of content analysis assigning psychological content to text elements depends on the agreement of independent coders, who are likely sensitive to the context of the given chunk of text, automated content analysis is blind to the context. It is also a difficult task to cope with homonyms and different morphological forms of a word, particularly in inflective languages.

Word frequency programs concerning personality

Pennebaker and colleagues (Pennebaker and Francis 1996; Pennebaker et al. 1997a; Pennebaker et al. 2001) worked out Linguistic Inquiry and Word Count

(LIWC) originally for the analysis of negative events of life and continuously re-written accounts. LIWC searches for words or stems. The vocabulary items were previously categorized by independent judges along seventy different dimensions. The categories included linguistic notions (e.g. word class), psychological categories (positive or negative emotions, cognitive processes, e.g. words expressing causation) and traditional contents (e.g. sexuality, home, work). The results of LIWC could be used to make inferences about the process of overcoming stress, or rather, the success of coping with stress. More recently the LIWC word frequency program has been used to study several forms of individual differences (for a summary see Pennebaker et al. 2003).

Thematic analysis

Traditionally, thematic analysis involves a process in which the analyser, when wishing to learn about a psychological category (e.g., anxiety) reads through a lengthy text corpus, manually selects and adds to a file all sentences or paragraphs in which the speaker – in the analyser's view – thematizes anxiety. The final result will be a collection of quotations which, however, cannot be analysed statistically but is interpreted and commented. There are several programs available for thematic analysis. The most widespread among them is ATLAS.ti (Muhr 1991).

Context analysis

Context analysis is the combination of the above two extremes, an area in content analysis that has been automated only to some extent. The essence of traditional computational context analysis is that a word search function is used to find all the contexts (lines, paragraphs, clauses or sentences) which contain – staying with our example – the thematization of anxiety. Thus, these programs have two kinds of output: different statistical results on the one hand, and the contexts of the search word dumped into a separate file on the other. Such programs include TACT (Bradley 1990) and in part ATLAS.ti (Muhr 1991) too, so the latter can do this as well, in addition to its main task, conceptual analysis.

Targeted interviews

Gottschalk and his group (Gottschalk and Gleser 1969; Gottschalk and Hambidge 1955; Gottschalk et al. 1958) and Weintraub (1981, 1989) made inferences about personality traits and states from the content features of random speech samples. All things considered, psychoanalytic interpretation is also built on the content analysis of the freely associated speech of patients, of course using well-defined concepts of personality dynamics. However, psychology uses not only spontaneous speech for content analysis but also conversations involving specific topics, whereby different mental constructions related to personality are studied. These conversations are called targeted, more or less structured interviews. The classic example of partly structured interviews is the so-called clinical conversation associated with the name of Piaget. In a clinical conversation Piaget raised problems with small children that they had already had some knowledge about. He asked questions like why is it dark at night, is the moon always round, or can you call a table by a different name. Progressing along the answers that the children provided and avoiding any suggestions, he put new questions to them, and on the basis of their answers he could identify several mental categories characteristic of children's thinking and world concept, for example child's animism, artificialism or realism.

The interview technique, including several hour-long in-depth interviews, has been widely used in the past few decades in the quest for psychological contents. However, the idea of content analysis directed at discourse form and the standardization of partly structured interviews appeared only in the 1990s in relation to the adult attachment interview.

The *adult attachment interview* technique was elaborated by Main and her colleagues for the study of transgenerational effects (e.g. Main and Hesse 1990). The interview sheds light upon the representational level of the attachment relation. Main assumed that the interview could be used to explore the 'mental state' of parents concerning attachment, especially from the point of view of reflexivity and elaboration.

In the course of the investigation a partly structured interview is conducted with parents. The interviewees are asked to characterize their own parents with five adjectives for each parent. The characterization should be justified by stories. There is a separate conversation about a separation or loss trauma of the interviewees and about the relationship between their own upbringing and the way they raise their own children.

So the parents should remember their early experiences in the interview, and recall and reflect on potentially traumatic events. In the meantime they should maintain a coherent discourse. The main criterion of content analysis is precisely the coherence of the conversation, measured by Gricean conversational maxims like relevance, quality, quantity and manner. A *free, autonomous attachment relationship* is characterized by active grammatical structures and a 'constructivist' position. The subjects are able to separate past interactions and their effects. They can separate what they experienced, thought and felt as a child from the way they see all these things in the present. The *rejecting* attachment relation is characterized by violations of quality (contradictions go unnoticed) and violations of quantity (little text, few memories, answers like 'I don't remember', etc.). Finally, the *overwhelmed* attachment relationship is characterized, in addition to violations of quantity (lengthy, grammatically confused sentences) by violations of manner (use of psychological jargon, childish manner of speaking) (Main and Hesse 1990).

Narrative interview

The narrative interview technique as a qualitative procedure investigating personal identity has been widely used in recent years (Lucius-Hoene and Deppermann

2002). In this interview subjects are asked to relate their life story. Unlike in a biography, the focus is now on the story-like nature of narration. (There are several different techniques that can strengthen the story-like nature of narrative. One common practice is to present a time schema in the instructions to support the temporal evolution of the story. After the introductory instructions the questioner puts only further questions that can move the story on, gives feedback to the subject that he or she understands the story, repeats what was last said if the subject gets lost, but never asks about causal relations, never requests additional information, and does not introduce new themes, as is common in partly structured or in-depth interviews.)

Narrative interviews can be used not just for the study of identity; in fact, they were developed and applied first in Germany in the 1970s in social psychology research on pressing social issues that played an important role in the personal life of the interviewees, and in relation to events that the interviewees were likely reluctant to formulate an open personal opinion about (Schütze 1977). The technique is based upon the assumption that a narrative can bring a type of knowledge to the surface that the narrator is unaware of at the time of the interview, either because of different instances of defence, or because the experiences have not yet been put together to form systematic knowledge. When the text of the interview is analysed, the interpretational horizons of the interviewee and the interviewer are merged, which requires a level of abstraction that goes behind the surface of textual utterances and significant theoretical efforts and meaning construction.

The narrative interview technique was further developed and published by Bauer (1993, 1996). Resistance against change is a delicate issue in most organizations, as it is often associated with negative properties. Therefore, people belonging to an organization do not like to be seen as resisting organizational change. It is quite likely that questionnaires or question–answer interviews produce responses that meet social requirements, in other words, subjects underestimate their resistance to change. In contrast, when events related to these changes are told, there is some chance that their hidden assessment and attitude will emerge.

The analysis of narratives involving both autobiographical and social problems may raise the question whether the interviewees, either deliberately or unintentionally, tell a faked or made-up cover story instead of the real one. The more knowledge and experience a person has concerning an event, the richer the story about it will be. This is desirable from the point of view of the analysis, but it has the risk that the interviewee communicates the story according to some sort of strategy. The analysis of narratives involving social issues told by 'knowledgeable' interviewees (e.g. politicians: see Jovchelovitch 1996) should also include perspectives in the interpretation that represent other background knowledge. In the case of life stories, where we can safely say that everybody knows their own life the best, this solution is less effective. The possibility of self-presentation can be decreased in an interview situation. At the same time, the events recalled in an interview situation and the way they are recalled can offer an opportunity to make inferences about identity even independent of communicative intent.

Summary

Psychology has been intrigued by the relation between language and human mind from its beginning. The most salient theories in this domain are Wundt's *Elements of Folk Psychology* and Sapir and Whorf's *theory of linguistic relativity*. Several attempts have been made to establish correlations between the use of different language forms and psychological states or traits. From the 1950s, psychological content analysis gained predominance. This chapter reviewed the types of content-analytic works in psychology and discussed the problems of automation of content analysis. Whereas in classic forms of content analysis assigning psychological content to text elements depends on the agreement of independent coders, who are likely sensitive to the context of the given chunk of text, automated content analysis is blind to the context. It is also a difficult task to cope with homonyms and different morphological forms of a word.

9 Narrative psychological content analysis

Methodology
— see pp. 39–40

As we have already stressed in the Introduction, narratology describes a finite number of constituents and a finite number of variants of these constituents concerning the composition of narratives. Each constituent, or their versions, can be reliably identified at the level of the text. At the same time meanings at the level of experience can be associated with the constituents of narrative thus defined. *Narrative contains a finite number of structural or compositional 'slots' that can be filled with an equally finite number of psychologically meaningful contents, while the surface text may show infinite variety.* This is what narrative psychological content analysis attempts to make the most of. Without attempting to be exhaustive, in what follows we will take a look one by one at the narrative components that can be equipped with psychological meaning.

Characters and their functions

As any story, episodes told by interviewees involve characters who perform various acts. Propp (1968) analysed a large number of Russian fairy tales. He discovered that characters and their functions from the perspective of the significance for the course of the action are stable elements in this corpus of stories: fairy tales are combinations of a limited number of functions or plot units. Moreover, the combination is patterned by rules. Functions are generalizations of characters' actions that may be entirely different in their surface form. *Harm-doing*, for instance, can be executed in the stories in twenty different ways, for example:

> The villain abducts a person, The villain seizes or takes away a magical agent, The villain casts a spell upon someone or something, The villain imprisons or detains someone, The villain seizes the daylight, etc.
>
> (Propp 1968: 31–32)

Propp identified altogether thirty-three functions, such as 'One of the members of a family absents himself from home. Prohibitive commands are addressed to the hero. The villain makes an attempt at reconnaissance, etc.' Propp also noticed that many functions logically join together into certain classes. These bunches of functions correspond to their respective performers. He termed them *spheres of action*, and identified seven such spheres that were fulfilled with the corresponding character types, such as *hero, villain, donor, helper, etc.* (Propp 1968: 79–80). The distribution of actions among the characters has three possibilities: one sphere of action exactly corresponds to a single character, one character is involved in several spheres of action, and one sphere of action is distributed among several characters.

The four short story excerpts below illustrate Propp's analysis and conceptual scheme.

* A tsar gives an eagle to a hero. The eagle flies the hero away beyond the mountains.
* An old man buys a horse for Sucenko. The horse carries Sucenko away to the dragon's cave.
* A sorcerer lends Ivan a boat. Ivan drifts in the boat to another kingdom.
* A princess presents the warrior a ring. Young men appearing from out of the ring lead the warrior to the place of combat.

(after Propp 1968: 19–20)

It is apparent that there are no identical characters and identical actions in the four excerpts. Nevertheless, the four plots are common in involving two functions: *the hero acquires the use of a magical agent* and *the hero is transferred to the whereabouts of an object of search,* and in employing three spheres of action or character-types: *the hero, the donor* and *the helper.*

Although Propp's analysis is not without psychological implications (there are motivations, dispositions and character traits behind each function; functions can be ordered into causal schemes – a feature which is heavily exploited by story grammars during the 1970s and 1980s), it is directed to the structural description of a given corpus of stories, in this case Russian fairy tales. However, the properties of narratives explored by Propp, with some modification, may offer a possibility to analyse intra-mental events too.

In narratives of autobiographical episodes the range of characters can be easily classified from a psychological aspect. Of course, in this respect narrative is not alone, since Mérei (1984) for example uses the repertoire of manifest dream contents to infer the order of significance in attachment. However, narratives, especially narratives of life history, have a special feature in that the characters in them, the partners not only swing the plot in motion by their social actions (that is, they do not have only functions related to the plot) but also represent interpersonal, psychological functions that are important for personality development and the state of personality too. The plot function of *providing assistance* or *protection* can be easily interpreted along the psychological function of *defence* and *security*, and it does matter whether this function is fulfilled by the parent against the child or vice versa. In the latter case we are dealing with the reversal of roles, which entails a relationship between parent and child that involves emotional burdens and insults for the child.

Thus, the psychological content analysis of characters and their functions does not simply take stock of freely chosen units in the text but builds on the properties, the characters and their actions that constitute the essence of the text by giving a psychological interpretation to these properties. This is the reason why it can be called psychological content analysis.

In regard to the psychological functions of characters Péley (2002), Ehmann (2000) and Hargitai et al. (2007) conducted some interesting research. Péley (2002) held interviews with young people using drugs and a group of youngsters leading a 'normal' life as measured along socio-demographic indices compared with the first group, using the technique of narrative interview. In this study she wished to verify the assumption that juvenile deviant patterns of behaviour are underlain by disorders in early object relationships and the mistaken compensation for these disorders. Accordingly, she asked her subjects to tell episodes in which their representations of early self-objects are expressed (for example, the first good or bad memory, a memory related to the parents), and in which defence and security (a threatening situation successfully controlled, a threatening situation unsuccessfully controlled), self-assessment, value and the corresponding internal efforts and assistance (memory of an achievement) appear. She divided the characters in the recounted episodes into four categories (roles): parents (father, mother), narrow family, extended family, non-relatives. She analysed the psychological functions of the characters by using twenty-one categories that could be described along confidence–distrust (e.g. 'traitor', 'enemy'), defencelessness (e.g. 'likely to leave/worry') and providing security (e.g. 'protective', 'supportive'). The distribution of the characters in the stories and the functions attributed to different characters in each story could be used to draw conclusions that clearly supported the initial hypothesis.

Analysing autobiographical interviews made with auto-immune female patients, Ehmann (2000) recognized that the characters of life stories are organized into three marked roles in the experience of interviewees, and these roles have a distinct psychological function within their experience. Two of the three role categories (supportive and causing damage) are also part of Propp's tale dramaturgy, while the third role, the category of a person likely to leave, stepping out of the life of the interviewee through divorce, moving out or death, is typically characteristic of the narratives of this particular sample. The emergence of persons belonging to each role follows the pattern shown below. Pre-morbid life cycle is dominated by people who are likely to leave and/or cause damage, although as a counterpoint, one dominant supportive person and several less important supportive characters are also present. When the illness is diagnosed, the thematization of persons likely to leave or cause damage radically decreases or is stopped altogether, and typically one or more new, dominant supportive individuals appear on the scene. From the date of the diagnosis up the present time of the narrative the subjects do not thematize people likely to leave or cause damage at all, or they do so only by distancing them and relegating them back to the past; however, they mention more and more persons with a supportive role. The 'split' world view of auto-immune female patients is especially aptly characterized by the attitude of distancing or making insignificant towards situations in which formerly supportive individuals left them or caused damage to them. On the basis of the results it seems that for the sake of making their life stories coherent, thereby making their intra-mental processes controllable, the subjects of the study insist on a tripartite division of roles, and within this division on populating their world with supportive individuals. And the desert of supporters that cannot be prevented at the perceptual level is defended at the level of experience.

Hargitai et al. (2007) analysed the life story of female patients suffering from colorectal tumour and major depression in the context of their results in a Szondi test. The test scores were in accord in several respects with the psychological functions of the characters appearing in their life stories. In the case of patients suffering from depression the high number of partners having a 'non-supportive', 'non-assisting' function is compatible with the result that depressed patients exhibit high saturation in positive h-reaction, that is, they cannot deplete this instinctive need, and as a result, libido accumulation takes place. Depressed patients constantly seek love and tenderness, but they fail to find them in their unsupportive, non-assisting interpersonal relations. Likewise, this factor reaction of depressed patients, which indicates the accumulation of rough tempers, anger, revenge, jealousy, etc. as far as affects are concerned, is reflected in the relatively high number of characters appearing in the enemy function in the life stories of these patients (the frequency of partners with the enemy function is three times as high as in the life stories of tumorous patients).

Control of spatial-emotional distance

It was some outstanding narratologists of the twentieth century that took notice of the role of concrete and symbolic space in the composition of literary texts. Bakhtin (1981) represents the chronotopos of romance by a pattern of recurrent motives describable in spatial relations: lovers *meet*, some obstacles prevent them from uniting, they *get separated* from each other, and finally they meet each other again and *are united in marriage*. Frye (1957) makes a distinction between 'fictions in which the protagonist gets isolated from society and fictions in which he gets assimilated into society.' The former would correspond to the myth of tragedy, the latter to that of comedy. In this view archetypal spatial symbolism is the equivalent of archetypal qualities of experience. However, archetypal spatial patterns constitute only a part of the spaces that organize text and can be found in the text. Examining literary, fictitious narratives, Kornélia Faragó (2001) made an attempt to define the concrete and metaphoric spaces appearing in texts and their significance. She highlights the topoi that can be mapped onto spatial motives and refer, on the one hand, to subordinate and superordinate spatial relations and, on the other, to coordinate relations in the text. The recurrent patterns of subordinate and superordinate relations can be formulated in terms of the mythic topoi of grinding poverty: rise–fall, glorification, and heaven–hell. However, from the point of view of interpersonal relations coordinate spatial relations also have a great importance: the 'game of from/towards something/somebody', which is realized in the spatial-emotional relationship of approaching versus distancing.

According to Frye (1957) two general directions of the movement of emotions are represented in approaching an object (e.g. in the form of pity) and in moving away from an object (e.g. in the form of fear). The dynamics of approaching–distancing in narratives of life stories implies the way how the relationship between the narrator as the protagonist of the story and other characters as partners is controlled, and how the emotions of the narrator are controlled.

Relying on theories of object relationship (Mahler et al. 1975) and theories of self-development (Stern 1995). Pohárnok et al. (2007) worked out assumptions concerning the psychological meanings of approaching–distancing. According to this there is an interpersonal inactive space that is always organized on the basis of the relationship between the self and the other thing: the two endpoints of the space are given by the self and the other thing, and their movement in relation to each other can be seen as a key feature of their relationship. On the one hand, the relationship of the self and the other thing can be described by movements in physical space: in the dimension of towards it (together with it) – away from it (without it). Here movement can be described in terms of actions performed by the other person (e.g. 'he came up to' or 'he left'). On the other hand, the relationship of the self and the other person can also be described from an intersubjective aspect by the states of sharing (understanding) and the lack of sharing (no understanding). This time the mental states experienced in relation to the other person – desires, emotions, intentions – indicate proximity versus distance, for example, 'I liked it' and 'He did not forgive'.

Pohárnok et al. (2007) compared narratives of the life stories of borderline female patients with similar stories of female patients of comparable age suffering from major depression. When studying the psychodynamics of personality organization Pohárnok started out using the interpretation by Mahler, who believes that pathology is caused by impairment in the process of separation–individuation. In the case of these patients, separation from the mother involved a crisis in which each instance of a distancing attempt evoked a sense of being left alone for good. However, proximity threatened them with their self-boundaries becoming blurred and losing their own identity. Borderline patients relive the crises of separation–individuation in their adult relations. The results confirmed Pohárnok's expectations. While there was no difference between the two groups in the absolute number of approaching–distancing, a significantly larger number of changes in approaching–distancing could be observed in borderline patients. These changes often appeared in a single statement, such as 'Well, it was such strong love, but I know that when it came true (*approach*), I felt it to be very strange (*avoidance*)'.

Narrative perspective

Generally, the narrator not only presents the events and the actions of story characters, but – in addition to this – he or she has a possibility to describe the events, actions and characters from different points of view. The concept of narrative perspective has a double meaning. On the one hand, it refers to psychologically interpretable phenomena, while on the other hand it could be defined as a linguistic concept. The linguistic concept of narrative perspective covers those linguistic markers that connect the story world – events, actions, characters and relevant circumstances – to that character of the story whose point of view the narrator takes. The narrative perspective or point of view commands an essential role in the analysis of the representation of the events of a narration, because it contains the states of consciousness related to the events of the story and to the characterization of the figures. Thus point of view has been considered by certain authors (i.e. Bakhtin 1981; Bal 1985; Friedman 1955; Genette 1980) as the key to the narrative composition (for a review, see van Peer and Chatman 2001).

Uspensky (1974) introduced two independent dimensions to systematize the various forms of narrative perspective. On the one hand, he differentiated between four conceptually independent forms of perspective: evaluative, phraseological, spatio-temporal and psychological. On the other hand, and mainly on the basis of psychological form of perspective, Uspensky distinguished the external and internal forms of perspective. This duality of internal and external perspective is applied to all four dimensions. According to Uspensky the various forms of narrative perspective could be investigated by the linguistic analysis of literary texts. As opposed to the abstractness of the evaluative dimension, the perspective manifested in the spatial–temporal dimension is relatively simple. The grounding of the spatial–temporal dimension is helped by the spatial metaphor of perspective: understanding the description of sights, we can infer the narrator's spatial position. Time perspective refers to the anchoring of the deduced order of subsequent events in a story. This can occur as two distinct types: presenting events in a synchronized way or in retrospect, which is exhibited in variations of verb tense (present versus past) or verb aspect (perfective versus imperfective).

Perspective at the psychological level means the method of introducing characters. The narrator – who is not necessarily identical with the author – can choose among the various methods of introducing characters. Character-painting might be limited to the description of behaviour. The contrasting alternative to the external introduction is the omnipotent narrator, who guides the reader through the inner world of the characters, describing their emotions, experiences and thoughts. Merging these alternatives, the author might choose to paint a character by referring to her or his inner states, but from an observer's perspective. In this case the narrator, through the acts of perceiving those states, merely supposes their presence (e.g. 'It seemed he thought that x'). The depiction of characters we have just described – going from the outside perspective towards inner states – is revealed in the verbal composition of the text. The narrator uses action verbs to describe the behaviour of characters, whereas in the description of the characters' mental states, verbs (*verba sentiendi*) descriptive of mental states are used. In the third, combined form the narrator connects the target's unobservable mental content with the so-called alienating expressions suggestive of the perceptions of an observer (e.g. 'one sees that x'). Another possibility of perspectivization at the psychological level is that the narrator directly interweaves a character's emotions and thoughts with the text without distinctly signalling it in the composition. In this case a narrator speaks as a character and not about a character.

Pólya (2007) has attempted in the context of narrative psychology to unravel and operationalize the psychological implications of the narrative perspective in autobiographical narratives. (The analysis of the evaluation and of the spatial–temporal dimension – even in autobiographical material – has several psychological connotations. Some of these will be mentioned later.) The dual role played by the fictional or non-fictional autobiographical voice – as a character in and narrator of the story at the same time – is however a unique characteristic of this form. The role assumed at a given time and the reflections made from one role onto the other can be identified in the text. This makes possible the extension of McAdams' concept of narrative identity with the aspect of self – reflexivity, while it also offers a more objective method for examining the identity states than the psychological content analysis used by McAdams (1985). Pólya's analysis is based on the premise that the narrator of a life story may choose one of two narrative positions: the narrator as 'the voice of the story' may relate the events as seen from the retrospective position of remembering them, or tell them as originally experienced at the time of living these events when the position of 'the voice of the actor within the story' is assumed. In order to separate the two positions Pólya uses the concept of a spatial-temporal system connected to the speaker (Harré 1983a; Lee 1997; Lyons 1995). This means that the narrator of an autobiographical piece, for example, may be seen linguistically as a subject in the centre of a three-dimensional system of coordinates. The deictic expressions referring to time, person or place are the dimensions of this system, thus among others the personal pronouns, the spatial and temporal adverbs and verb tenses. The analysis is built on the fact that the meaning of deictic expressions may be determined only with knowledge of the context they are used in. Taking the sentence 'I'm here now' as an example, we can ascertain who the 'I' personal pronoun refers to, or what time, place or state the adverbs 'here' and 'now' and the present tense verb 'am' refer to only if we are aware of the context the sentence was originally used in. The position of the autobiographical narrator may be defined with the help of the concept of the three-dimensional deictic system. It helps us determine whether the narrator appears as the 'narrator of the story' or as 'narrator as part of the story'. When the narrator begins to relate a story the deictic centre of the text is usually connected to the situation of the narrative. This means that the singular first person pronoun in the text refers to the narrator's position, and the deictic expressions referring to time and place maybe 'proximal' (at this time, here etc.) and deal with the actual position of the narrative, or distant (then, at that time, there etc.) in which case they refer to the events revoked. However, when the narrator takes the position of the character the 'proximal' deictic expressions referring to time and place and the present tenses refer to the events revoked and told and not to the actual circumstances of the narration or remembering. As the personal pronouns, unlike the spatial and temporal adverbs and verb tenses cannot be divided into two formally distinguishable categories – proximal and distant – we infer the switch in personal pronouns between the positions of narrator and narrator as character from the above proximal/distant distinction of the adverbs and the change of the verb tenses.

More recently, in accordance with the criteria of functional studies of the organization of experience and self-reflexivity, Pólya et al. (2007) emphasised the temporal plane of the narrative perspective instead of narrative positioning. Narratives of life stories deal with minimally two temporal planes of events (with a few exceptions they do not handle any more than that). One is the temporal plane of the narrative situation; the other is the narrative plane of the events told in the life story. In accordance with the two temporal planes there are four versions of the narrative perspective. In a retrospective narrative perspective the narrative viewpoint is temporally related to the narrative situation, while narrative content is connected in time to the narrated events. In an experiencing narrative perspective both the narrative viewpoint and the narrative elements are localized at the time of the narrated events. In a re-experiencing narrative perspective both the narrative viewpoint and the narrative elements are connected to the narrative situation. The fourth variant practically never occurs.

The analysis tools that are used to describe the embedding of biographic events into the content of consciousness through capturing the narrative perspective build on well-definable linguistic properties of the text. Thereby, they offer a possibility to investigate identity states. Pólya (2007) prepared a narrative interview with young gay people and with women who participated in IVF programmes about some critical episodes of their lives. In the first case subjects were asked to speak about the time when they told their family that they were homosexual. In the second case subjects spoke about the situation in which they learned that they could not have a baby. Both cases concern the central category of identity, so the way in which the events connected to the subjects were organized could be used to draw inferences about their identity states, especially concerning the emotive content of identity. To verify the correctness of the inferences, when taking the interviews Pólya also administered questionnaires to measure identity states. The two sets of data, one concerning the use of the narrative perspective in telling stories of life and the other concerning identity states, showed strong correlation. The retrospective narrative perspective entails an emotionally balanced identity state, while in the case of experiencing and re-experiencing perspectives the data of the questionnaires indicated insecurity of identity and an unbalanced emotional state.

The role of time in the narrative

The relationship between time aspects of the narrative text and psychic processes were investigated from two sides. From the side of the reader, an intricate relation between story emotions and reading time was demonstrated (Cupchik and László 1994; László and Cupchik 1995), and this was used for characterizing the meaning-creating processes in the reader's mind. From the side of the storyteller or the author, such studies were performed in the scope of modern psychoanalytical art psychology, whose interest lies not as much in the personal sources of the contents, but rather in the origin of psychic attitudes responsible for the use of different forms. In case of Proust, for example – beyond the explanation of the relationship between autobiographical and personality development aspects and the lifetime writing flow – explanations were suggested to the peculiar narrative technique which, breaking the 'ordinary' or canonical time sequence of the story, focuses on the writer's (the main character's) experience and internal states driven by associative, involuntary memories. These investigations found that the function of the disclosure of past experience and the associative time handling was the repeated recall of maternal love and the related positive self-sensations (Kohut 1971).

Time structure of the narrative is an intrinsic property of non-literary autobiographical stories as well. This, as with the above narrative characteristics, seems to appear as an indicator of intrapsychic processes and conditions. Time structures may be analysed along the following aspects:

• The relationship between narrated event(s) and the real (biological, psychological and social) chronology of life story. Which life segment(s) the event(s) come from?
• 'Density' of the story, relationship between the real and narrated time extension of the event (e.g. arresting or dilating the time flow).
• Time perspective of the story and its changes (present, past, future).
• Chronological pattern of the story: deviations as to the linear sequence, and phenomena bound to time fluctuations.

Below we refer to two of our studies connected to the last two aspects. Time perspective of the story may be identified relatively easily at the level of the text, for example by adverbs, verb tenses and action directions of verbs (e.g. plans: future-directed, finishes: past-directed). Based on this, and on a feature of stories that they always imply some kind of judgement, which can also be identified (see below), we content analysed therapeutic diaries of addict patients from the point whether they allow for conclusions as to the healing or the future outlook of the patients (Stephenson et al. 1997). Actual improvement was judged by psychiatrists and psychologists in a five-score scale at the end of the therapy and also one month later, independently of the content analysis.

The diaries were kept for thirty-two days by the patients in therapy. Accordingly, we divided each text of each patient into four chronologically equal parts, and coded the time direction (past, present, future) and the quality of evaluation (positive, neutral, negative) in each of the four segments. The evaluations in the diaries could be ranged into three main groups, such as the self, the therapy and 'external' persons (e.g. family members). As to chances for improvement and permanent healing, the analysis showed marked differences along time perspective and evaluated thematics. The highest healing chance was found in patients with present and future oriented, positive evaluations. The results were even more articulated by the fluctuations of the three evaluated thematic contents: chance for healing was improved by a decrease in the negativity of self-referred evaluations as well as their turning into positivity from segment quarter to segment quarter, provided it showed positive correlation with an increase of positive evaluation of the therapeutic programme.

As to the chronological pattern of narratives, an analysis of interviews with second generation Holocaust survivor Jews (Ehmann and Erős 2002) called attention to a finding that the chronological linearity of the story will be broken whenever the subject comes to disclosing a trauma-laden event in the story. At this point the narrative time starts to 'jump', the clock of the narrative will 'pendulate' several decades back and forth even within a single sentence. Consequently, the chronology of autobiographical stories and trauma handling seems to be closely interrelated (which, in turn, calls for a new look at the problem of narrative coherence as well).

Time experience

Another relevant temporal feature of life narratives is subjective time experience, that is the way the person experiences time. Time experience has already been measured by the LIWC (Pennebakeret al. 2001). However, the time category receives little emphasis in LIWC. It is located in the domain of 'relativity', together with 'space' (up, down, inclusive, exclusive) and 'motion'.

Though no one has yet devised a compelling psychological theory of word usage, the word use approach is a sharp edge in contemporary psychometry (see Pennebaker et al. 2003). In our approach, narratives of personal life experiences refer to self and identity. Following the non-essentialist self theories (e.g. Bruner 1990; Erikson 1968), which derive self from life narratives, we may use temporal features of these narratives to characterise the qualities of the narrating self. Consequently, we may use narrative self theories for a theoretical explanation of the so far unexplained psychometric correlations. Moreover, when using narratives as more or less organized texts, we may go beyond word level analysis and use language patterns that depict time experience (Ehmann et al. 2007).

In psychological literature, various aspects of time experience were given interpretation.

- *Relationship between time and the unconscious.* Although the cornerstone of psychoanalytic theory is that the unconscious is timeless, most papers dealing with time pathology refer to an article and a subsequent discussion between Sigmund Freud and Marie Bonaparte (Bonaparte 1940), where the old Freud argued that the lineal, abstract temporality characteristic of the functioning of the conscious system is not prevalent in the unconscious system, but finally, he did 'not rule out the possibility of other forms of temporality in the unconscious' (Boschan 1990: 338). This event is interesting for us not because it has served for psychoanalytical authors as a justification for any considerations about the unconscious aspects of any time pathologies. It is more important that the non-linear nature of narrative chronology that can be empirically well analysed in written texts may as well be explained by the impact of the speaker's unconscious processes: when subjects recall life stories with multiple time loops back to previous events, or with embedded sub-stories, this may be informative about the psychological process of trauma elaboration, for example.

- *Matte-Blanco's theory* about the 'symmetrical-asymmetrical bi-logic structures' in the conscious and the unconscious. These bi-logic structures are constituted by (1) symmetry, with its disregard for time, space, and (2) asymmetry, with all its object distinctions given by the existence of time, space and a clear difference between the whole and its parts, which permits the conceptualization of past, present and future (Fink 1993; Matte-Blanco 1988, 1989).
- *Fraser's 'Umwelt' theory on the external and internal reality of time.* This theory uses a visual metaphor of the time arrow to conceptualize various forms and pathologies of subjective time experience along the stages of nootemporal, biotemporal, eotemporal, prototemporal and atemporal 'Umwelts', that is 'perceived realities' (Fraser 1981).
- *Anniversary reactions.* The pathology related to recurring dates, such as personal, religious, and national holidays, and the anniversaries of severe psychological traumas is a favourite topic in psychotherapeutic literature (Mintz 1971).
- *Fragmented time.* Hartocollis claims that many borderline and narcissistic patients suffer from a pathologic condition when the subjective perception of the past and the future splits from that of the present, and even the present is fragmented into smaller parts (Hartocollis 1978). (This phenomenon is similar to Fraser's eotemporal Umwelt.)
- *Types of traumatized time.* Terr (1984) summarized the types and disorders of subjective time experience in survivors of extremely severe traumatic events. The main groups of disorders and distortions are treated under the titles of short time sense, duration, simultaneity and succession, and temporal perspective (Terr 1984).

Time experience was related to psychopathology by the Time Perception Scale in Experiential World Inventory, a psycho-diagnostic test developed by El-Meligi (1972). The test measures changes in the experience of time flow, time orientation, and experiential age. The general lesson of the subsequent investigations of subjective time experience is that the more pathological a personality, the more disturbed/distorted his or her subjective time experience.

Narrative evaluation

The evaluative-ideological plane is one aspect of the narrative perspective in Uspensky's (1974) system. It shows how and from which position the narrator evaluates the world that he or she depicts. The vantage point can be that of the author, of the narrator (who is not identical with the author), or of any of the characters. As Uspensky (1974: 17) suggests, evaluative-ideological perspective is the least amenable to empirical study. Its analysis demands lots of intuition. For instance, when we connect certain evaluations to certain positions on the basis of evaluative adjectives, we often do it by using our previous knowledge of how different people and institutions use the adjective in the given context.

Narrative evaluation, however, has another aspect, which is also a necessary ingredient of stories. This aspect has been discussed by Labov (Labov 1972; Labov and Waletzky 1967). Labov asked adolescents questions like 'Were you ever in a fight with somebody bigger than you?' or 'Was your life ever in danger?' and let them tell the story if they answered yes. Although Labov was primarily interested in the relation between the sequence of events and the sequence of the story, he noticed that narrators consistently exert an effort to make the point of their story salient. They were not concerned with reporting a sequence of events but rather telling a story that will not be seen as pointless. The way that narrators achieve this is infiltrating evaluation into the story. Evaluative clauses intrude into the sequence of narrative clauses. But the most powerful evaluative elements are not comments external to the action but embedded in the action itself. One can emphasize the reportability of a story by narrating as an event an evaluative comment: 'And when we got down there her brother turned to me and whispered "I think, she's dead, John!"' (Labov and Waletzky 1967: 39). Even a narrative clause itself can be an evaluation, as the following sentence shows: 'I never prayed to God so fast and so hard in all my life!' (Labov and Waletzky 1967: 37).

Emotional and cognitive evaluation of an event in narratives, however difficult it can be to detect and identify it at the text level, may be an indicator of internal processes and states relevant to the event. Evaluation indicates what events mean to the person (Linde 1993). A rudimentary form of analysing narrative evaluation is using emotional dictionaries such as the Harvard General Inquirer Emotion Dictionary or the relevant dictionaries of the LIWC text-analysis program (Pennebaker et al. 2001). Given that these programs regularly miss the narrator's perspective and are not able to relate the object of evaluation with the evaluation itself, it seems to be more adequate to stick closer to the text in the content analysis that is aimed at evaluation. It is reasonable therefore to focus on whole utterances which evaluatively refer to the self, to the partners and/or to the situation of the action. This is exactly what Stephenson et al. (1997) did when they analysed diaries of addict patients who participated in a therapeutic programme. They coded self-positive (e.g. 'This day I felt better than ever'), self-negative (e.g. 'I think I am brain dead, I am so tired I want to sleep forever'), programme positive (e.g. 'I enjoyed K's collage'), programme negative (e.g. 'With the meeting this morning I was just on the verge of moving out'), outside world positive (e.g. 'I got a Valentine's card from the wife, nice to know she still loves me after all the crap') and outside world negative (e.g. 'I am not expecting my family to be different when I leave Promis') statements and from the distribution and change over time of these statements they were able to infer with high reliability to the chances and permanence of recovery.

Finally, a possible method of the study of narrative evaluation is introducing the evaluative perspective by instruction when soliciting the narrative interview or narrative task. In a study (László et al. 2002) we investigated the development of national identity by asking stories about positive and negative events in Hungarian history. By relating the properties of the narrated events to the evaluative dichotomy, the stories revealed what positivity and negativity means in the representation of history for the target sample. This research also shows that narrative psychological content analysis can be applied not only to life-historical narratives, which refer to personal identity, but also to the study of naive histories as social representations which are constituents of social identity.

Narrative coherence

Stories present the events of the outside and inner world in rational order. Narrative techniques of postmodern literature that deny the conventional logic of action do not contradict this statement, since imagined, possible worlds always refer in some way to the shared, consensual world. This is why even the most excessively absurd story can be endowed with coherence.

Study of story coherence became an issue for psychology in memory research. Kintsch (1974) suggested that the minimal criterion for coherence in a text is the occurrence of common objects, persons and/or concepts in the text-statements. However, as Black et al. (1984) pointed out, for narratives it is not enough. Although there are three concept-repetitions in the following sequence, the sequence is quite incoherent: 'John took a psychology course at Yale. Susan registered for a psychology course at Yale. Rita dropped a psychology course at Yale.' The reason is that it is difficult to make causal inferences between each sentence.

Black et al. (1979) proposed that maintaining a consistent point of view contributed to the sense of coherence. The sequence 'John worked in the front yard. Then he went inside' maintains a consistent point of view, because John is the actor in both sentences and the actions are described from a location in the front yard. This sequence took a shorter time to read than a similar sequence which changed the point of view by replacing the verb 'went' to 'came'.

The degree of narrative coherence in episodes of life history and in narratives of life history themselves appears to be a sensitive indicator of intra-mental occurrences. According to Antonovsky (1987) people's general state of health is also related to how coherently they experience their life story. At the same time, it is also obvious that it is rather difficult to capture the coherence of narrated life stories operationally at a textual level, since even at the level of the plot there are complex causal chains connecting very simple stories, and at this level we have not yet considered either the previously analysed further factors of coherence or the harmony between the plane of action and the plane of consciousness. Barclay (1996) suggested an analysis schema for establishing the coherence of texts of life stories; however, this schema can be used mainly for identifying the components that play a role in creating coherence rather than for measuring coherence. Research on the measurement of textual coherence in narrative is conducted at the University of Memphis in a research group headed by Art Graesser. The COH-METRIX text analysis program developed by them is built on the text reception model of Kintsch and van Dijk (1978). The program, which is in an experimental state, contains a coherence analyser module for measuring causal, intentional, temporal, spatial and structural cohesion, so it handles coherence indicators characteristic of narrative on the basis of 250 linguistic markers (Dufty et al. 2004). Nevertheless, the only procedure available for establishing story coherence at the moment seems to be a global estimate, using independent evaluators to assess a text from the point of view of coherence. This procedure was used by Pennebaker (1993) when he asked patients suffering from emotional disorders to narrate in writing certain traumatic or stress-generating events. The patients were asked to repeat the written narratives through three to five days. Pennebaker checked the change in mental and physical state of health by using several variables and compared them to a control group writing about a neutral topic, for example he tested changes in immune activity, checked the number of days spent on sick-leave, and so on. In addition to performing a content analysis of the written narratives, looking for words that refer to cognitive and emotional operations, he used independent evaluators to assess the story coherence of the narratives written day after day. While writing about tension-generating experiences generally led to a positive change in the state of health as compared to the control group, the most significant improvement took place in the case of patients whose emotionally negative and less coherent story shifted towards a positive emotional direction and became more coherent by the fifth day.

We used a similar procedure in a study in which career starters with no job, steadily unemployed young people and previously unemployed youngsters who managed to find a job were tested on their attitude towards the unemployment situation and the psychological components of their career possibilities (László et al. 1998). In this study, among other things, we asked the subjects to tell an episode of their life in connection with their parents' work and then another one in connection with a sense of achievement and a sense of failure. (The choice of episodes was determined by patterns of motivation for work in the family and the relationship to achievement.) Among other things, the stories were evaluated in terms of their coherence. The results showed that finding a job was most strongly correlated with the coherence and structured nature of the stories. The story coherence results of nearly half of the jobless career starters – in accord with other results concerning attribution patterns, for example – were similar to those of the already employed subjects; while in another group of career starters the value of story coherence and structure matched those of the steadily unemployed subjects. This result was in strong correlation with their indicators of finding a job later.

In Hungary Mészáros and Papp (2006) made an attempt to identify the coherence of life stories at the textual level. Their model relies on the principle of co-referentiality; that is, the degree of text coherence is indicated by the density of words with similar or identical reference in the text. Even at the level of words it is pretty difficult to measure coherence. Repetition, which is the most obvious way of realizing co-referentiality, has a number of hidden forms, from variations to antitheses (Fónagy 1990).

Psychological interpretations of self-reference

Narratives of life stories are by necessity self-narratives in that the narrator and the main character are by definition the self. Narrative is about the experiences of the self. However, it is not inevitable that narrators should give an account exclusively of their subjective experiences when recalling the events of their life, while ignoring the experiences of their partners. However, it is quite possible that a narrative lacks the experiences of the self; the self, as it were, is left out. At the textual level of narrative the presence of the self manifests itself in self-references. Hargitai et al. (2007) review the possible psychological interpretations of the presence or absence of the self, relying on the concepts of Szondi's fate analysis. The self-theory of fate analysis built the self on two opposing poles of self-instinct factors: one is the *instinctive desire for possession*, that is, the contraction of the self, while the other one is 'becoming everything', that is, the expansion of the self fed by the *instinctive desire for being*. Within the above factors there are two contradictory tendencies (introjection versus negation; projection versus inflation) that ensure a person's self-preservation, autonomy, adaptation and integration to reality.

The predominance of certain tendencies without any compensation may lead to special forms of mental disorders: for example, the hypertonia of introjection – its accumulation to an extreme extent – may be manifested in an excessive form of the will to possess everything (values, concepts, internal and external contents). Furthermore, it may also indicate a dangerous increase in narcissism and autism too. Inflation, that is, the dominance of the extension of the self's existence may also suggest a danger: it may manifest itself in megalomania, querulousness, religious fallacies and paranoia alike. In these cases the true source of danger is crossing the border of reality.

In the sense of the above approach, considering the fine ratios of linguistic markers concerning the self only, we can make a distinction between mental states characterized by the dominance of possession and being and a radical decrease of a sense of the self, an intense sense of being impoverished and the narratives of life stories that, as a matter of fact, represent them.

Negation

Forms of negation often pop up in narratives of life stories. The psychological interpretation of the negation of time (e.g. never, at no time) has already been touched upon in connection with traumatic experiences. In certain cases negation represents ambivalence, for instance it turns meaning over or highlights one or another pole of the given construction, but it does not negate the phenomenon itself. *Ambivalent negation* (e.g. no, neither, negation by a privative) implies the existence of an alternative perspective, thereby representing an inhibition-like mental adaptation. In contrast, so-called *eradicating* or – using Bakhtin's term – *abstract negation* (e.g. nowhere, never, nobody) does not negate one or the other pole but eradicates, cancels, as it were, the construction itself. This sort of eradicating negation implies a danger for the self, destruction.

In the discursive theory of suicide, Kézdi (1995) views negation as a linguistic marker of psychological crisis. Negation is part of the negative code described by Kézdi, which in Hungarian culture controls fields of action that can be connected to a crisis. According to Kézdi (1995) the problems arising in the prevention of suicide and crisis intervention derive from obstacles that prevent the detection of crisis: in Hungarian culture the 'background noise' of the negative code conceals the forms of negation increasing in number in the communication of people undergoing a psychological crisis.

Hargitai et al. (2007) reviews the depth-psychological interpretations of negation. These interpretations do not present a unified picture. Freud viewed negation as the intellectual, conscious function of judgement making, where *judgement is an intellectual substitute for suppression*, that is, negation is, in a way, the intellectual acceptance of suppressed contents of consciousness. In his later works negation appears as the most fundamental, most primitive mode of defence quite common in everyday life. Freud makes a distinction between the notions of *Verneinung* and *Verleugnung*, where the former implies that somebody utters a statement in a negative form, while the latter can be used when we believe something to be non-existent that we are, as a matter of fact, aware of.

According to Szondi's (1956) self-theory of fate analysis negation is not an intellectual process but rather the most general, most human and – in some cases – most fatal *position* taken by the self. The form of this 'saying no' and especially its degree often determine the relationship of individuals and the community: the negation function ensures accommodation to the environment of healthy people and to moral standards; this is what guarantees the functionality of society through the suppression, inhibition and alienation of certain instinctive aspirations. However, 'saying no' may also appear to an extreme extent: what underlies the predominance of negation is the depreciation of the world, which implies dangers for the self in every case. In this case, the predominance of negation is equivalent to the contraction of the pre-suicidal syndrome and the negativism of auto-aggression that arises as a result of alcoholism or drug habit. At this point psychoanalysis and the theory of fate analysis communicate with each other, since according to Freud negation – as a successor of replacement – feeds on the destructive instinct.

The computerization of content analysis in narrative psychology

One important condition for a research and theoretical strategy based on narrative psychological content analysis is to develop computer programs, which can relatively safely identify narrative categories carrying psychological content in large databases. The programs should be able to register hit frequencies in an ordered format and make the data available for statistical analysis. Most importantly, the programs should be able to identify not only individual words (and perhaps their morphological variants), but linguistic patterns of narrative composition which carry psychological content. When developing these programs in Hungarian, we used the language technological devices of MorphoLogic Ltd, which provided us with a complete morphology and grammar. For those who are interested, technical details are given in the Appendix. This type of program development required a heavy support from the computer linguists. More recently *Nooj*, a public language technological device, is available on the internet (Silberztein 2006), which enables users to compose local grammars in quite a simple way. Of course, so as to arrive at programs which can catch narrative components of a text, users cannot save morphologically annotated dictionaries on a given language, but further annotations and construction of local grammars are relatively simple in this system.

Reliability and validity studies of the narrative content-analytic programs

What has been said so far about the relationship between the narrative categories identified in life stories and the ways the experiences of narrating individuals are organized, however logical they may appear to be, is, after all, just a hypothesis. It is an assumption that needs to be verified. In the same way, it has to be verified whether the content analysis programs developed for measuring narrative categories can find the linguistic structures that correspond to the targeted narrative categories in various texts; that is, how reliable these procedures are. Our research group has conducted a series of studies to test the reliability and validity of the programs measuring narrative perspective, time experience, control of spatial-emotional distance, self-reference, and negation (Ehmann et al. 2007; Hargitai et al. 2007; László et al. 2007; Pohárnok et al. 2007; Pólya et al. 2007).

What do we measure when testing validity?

From specific narrative patterns of thematically targeted life episodes, we want to conclude with several aspects of the identity of the narrator. These aspects can be general, like coherence, complexity, stability or emotional regulation, or more specific, such as how the person experiences time or to what extent can the person be characterized with depression. Consequently, the psychological constructs and the measures we used for validity studies were derived partly from identity research, partly from the study of personality traits and disorders. For the latter, we assumed that personality traits and states as measured with personality questionnaires and tests are associated with identity construction, therefore they are apt to study the external validity of our measures. In other words, we do not want to confuse identity as a concept of psychosocial adaptation (Erikson 1959) with the concepts of personality, which refer to individual ways of bio-psychological adaptation, nevertheless we think that the former concepts are related to the latter ones and this relation provides ground for validity studies (see McAdams 2001; McLean and Pasupathi 2006). In order to demonstrate the procedure of the validity testing of the programs, some of our results are presented in the Appendix.

Summary

This chapter outlined the categories of the narrative psychological content analysis, introduced the idea of automation of the search for these categories and argued for the necessity of validity and reliability studies. The sample of narrative categories, such as characters' functions, narrative perspective, narrative time, control of spatial-emotional distance, self-reference, negation, narrative evaluation and narrative complexity, which can and will be extended, were linked conceptually to psychological processes of identity construction. When speaking about automation of narrative psychological content analysis, it should be stressed that in contrast to other kinds of content analysis, the above content categories are not at all or only moderately context sensitive. Relevance of content words, which constitute them can be adjusted to targeted syntactic or thematic contexts by local grammars.

Progress in developing narrative psychological content analysis can also be made in another direction, to be detailed in the following chapters. So far, content analysis in narrative psychology has been used for learning more about the mental life of individuals and about the states of identity and personality. However, we have duly emphasized in the introductory chapters that we consider scientific narrative psychology to be applicable to the explanation of social-cultural processes and the psychological phenomena of social groups. In subsequent chapters, narrative analysis will be extended to a specific form of group identity, to national identity.

10 Social memory and social identity
The social psychology of history

There is quite a lot of affinity between psychology and the historical sciences, both being involved in studying the key drivers of human action, though there is little practical interaction between them. History has been the terrain of the historical sciences for centuries. Naturally, this does not mean that analyses of a social psychological nature concerning the mental state of social groups, which related phenomena of social psychology to historical processes, have not been carried out at all. Suffice it to refer at this point to one example, the work of István Bibó, especially his selected papers entitled *Democracy, Revolution, Self-determination* (Bibó 1991). There has been some research on historical events, eras and characters too, which explored the picture that society had about these historical subjects, starting out with the presupposition that we can infer social predispositions, judgements, and in the final analysis, expected behaviours from the organization of these views (see Hunyady 1998; McGuire 1993). These examples show that in contrast to the historical sciences, where the object of explanation is the historical process itself (and occasionally aspects of social psychology may also have a place in this explanation), history in social psychology appears as a synchronic form of representation, a piece of knowledge whose forms of organization are used to predict and explain expected patterns of social behaviour.

Types of explanation

Theory construction and research in mainstream social psychology are based on the principle of scientific causal explanation. It assumes that an event to be explained, for instance making judgement or behaviour, can be derived from a limited number of causal factors, such as from the organizational patterns of historical views. This kind of causal thinking can also be observed in the historical sciences where beyond presenting historical events there is a need for presenting the relationships among various events too. One classic example of causal explanations in historiography is the work of Alexis de Tocqueville (1969 [1935]) on American democracy in which there are numerous examples of explanations derived from empirically generalized rules. Elements of a causal chain concerning the establishment of American democracy include for example the physical environment that proved to be a hard test for the settlers, the simple social world they had to face, the lack of government institutions, which altogether urged citizens to form alliances and work together. The voluntary associations established for the sake of achieving common goals then created the skills and techniques that were essential for democracy. Tocqueville's work is not without psychological generalizations either. The beneficial effect of uniting in an association for example is captured by him in the following psychological consequences:

> When some view is represented by an association, it must take clearer and more precise shape. It counts its supporters and involves them in its cause; these supporters get to know one another, and numbers increase zeal. An association unites the energies of divergent minds and vigorously directs them toward a clearly indicated goal.
>
> (Tocqueville 1969: 190)

The so-called 'rational' form of scientific explanation, which, instead of using empirical laws, views the grasping of an idea expressed in events as the explanation of events, emerged in Wilhelm Dilthey's history of ideas. According to Collingwood (1947) the subject matter of historiography is not the historical event, but the thought expressed in it. Discovering the thought means understanding it. This kind of understanding targets not only the relationships between events but also the relationships between actors' dispositions and intentions; that is, the main goal is to establish what makes a historical action *rational*. While the history of ideas became a significant trend in the historical sciences, Dilthey's psychology based on understanding did not have much to expect, and as a result, mutual reflections by the two disciplines were practically out of the question in the paradigm of rational explanation.

In Chapter 1 we have already addressed the issue, and at this point we will discuss it in some more detail, that the narrative features of the explanation of historical knowledge are given an increasingly stronger emphasis within the historical sciences too. The principle of narrative explanation, put in a polarized way by Hayden White (1981: 19) states that 'the reality of these events does not consist in the fact that they occurred but that, first of all, they were remembered and, second, that they are capable of finding a place in a chronologically ordered sequence'. In this sense, a narrative produced by historians is an historical explanation by itself.

According to what has been said above, historical narrative is the product of social construction, but it is a construction that uses narrative as a cognitive tool with its own rules and laws. The validity of narrative hinges on its credibility, authenticity and coherence, which in turn are dependent on the proper use of narratives – time, plot, characters, perspective, narrative intentions and evaluation. The paradox of narrative is that it is a universally valid human cognitive mechanism and, at the same time, a form of knowledge created by this mechanism that is validated and maintained socially. This dual nature of narrative has for the first time created some productive contact points between history and social psychology since Dilthey's attempt in the history of ideas. It makes it possible to introduce cognitive structures with psychological content into the analysis of historical narrative as explanation or interpretation: the analysis of historical discourse is fed back to empirical data.

The shortcoming of the theory of collective memory and related research areas is that they have not created a methodology that can repeat, compare and verify experiments. One important goal of the research conducted by our group is to link the processes of historical memory and identity construction to exact properties of historical narrative identifiable at a textual level.

History, narrative, identity: construction and reality

Since fiction is considered to be the proper category of narrative, the narration of historical events unintentionally falls under the suspicion that by having the aesthetic criteria of the 'goodness' of narrative in mind, it blends fiction with the reality of depicted events. (It is noted here that the attempts to replace narrative causal explanation used in the historical sciences by scientific (Hempel 1942) or rational (Collingwood 1947) explanations, have not met with much success. Doubtless, it is a fact that ever since history abandoned annals and chronicles and included simple facts in the narrative network of human intentions and goals, reconstructive operations have inevitably been coupled with construction. The question is whether history will thereby have no choice but to lose its relation to reality and, through a construction that is boundless and unverifiable, end up in the realm of fictionality or, as is called today, factionality.)

According to the continuity theory (Carr 1986), historiography does not force events into unrealistic fictional structures, because the narrative function precedes actual narration; it exists under the level of historical narratives as the fundamental mode of experiencing time (Ricoeur 1984–1989). There is no 'aboriginal' reality before or outside the narrative: events are perceived or comprehended in narrative structures both in the common sense and in the historiography. As Mink (1978: 128) writes: 'Narrative is an irreducible form of human comprehension, an article in the constitution of the common sense.'

Current psychological theories are consistent with the above position. Evolutionary psychology has pointed to the phylogenetically evolved capacity of attributing mental states – intentions, goals, beliefs, emotions – to the partner, which is the prerequisite for developing narrative thinking (Pléh 2003b; Tomasello 1999). Developmental studies have shown that 'reading' environmental events in terms of intentionality is there already in infancy (Gergely et al. 1995; Leslie 1991) and proto-narrative structures are observable in early mother–infant interaction (Péley 2002; Stern 1995).

Jerome Bruner (1986) speaks about two natural forms of human cognition: the logico-scientific thinking and the narrative thinking. He claims that neither of them is superior to the other. They are complementary and not reducible to one another. They organize experience and represent reality differently. Paradigmatic or logico-scientific thinking operates with abstract categories, procedures of formal logic, and strives to meet scientific causality and universal truth conditions.

Narrative thinking is more mundane. It is built upon concern for the human condition. Causality for narrative thinking is finding plausible or lifelike connections between two events. It establishes not truth, but verisimilitude and coherence. If one accepts that narrative is a particular mode of experiencing the world, it is not difficult to agree with Bruner (1986: 43), who looks at the narrative as the medium of constructing the psychological and cultural reality, in which the participants in history actually live. Studying how people tell and understand stories, including stories of the history enlightens how they create a reality of their own.

Social, collective and cultural representation

We have dealt in detail with collective representations and the theory of social representations in Chapter 6. We have pointed out that the theory of social representations is a continuation of Durkheim's intellectual tradition, although it substantially deviates from the theory of collective representations. Durkheim established sociology as a discipline by introducing the concepts of social fact and collective representations, thereby eliminating psychological facts from the explanation of social behaviour. Moscovici has developed his theory in the intermediate level of the organization of social behaviour, where representations evolve and are shaped by the processes of social dynamics. In order to stress this social psychological aspect of representations, he coined the term social representation instead of the collective representation.

Thus, social representation theory is interested in uncovering the conditions of the representation process in each – individual, social or group, and societal – level (Doise et al. 1992). Integrating psychological and social phenomenal levels has been earlier attempted by Maurice Halbwachs, a student of Bergson and Durkheim. Instead of collective representation he speaks about *collective memory* or social frames of memory.

Collective memory and social representations

It is not a mere play with words if we say that Halbwachs' collective memory and Moscovici's social representations can be translated into each other. Both concepts have been worked out following Durkheim's lead, explicitly contrasted to Durkheim's collective representation concept (Durkheim 1947 [1893]). Whereas collective representations, as social facts, were instrumental for Durkheim in detaching sociology from psychology, both Halbwachs and Moscovici try to conceptualize the interplay between social and psychological phenomena. This psychological leaning is reflected in coining the term 'memory' instead of representation by Halbwachs, and 'social' representation instead of both collective (sociological) and individual (cognitive) representations by Moscovici.

This psychological stance is obvious when they more or less explicitly refer to the human cognitive capacities when talking about the material of the representation. Halbwachs emphasizes that as opposed to the abstractedness of thinking, memory is always concrete. Halbwachs (1941: 151) says that 'Any truth should take the form of a particular, concrete event, person, or space, concept and image should merge, so as to be preserved in collective memory'. Moscovici (1984: 33) emphasizes that concept and image are undetachable two sides of the same coin in social representations.

For both Halbwachs and Moscovici, representations are constructed around a central pattern. Halbwachs describes it as image, Moscovici, as figurative nucleus. It is clear, however, that they allow other organizational forms as well. Halbwachs explicitly writes about the preserving and organizing force of narrative. Moscovici is rather implicit on the narrative function, however, when talking about 'finalities' or goals in social representation process, he refers to the essential narrative category of intentional or goal-directed action (see László 1997).

There are, however major differences between the two approaches. One of these differences, I think, explains the different affinity of the two theories exhibit towards the problem of group identity. Although memories or representations are constructed in social communication according to both theories, Halbwachs' collective memories encompass the whole past of the group, whereas Moscovici's social representations are clearly directed toward the 'new' phenomena, that is the present life of the group. Halbwachs contrasts collective memories with scientific knowledge, but he is not interested in communication between the two knowledge domains. He concentrates exclusively on the accumulation and preservation of group experiences. On the contrary, social representations theory is preoccupied with transformation (or 'familiarization') from scientific knowledge into everyday knowledge. As Moscovici notes, novel phenomena are produced and/or first being tackled by sciences in modern societies. This knowledge is transformed to everyday knowledge by social representations. (In earlier centuries the route was reversed: scientific knowledge was fuelled from common sense.)

Both Moscovici and Halbwachs imply a relationship between representational processes of the group and functions of constructing and maintaining group identity. However, it was Assmann (1992) who offered a synthetic theoretical framework, which explicitly relates past and present representational processes to group identity. Assmann distinguishes *cultural* from *communicative* memory (see Table 10.1). The communicative memory embraces memories from the proximate past, shared with contemporaries. A characteristic example is the generation memory. It emerges in time and it decays with time, with the decay of its carriers. The span of communicative memory is about eighty years, three or four generations. Several interesting and so far unexplained phenomena were observed in autobiographical memory studies that concern communicative memory of a society from the perspective of the individual. For instance, regardless of the type of event, those events prove to be the most memorable for each generation, which they experienced in their late adolescence to early adulthood (between age 15 and 20: see Rubin 1996). Forty years, that is half of the communicative memory period, is again a critical threshold. After elapsing forty years, those who experienced a significant event in their adulthood, fearing that their memories will disappear when they are departing, feel motivated to record and transmit their experiences. An example is the proliferation of Holocaust literature during the mid-1980s.

Table 10.1 Characteristics of communicative and cultural memory (after Assmann 1992)

	Communicative memory	*Cultural memory*
Content	Historical experiences in the individual life course	Myth of origin, archaic history and absolute past
Form	Informal, natural, based on interpersonal communication	Formal, festive, ceremonial
Media	Human memory, immediate experiences, oral tradition	Recorded, objectified in writing, dancing, pictures, etc.
Time structure	80–100 years, 3–4 generations	Absolute past to the mythical times
Carriers	Contemporaries	Professional carriers of tradition

Source: after Assmann 1992.

Cultural memory goes back to the origin of the group. Culture objectifies group memories, which have proven to be important to the group (e.g. encodes these memories into stories), and preserves them in this way. It makes it possible for new members to share group history.

In terms of communicative and cultural memory, Halbwachs' theory is more directed to cultural memory, Moscovici's theory to communicative memory.

Group narrative and identity

The concept of identity has at least two meanings. Originating from the Latin *idem* and *ipse* categories, it means identity or perfect similarity with something on the one hand, and identity or 'sameness' in time and space on the other. For distinguishing these two aspects of identity, Ricoeur (1991) suggests to use the category *ipseity* for the latter. In social psychology a similar distinction is made with adjectival constructs. *Social identity* designates belongingness to a social group, sharing its norms, getting value and security from the group. Stability and continuity of the self despite the manifold changes in one's life course is expressed by the term *personal identity*, a concept suggested by Erikson (1968).

Individual and group identities are closely interrelated. D'Azevedo (1962) provides an example of how group history, as cross-generationally sustained oral group narrative, contributes to construction of group and individual identity. The African Gola have a special status for members of a family or group of families who know the genealogy of their ancestors. These special family members can narrate stories that align presently living members of the family and derive them from the ancestors in a historical line of descent. The stories do not simply enumerate ancestors but are organized to give historical meaning or significance to what is told. Among the Gola, the general idea is that individuals cannot know their place in society or appreciate fully the kind of person they are unless they are familiar with the genealogy of their family. A member of the group not only learns about a large number of living kin, and so has the security of being from a large family, but also learns that one comes from a family that can offer its young members a sense of pride and security in a clearly defined tradition. The Gola genealogy oration provides a group-building exercise, with the group constituting itself by its stories about itself (d'Azevedo 1962).

Specialists, like *griots* in African tribes, were trusted to preserve and narrate history of the group. Ceremonial history performances were usually accompanied by music and dance (Assmann 1992). Specialists in group memory enjoyed privileged status in the group hierarchy. They played a central role in the initiation rites, in which adolescents acquired adult identity partly by 'merging' into the group's history (Leach 1976). Historical consciousness or the 'sense of the past' (Shils 1981) thus is not the invention of literacy.

In cultures with literacy, cultural memory is largely transferred by texts. These texts are typically produced by specialists, such as historians and writers. Although with the emergence of literacy the need for interpretation immediately appeared (which at times, in the case of history, may lead to the rewriting of events), as a counter-effect, there was some pressure for canonization too (see e.g. the text of the Bible). Nevertheless, written narratives about group history preserved a lot of their role in the construction of group identity. Issues of national history or political history, including questions of power, leadership and territory have become the main themes of historiography not only because they are easy to tell but also because they have contributed to the cultural memory of a nation and thereby to its national identity. However, it is well known that this type of historical-cultural memory embodied in history textbooks, historical monuments and celebrations is itself exposed to change in socially and ideologically articulated societies, that is, in change-oriented cultures called 'hot' by Lévi-Strauss. Not only events of the recent past become part of actual social communication and develop towards a canonized form of cultural memory (in this context Pennebaker et al. (1997b) published a seminal volume in which, among other things, they studied – on approaching the critical eighty years – the fate of still living memories of the Spanish Civil War) but stories of several century-old events buried in cultural memory may also be revived and changed from time to time, often without any new evidence or document being brought up. It has been shown by historians that Lincoln's speech delivered in Gettysburg, which offered a new history to the American nation, does not contain any new element – the superior rank of the Declaration of Independence with respect to the Constitution of the States for example was demonstrated by Daniel Webster as early as the 1830s (Carr 1986) – still, the place, the time and the force of rhetoric made this speech the guiding principle of American history.

The other example comes from anthropology again and shows in a duly extreme form how the needs of a group can reshape history. The Gonja nation of Africa was studied by anthropologists as early as the beginning of the twentieth century. The land of the Gonja then consisted of seven main regions. Anthropologists recorded a story of origin of the Gonja nation according to which once upon a time there was a great and famous chief who conquered the country and

divided it among his seven sons. Later the British colonial administrative authority reduced the number of regions to five. After a few decades the Gonja people
still told the same story of conquest with unbroken pride, with the slight difference
that the great chief had five rather than seven sons (Goody and Watt 1963, quoted
by Hilton et al. 1996). This sort of 'rewriting' is quite common in the history of
European nations too, and can be observed at a time of rapid social changes.

National identity in the mirror of history

Biographical narratives or narrated life histories are good reflections of personal
identity; in fact, they are occasionally inseparable from personal identity (Bruner
and Lucariello 1989; Erős and Ehmann 1997; Greenwald 1980; McAdams 1988).
According to McAdams (1985: 18) individual identities can be categorized into
different classes through stories, so the stability of identity goes hand in hand
with the longitudinal consistency of a narrated life story. The transformation of
identity – the crisis and change of identity – brings about the revision of an auto-
biographic story. The mildest form of rewriting involves small changes in some
obscure chapters of an individual's life history. In extreme cases even the entire
text may be 'rewritten': the subject, the cast, the scene, the plot and the theme
itself may all change. The author also points out that the problem of identity
suggests that in accordance with the direction of the process the life history that
eventually unfolds should make sense in a sociohistorical matrix embedded in a
larger framework. The parameters of life history are set by the individual's world.
In this sense identity is a fully psychosocial phenomenon.

The other constraint is that the impact of life narrative on the social world
springs from the individual's own group. Life narrative must be shared with members of the group who the individual meets face to face. As was put by Bruner and
Fleischer-Feldmann (1996):

> The story of a life, when all is said and done, must be shared with one's
> 'miniculture,' with the proximal group(s) on which one's cultural existence
> depends. ... What is plain is that the accounts given by individuals constitute,
> in some important sense, the group's identity.
>
> (Bruner and Fleischer-Feldmann 1996: 294)

National identity and historical narrative

Our present standpoint does not require a detailed discussion of the debates concerning the notion of nation: What criteria define a nation? When did it come into
being historically? Is the term legitimate at all? What we consider to be a nation
is a mental unity that by means of language, culture and a common past provides
a group of people with a sense of belonging to a group. The concept of nationalism has its roots in the French Revolution and German romanticism, especially
Hegel and Herder. While also being a positive driving force promoting progress
in the nineteenth and twentieth centuries and contributing to the independence of

several European states, nationalism has caused wars and extreme pain to human-kind. Nationalist ideas aside, attachment to language, culture and the past is an important aspect of social life and personality development not only in the western world but universally too.

Nations are well-defined social groups that generally live within the border of a state. Some European nations have evolved over centuries, some of them are products of the nineteenth or even the twentieth centuries. The modern state evolved in western Europe between the fifteenth and seventeenth centuries in a process where the former symbolic central power more and more firmly control-led the political life of the newly emergent nations. A process of unification took place whereby the country became a unit not only politically and legally, but also administratively and economically. In this process, national consciousness gradu-ally ceased to be the privilege of the nobility. The growing bourgeoisie and intel-ligentsia increasingly participated in its evolution. Simultaneously they endowed the state with warm and immediate emotions that the bourgeoisie had developed in their close communities. In this way, national and democratic feelings became intimately linked in the social development of western Europe with increasing predominance of democratic over national feelings.

István Bibó's works clarify that the situation was entirely different in central and eastern Europe. Modern democratic nationalism had neither the power nor the will to take possession of the existing state-frameworks (i.e. Habsburg Empire, German and Italian small states, Ottoman Empire). Nationalism turned, instead, to frameworks of an historical nature (the German Empire, unified Italian, Polish, Czech, Hungarian and other kingdoms) that continued to exist only as shadowy institutions and lived on mostly in symbols and memories. Thus, national frame-work in central and eastern Europe was not a stable, taken-for-granted, indisput-able entity. It was something that had to be created, or restored or had to be fought over, and something about which one could be anxious. These historical anteced-ents bear significance to the development of national and citizen identity, which, in turn, are expressed in national histories. Other more recent dramatic examples are in the dissolving Soviet Union and Yugoslavia (see László and Farkas 1997).

The stories for the nations' past are produced by professional historiographers at least since the nineteenth century (White 1981), but from the point of view of national identity, folk histories – representations of the past in various groups of the nation – are more informative. These representations, just as 'official histor-ies', take narrative forms. They involve settings, characters, conflicting goals, means to achieve goals, outcomes, moral evaluations, and several other narrative qualities that can be related to identity. From the point of view of identity, it is equally important that

> we can comprehend the appeal of historical discourse by recognizing the extent to which it makes the real desirable, makes the real into an object of desire (in Lacanian sense) and does so by its imposition upon events that are represented as real, of the formal coherency that stories possess.
>
> (White 1981: 20)

Despite the plausible relation between national histories and national identity, number of works intending to uncover this relationship is surprisingly little. Whereas social psychological inquiry has recognized the salience of the concept of nation, its study, until recently, has been limited to developmental aspects (e.g. Jahoda 1963; Piaget and Weil 1951) or to national identity expressed in preferences or attitudes (Lawson 1963; Tajfel et al. 1970; Vaughan 1964). Hilton et al. (1996), who assumed that national histories are social representations which underpin socio-political attitudes and studied how social representations of history predict attitudes to European unification, reviewed the field. They remarked that even the most thorough study on the relationship between personal identity, national identity and international relations (Bloom 1992) does not have references on how representations of history may play a part in forming national identity. They found references to the role of history in shaping current attitudes in works of Hobsbawm (1992) and Hewstone (1986), but these approaches do not deal with either the representational aspects or the identity functions of national history.

Characteristically, there is consensus in very different ethnic groups as to what can and should be told of the history of a group, which events and persons are important from the point of view of a nation's history (László et al. 2002a; Liu et al. 1999). Likewise, it is interesting to see that – although made somewhat more colourful by various cultures – the same can be observed in world history too (Liu et al. 2005; Pennebaker et al. 2006). At the same time, the meaning of each event, their relevance for the present and the future may be viewed differently by various social groups, and the construction of national identity often takes place in the crossfire of debates. The social representation of events is largely determined by group interests and knowledge about a particular event. Accordingly, we can distinguish *polemic* (competing social representations of different social groups), *emancipated* (social representations that fit on the basis of a few criteria) and *hegemonic representations* (unified social representations widely accepted in a society). Following Bakhtin (1984, 1986), Wertsch (2002) claims that representations develop dialogically: they are shaped by the concurrent 'voices' or representations which are present in the society.

The social representations maintained in the present time of a society are not static but dynamic entities that change in accordance with the changing demands of the present. As Liu and Hilton (2005) put it, 'past weighs on the present'. This is especially true of representations concerning negative historical events that are characterized by a special kind of dynamism. According to Gregorio Marañon, three generations are needed to process traumatic events (Pennebaker et al. 2006). Approximately eighty to ninety years are needed for a generation to get sufficiently far from a traumatic event emotionally and temporally so that it can deal with such an event properly. The results of research on the Spanish Civil War show that groups with different political views have different (polemic) representations concerning the civil war. However, these representations tend to converge by the third generation; polemic representations turn into hegemonic representations (Páez et al. 2004).

Hegemonic historical representations can be produced artificially too. This is exemplified by George Orwell's novel *Nineteen Eighty-Four*, in which the Ministry of Historical Truth makes sure that a history that is desirable for the regime is created. However, the shaping of history in terms of particular social needs is not the privilege of totalitarian systems only. In this context Hobsbawm (1992) speaks about 'invented traditions'. A special issue of the *Journal of Contemporary History* published in 2003 is concerned with the adaptations of history observed at the time of political transitions. All the authors agree that the use of history for the legitimization of a particular political regime is a universal phenomenon which manifests itself the most clearly at the time of a political transition. The criteria of usable past are listed by Gyáni (2003):

1. Historiography should satisfy the need of the elite for legitimizing its own power by the force of national myths and invented traditions. *2.* Occasionally, historiography should provide a reference framework, some positive archetypes for the elite so that it should promote the acceptance of inevitable, often unpopular innovations. *3.* The task of historiography is to present behavioural models of the community's past to be followed as clearly and explicitly as possible so that particular developments in the present could be seen as the embodiment of classical virtues and values (or their revival, as it were). *4.* At the same time, historiography acknowledges that it is responsible for justifying political demands on the basis of the community's past built on historical rights in case territorial disputes arise with other countries. *5.* Finally, as for its political usability, the almost boundless possibilities of historiography partly derive from the fact that the past is an overly plastic entity, therefore every age and every generation can shape history for their own benefit. This is served by the notion of the golden age whose role is to restore the roots, continuity, credibility and dignity for the people that constitute a nation, thereby becoming the guiding line and model of national fate.

(Gyáni 2003: 62, my translation)

The 'affordances' of historical events (Liu and Liu 2003), that is, the symbolic contents and emotive qualities of identification potentially expressed by them, identity policy and the real identity needs of society collectively determine the present representations of history. In a study carried out in New Zealand, Liu et al. (1999) found that the cultural renaissance of the Maori aboriginals and their struggle for equal political rights integrated those events of the common history of the aboriginals and the European immigrants and those interpretations of these events into the social representations of the present which suited the social goals of each social group (pro-integration Maoris, pro-isolation Maoris, pro-integration Europeans, pro-isolation Europeans) and the social identity providing a foundation for these representations in the best possible way.

The classic example of narrative restructuring is the revival of the history of the Masada fortress at the time of the foundation of the Israeli state. In 72–73 BC the Romans stormed the Masada fortress defended by the Jews. The Jews defended their fortress heroically for several months, and when they saw that they had no chance left against the superior power of the enemy, they committed group suicide in order to avoid being captured. This event had been dormant in the historical memory of Jews for a long time, but when the State of Israel was founded in 1948, the founding fathers made it the cornerstone of Jewish history. The conscious step of identity policy was also motivated by a social psychological need to restore the self-esteem of the Jewish nation that had become a victim of the Holocaust, in other words, to ensure that Jews could identify with the idea of active resistance and heroism. This interpretation is confirmed by simple facts like the erection of the monument commemorating the Masada incident took place much earlier than the erection of the first Israeli Holocaust monument (Klar et al. 2004; Zerubavel 1994).

The relationship between national history and national identity has been neglected for two reasons. On the one hand, the two most competent areas in which the phenomenon has been studied intensively, social representations theory (Moscovici 1984) and social identity theory (Tajfel 1981) have developed independently of each other, and on the other, narrative metatheories (J. Bruner 1986; Sarbin 1986b), have previously had relatively little influence on theorizing in social psychology. At present, however, there are several theoretical endeavours to integrate social representations theory and social identity theory. The general idea that representations existing in groups by necessity fulfil some sort of an identity function is increasingly gaining ground (Breakwell 1993; de Rosa 1996; Elejabarrieta 1994; Vala 1992). Starting out from omnipresent narrative discourse (Bahtyin 1981; Barthes 1977; Halbwachs 1925) and the idea that human thinking takes place in a narrative mode (J. Bruner 1986), as has been discussed in detail in Chapter 1, there emerges a narrative view of social representations (Flick 1995; Jovchelovitch 1996, 2001, 2006; László 1997, 2003). This integrated approach argues that stories about history are suitable for the study of national identity in social psychology (Liu and László 2007). The narrative-based content analysis of stories of the national past may be able to explore all the social representations – symbolic constructions – that mark the place and role of a group in the world, and it may also be able to give an outline of the emotive structure of group identity in a clear way. In this book we offer some conceptual and narrative tools of content analysis for these aspirations which can be used to identify some relatively stable properties of national identity and its actual state: *the social psychological processes of identity construction through history.*

It has been established that from time to time collective memory and the social representation of history are revised in communicative memory. These representations appear in a narrative shape and work as naive history-stories, folk histories in accordance with the actual identity needs of groups. However, stories often reveal more than that about identity. Narrative is not merely a natural, economical cognitive tool for preserving information, but at the same time it is a form that is suitable for establishing a personal relation and identifying oneself with something. As Ricoeur (1991) writes, identifying ourselves proceeds always through identification with others – through history in reality and through fictional narratives in the plane of irreality. By means of empirical studies we can draw conclusions that reveal the characteristic features of group identity in the language of social psychology from professional and folk historical history-stories, the literary portrayal of history or pictorial narratives. Thus, the question is not in what way and to what extent these stories correspond to a scientifically reconstructed reality (although from another aspect it may also be an interesting question); what we want to know is what psychological state of being balanced or imbalanced, what sense of security or being threatened, what sort of continuity or discontinuity, temporal orientation, inter-group relationships, motivation and evaluation are reflected by the stories.

Two examples: study of Hungarian national identity in the light of folk-historical narratives and of history books

In order to show how to infer to identity states and identity processes from historical narratives, two studies on Hungarian national identity will be presented. The first study was done with folk-historical narratives told by students on positive and negative events in Hungarian history (László et al. 2002a). The second study compared the story of the Austro-Hungarian monarchy in contemporary Austrian and Hungarian history school books (Vincze et al. 2007).

In the first study, a total of 132 Hungarian students in three age groups (secondary school pupils, 30 per cent of the sample, aged 10 to 12 years; high school pupils, 40 per cent of the sample, aged 14 to 16 years; and college students, 30 per cent of the sample, aged 20 to 25 years) were asked two questions related to Hungarian history. Sex distribution was 40 per cent males and 60 per cent females. The questions were as follows:

1   'Describe a historical event which is your favourite one, which you are proud of, in which you would have been glad to participate' (*positive event*)
2   'Describe a historical event which is the most terrible for you, which was the worst for the country, which should not have happened at all' (*negative event*).

Some vignettes are shown as illustrations of the texts given by the subjects. (The complete textual volume is filed with the Oral History Archives of the Institute for Psychological Research of the Hungarian Academy of Sciences.)

HIGH SCHOOL FEMALE POSITIVE I would be glad to live in the era of King Matthias because he was trustworthy. I have heard a lot of stories about him: he was generous to the good folk, and punished the evil folk. He supported the poor. He wandered all around the country, disguised as a poor man, and thus he experienced how the peasants were treated.

SECONDARY SCHOOL MALE POSITIVE The year of 1456. The siege of Nandorfehervar. The Ottomans attacked the Hungarians. Our leader was

John Hunyadi, the Ottoman-beater. The town was almost lost, the crescent flag had already been set on the castle wall, when a great hero, Titusz Dugonics, threw himself down, dragging the Ottoman flag with him into the abyss. That was how he defended his homeland, his own honour and the future of the Hungarian nation.

HIGH SCHOOL MALE POSITIVE The best was the 1848 freedom fight, because the Hungarian nation was fighting for the homeland. Outnumbered and outgunned by the Austrian and Russian armies, they were not frightened. Even poets fought bravely for the homeland. Whose main weapon was the pen, as we know.

COLLEGE MALE NEGATIVE Trianon Treaty. The land of our country, loser of the First World War, was laying as a bleeding titbit at the foot of the winning nations. With no regard to economical structure, to ethnic or territorial labour distribution, arbitrary borders were drawn deep inside the body of Hungary. By this act, families, friends and economical regions were fully separated. The real problem was the rigidity of the borders.

HIGH SCHOOL MALE NEGATIVE I think the Second World War was the most terrible event. My grandma has told me a lot about it, because she survived those horrible years. She told stories that the country was invaded by plundering soldiers. My mom's dad was taken to the front and died there. My mom was hiding a lot from soldiers and their dogs. I cannot imagine that innocent people were executed by cold-blooded soldiers. People have lost everything. My mom said this terrible event should not have happened at all!

Methods of analysis

As a first step, the handwritten stories from each subject were typed into a computer, and two 'giant files' were made of them: Positive Stories and Negative Stories. Codes of age group, sex and story type were assigned to each story. The two giant files were processed by computer-aided content analysis (ATLAS.ti software: Muhr 1991) in which we simply counted the type and frequency of historical events mentioned spontaneously in the sample. Each story was handled as a whole entity. The assigned codes were merged into higher rank ones. (For example, codes 'King Stephan', 'King Lewis the Great', 'King Matthias' were amalgamated into code 'Great Medieval Kings'. Code 'Anti-Ottoman Victories' was generated in a similar way.) Computers were used in the process of making files derived from the complete text according to higher rank codes and calculating frequency data.

For positive historical events a total of five merged codes emerged:

- *Conquest of Homeland*: spontaneous utterances were found in 21 per cent of the sample, and their frequency showed a decreasing trend with advancing age (high school pupils 31.1 per cent, secondary school pupils 19.2 per cent and college students 11.4 per cent).

- *Great Medieval Kings*: emerged in 17.4 per cent of the sample, most frequently among secondary school pupils (21.2 per cent); occurrences were of nearly similar frequency among high school pupils and college students (15.6 and 14.3 per cent, respectively).
- *Anti-Ottoman Fights*: occurred in 26.5 per cent of the sample, most saliently among high school pupils (37.8, 21.2 and 20.0 per cent).
- *Anti-Austrian Fights*: total frequency was 24.2 per cent (respective percentages with advancing age were 15.6, 28.8 and 28.6 per cent).
- *1956 anti-Soviet Revolt and 1989 Change of Political Regime*: these two codes were merged because they did not show salient frequency in themselves, but in this merged form they represent some anti-Soviet quality and the only reference to the nearest historical past (sequential group percentages were 0, 7.7 and 14.3 per cent; total frequency was 6.8 per cent).

Spontaneous thematization of negative historical events was dominated by a total of six codes.

- *Ottoman Occupation*: a total of 21 per cent of the sample; decreasing tendency with advancing age (31.1, 9.2 and 11.4 per cent).
- *Failure of the 1848 Anti-Austrian Freedom fight*: it was mentioned by only a total of 4.5 per cent of the sample; no utterances were found in the college students group.
- *First World War*: total frequency was 25.0 per cent (sequential frequencies were 15.6, 38.5 and 17.1 per cent.
- *Trianon Treaty*: this event was of the second highest frequency behind the Second World War (28 per cent). A dramatic elevation was seen with advancing age (8.9, 32.7 and 45.7 per cent).
- *Second World War*: this was mentioned in the highest frequency (41.7 per cent). Age distribution was 44.4, 46.2 and 31.4 per cent.
- *Soviet Rule in Hungary*: a total of 10.6 per cent of the sample mentioned this as the most negative historical event. It is interesting that nobody thematized it in the high school pupil group (sequential percentages were 0, 17.5 and 14.5 per cent).

Life trajectory of a nation

A glimpse of the data ordered in decreasing frequency shows that in Hungarian history the 'best' was the anti-Ottoman fight, then the two anti-Austrian freedom fights, the conquest of homeland, the great medieval kings, the 1956 anti-Soviet revolution and the 1989 change of political regime. The worst events were the Second World War, Trianon Treaty, First World War, Ottoman occupation, the Soviet rule and the failure of the 1848 anti-Austrian revolt.

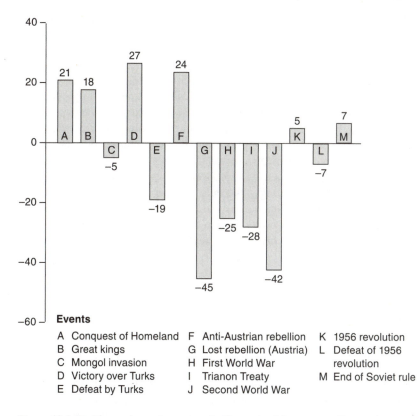

Figure 10.1 Positive and negative events in Hungarian history according to the frequency of recall

Age-related characteristics

There is an interesting trend with age in the type of positively and negatively classified events. Whereas younger pupils focus more on the historic past, older students for both positive and negative events look more for the not too far or immediate past. A clear example is that one-third of the high school students and half of the college students mentioned the Trianon Treaty as the most negative historical event, whereas the percentage in the secondary school group was only 9 per cent.

Distribution of positive and negative historical events is shown in Figure 10.1. The figure suggests that the majority of positive events had occurred in the distant national past. It seems to be that not only individuals, but also nations have a 'life trajectory' (Frye 1957; Gergen and Gergen 1988). If the frequency of spontaneous thematizations is regarded as a measure of positivity or negativity ('Second World War was twice as bad as First World War, and Trianon Treaty was almost as bad as Second World War'), then a kind of a national life history trajectory emerges from the data. It suggests that according to folk history, the good events belong to medieval history, and after long centuries of negative events, Hungarian history shows again an upward – though a very modest – tendency since the end of the Soviet regime in 1990.

This historical trajectory as it is reflected in folk histories is certainly related to the overall familiar Hungarian pessimism. Positive events, with the exception of the 1848–1849 revolution, seem to have ended in the sixteenth century, the distant past. Although it would be difficult to debate that many negative, even tragic events happened to Hungary in the past three or four centuries, this period also included successes, just as earlier times included dawns. However, such events of the latter type, like the Ottoman invasion, were represented positively by focusing on local victories. Interestingly, the only positive event from the nineteenth century, the 1848–1849 revolution, was finally repressed. This, again, was not reflected in the stories. These results point to what Bibó (1991) has termed *historical illusionism* as opposed to *historical realism* as a characteristic feature of the Hungarian national identity.

Folk-historical schemes

A further interesting feature of the data is that several events can be paired.

Table 10.2 seems to outline four marked clusters. (1) *Victory only* (Conquest of homeland, Great medieval kings), (2) *Failure only* (World wars, Trianon Treaty), (3) *First victory, then failure* (Ottomans, Austrians), and (4) *First failure, then victory* (The Soviets). These results can be analysed in terms of *folk-historical schemes*. Wertsch (2002) proposes that certain peoples derive cognitive narrative templates that summarize in a general way the major historical dilemmas that have faced them throughout history. According to Wertsch (2002), schematic narrative templates emerge out of repeated use of standard narrative forms produced by history instruction in schools, the popular media, and so forth. The narrative templates that emerge from this process are effective in shaping what we can say and think, because they are largely unnoticed, or 'transparent' to those employ-

Table 10.2 Clusters of good and bad events in Hungarian history

Good event	Bad event
Conquest of homeland Great medieval kings	
Ottomans Austrians	Ottomans Austrians
	First World War Trianon Treaty Second World War
Liberation from Soviet rule	Soviet rule

ing them, and they are a fundamental part of the identity claims of a group. They can be said to impose a plot structure on a range of specific characters, events and circumstances. His work, focused on the former Soviet Union, has identified the following sequence of moves in a cognitive narrative template for Russian history: first, an initial situation in which the Russian people are living in a peaceful setting where they are no threat to others, disrupted by, second, the initiation of trouble or aggression by alien forces, which leads to, third, a time of crisis and great suffering for the Russian people, which is, fourth, overcome by the triumph over the alien force by the Russian people, acting heroically and alone. This template has been used to provide explanatory insight into the actions of Russia in signing the Molotov–Ribbentrop pact partitioning the states between the Soviet Union and Germany at the beginning of the Second World War; Stalin was not being malevolent or aggressive, just acting defensively to bide his time before the inevitable battle with Hitler for the survival of the Russian people. This template can be applied to make sense of any number of conflicts involving Russia, from the Second World War to the Napoleonic Wars to wars with the Mongols, Poles and Swedes.

The relative obliviousness towards the Soviet period also deserves interpretation, particularly if we look at the central place of the symbolic field of *fights for freedom and independence* in the stories. The end of the Soviet period might have been a historic milestone that had opened a new perspective for future development of the country. Part of the explanation for the lack of inclusion of this period in the array of positive events can be that contemporary history has not yet entered into the historical consciousness of children, but this explanation does not necessarily hold true for high school and college students. On the one hand, the relatively low occurrence of the Soviet period as a negative event or its end as a positive event may be the consequence of the peaceful, non-dramatic transition. On the other hand, the overall evaluation of that period may not be black and white, or the perspective that has opened up not so attractive.

There is, however, a third option which we favour in the explanation. It is related to the folk-historical schemes described above where we found four subjective clusters: (1) *Victory only* (Conquest of homeland, Great medieval kings), (2) *Failure only* (World wars, Trianon Treaty), (3) *First victory, then failure* (Ottomans, Austrians), and (4) *First failure, then victory* (The Soviets). We argue that the 1989 change of political regime has no previous schemes in Hungarian history, because the 1956 revolt fits well into the traditional 'First victory, then failure' category, but its opposite, the 'First failure, then victory' pattern is unprecedented in historical consciousness. In the terminology of social representation theory, we may say the fourth cluster simply cannot be anchored to any earlier schemes. Furthermore, no pictorial core, no central nucleus can be formed about this historical event. Even if we wanted to form some central nucleus – e.g. 'the last Soviet tank as it is leaving Hungary at the eastern border' – this nucleus was a mere lack of something. And no stories can be built on a mere absence, on a 'zero narrative'.

The lack of a narrative schema and an image-like core concerning political transition is due to the same reason. The reason why this image-like core has not been established is not purely because the event is so close in time but because this sort of historical event – the narrative schema of 'We have lost but eventually we have won' – is unprecedented in Hungarian folk history. It would facilitate the balanced nature and security of Hungarian national identity if such a narrative schema could develop in the decades to come, and members of the group could rely on this story when constructing their own identity.

What was missing from the stories

For symbolic fields, it is also informative what was missing in the stories. From this perspective, there was a characteristic lack of the theme of cooperation in all age groups. All the ethnic groups, apart from their own national group, were depicted as adversaries or enemies. There has been nobody who could have helped or cooperated with the Hungarians. Although occurrence of competing groups and the theme of conflict may well be explained by the dramatic requirements of narratives, the 'Helper' role, which was empty in our material, is also a dramatic function in stories, as Propp (1968) showed with Russian folk tales.

The symbolic field of 'living in peace' was also almost empty. As an explanation of this result, we might again refer to Pennebaker's studies (Pennebaker and Banasik 1997), which argue that social memory preserves social-political changes having long-term impact. Nonetheless we know that there have been significant changes in Hungarian history that resulted in long-term peaceful periods (e.g. reconciliation with Austria in 1867). Still the topic of Peace was fairly underrepresented in our sample. This was controversial, because we saw that Peace was saliently mentioned, not among the good, but among the bad historical events. It was the Trianon Peace Treaty and its impacts on the country. Pennebaker and Banasik (1997) were, therefore, right: collective memory has preserved the long-term effect of a political event. Thus, peace is exemplified with the traumatic experience of the Trianon Peace Treaty, which is mentioned as the most negative historic event more and more frequently with growing age. The meaning of this peculiarly Hungarian event seems to have superscripted the original, good connotation of peace, and has turned its symbolic representation from positive to negative.

Group agency and responsibility

In the foregoing analysis we have investigated the content of narrative schemas and drew indirect conclusions from them concerning the relationship between the representation of national history and national identity. In the analysis to follow we will use a negative historical event to show that narrative psychological content analysis based on the fundamental features of narrative construction is suitable for gaining direct information concerning the social psychological aspects of identity. When we asked our subjects to mention positive or negative events of European history, the frequency of occurrence of the Second World War among negative events was very high as an event of both European and Hungarian history. Narratives about the world war also included the Holocaust, but its frequency of occurrence was significantly different in narratives about Hungarian history than in those of European history of the Second World War (see Table 10.3.).

The Second World War is the most frequent event among the negative events for both Hungarian and European history. The number of people mentioning the Holocaust, however, sharply differed between the Hungarian and the European Second World War stories. Whereas in the 'European' Second World War stories, 22 per cent of the subjects mentioned it, in the 'Hungarian' stories this percentage was only 6 per cent. This result would speak for itself, if further results of the narrative analysis did not contribute to the interpretation. Narratives necessarily involve causal explanation of actions. It implies the attribution of responsibility for the actions. In accord with the classic Heiderian view, this attribution can be internal (own group's, i.e. Hungarian responsibility) or external (other groups or external circumstances are responsible for the action). For both European and Hungarian Second World War stories, the cause of the Holocaust (if this element of the war is mentioned at all) is almost exclusively the German fascism: Hungarians, even Hungarian fascists, do not have any share in it. Since agency is a core element of a group's identity (Castro and Rosa 2007) and group perception (Hamilton 2007), we can, of course, further think of the productivity and functions of this type of defence, but it certainly impedes agency potential of the group, in this case, Hungarians as a group.

Table 10.3 Agency in Holocaust stories

Europe		Hungary	
22%		6%	
Agent Yes	Agent No	Agent Yes	Agent No
64%	36%	12%	88%

Further steps towards the automated narrative psychological content analysis

Given that agency is mostly expressed in active verbs, we built a program based on this type of verb for measuring agency in a narrative. First, we compiled a dictionary of verbs with semantic content of activity (e.g. initiate) and another one of passive verbs (e.g. accepts). We built local grammars around these verbs so as to assure that only their use in the activity–passivity meaning will be considered. We also incorporated into the program the grammatical features of activity–passivity (e.g. active voice and passive voice). Finally, we endowed the program with a grammar, which assigns thematic roles (e.g. agent versus recipient) to the characters and also has the capacity of resolving anaphora and ellipsis (when the name of a character is substituted by pronoun or omitted, respectively) within a paragraph. Running this program on the Holocaust text base showed 87 per cent correspondence with the manually coded results.

The representation of common history

School textbooks of history do not merely offer knowledge about national history but patterns of identification as well, and they also fulfil the function of regulating national emotions. There is no need for a lengthy discussion as to whether the course of history depends on the actions of particular individuals or on the operation of institutions, and it would be a mistake to openly declare what is true in unsettled questions of history. This sort of function is fulfilled excellently by the rhetoric, that is, formal-structural properties of historical narrative. To illustrate what has been said above, we will take a look at some results taken from the content analysis of the chapters of three Austrian and three Hungarian secondary school textbooks of history dealing with the Austro-Hungarian monarchy (Vincze et al. 2007). We analysed passages dealing with the period from 1860 to 1914, taking into consideration events leading up to this period too. The passages are not lengthy; all the textbooks devote only a few pages to the period under discussion. In some textbooks political history is mixed with history of culture; we have focused only on passages dealing with political history. Above all, we were interested to see the ratio of narrative statements involving action or consciousness (for example: 'Without a Parliament Austria-Hungary began a war that soon turned into a world war' and 'He knew that Franz Joseph, in full conformity with his petty-minded character, would reject the proposal') as well as the ratio of the establishment of facts. An example for the latter: 'The February Patent of 1861 was a centralistic constitution meant not only for the provinces but for the entire Monarchy.' The first row of Table 10.4 shows that there are significantly more facts in the Austrian texts as compared to the Hungarian ones.

There are also significant differences as to who the actor is when it comes to acting or taking some measure. The second to fifth rows of the table show that the Hungarian textbooks far outdo the Austrian textbooks in terms of the number of

Table 10.4 Results of the history school book analysis

Codes	Frequency	
	Austrian history books	*Hungarian history books*
Fact, statement	120	78
Action of Hungarian institution	2	52
Action of Austrian institution	30	11
Action of Hungarian person	1	57
Action of Austrian person	38	15
Action of other nation	15	10
Mentalisation of Hungarians	1	21
Mentalisation of Austrians	12	5

actions performed by individuals and by institutions alike. The objective nature of the Austrian textbooks is also demonstrated by the data in the seventh and eighth rows, which concern the frequency of occurrence of narrative statements consciously formulated about the internal states of characters. Statements of this kind occur in exactly twice as many cases in the Hungarian textbooks as in the Austrian ones. However, in the Austrian textbooks, as shown by data in the sixth row, other nations of the monarchy or their representatives are more frequent agents performing an action, and are also more frequent partners in or patients of actions performed by other nations of the monarchy or their representatives.

The results shown here as a small sample indicate that the same common history is presented differently in Hungarian and Austrian history textbooks, and as a result, the relationship to history is also formulated differently. If evaluation is added to all this, which is clearly done from the point of view of democratic development in the Austrian textbooks, while in the Hungarian textbooks equal emphasis is put on aspects of independence, we can see that the Hungarian textbooks devote relatively little attention to the standpoint of other nations, tend to personify history and make it more easy to experience. In this respect they promote the transmission and deepening of traditional national identity. In contrast, the Austrian textbooks tend to reinforce the citizen identity of students.

A methodological amendment to these results is that, similarly to the agency program, we collected different types of mental expressions into dictionaries, built local grammars around them, which assured that the use of a given expression would be measured only in the targeted context, and we assigned the mental acts to thematic roles (filled in each sentence either by Austrians or by Hungarians) by grammatical means. Using this program resulted in 85 per cent correspondence with the manually coded results.

Summary

This chapter discussed the affinities between social psychology and historical sciences. Narrative metatheory emerging in both fields in recent decades has considerably strengthened the earlier non-existent or very sporadic intellectual links between them. The chapter argued that group history conceived as narratively constructed and represented social memory is a constituent of group identity. When presenting different forms and theories of social memory, the chapter pointed out that historical representations develop in relation to the identity needs of groups, consequently, content and forms of historical representations are indicative of group identity. The chapter included a study of Hungarian national identity, which applied concepts and methodologies from narrative psychology. In contrast to studies that investigate the formation of the concept of nation (e.g. Jahoda 1963; Piaget and Weil 1951) or national identity expressed in preferences or attitudes (Lawson 1963; Tajfel et al. 1970; Vaughan 1964), a social representational approach was used. We assumed that social knowledge embodied in folk history was acquired and reproduced during socialization. Shared national folk-history narratives both *construct* and *reflect* social identities of peoples belonging to a given nation. The change and development of the structure and content of these histories are characteristic to the social group. Thus, folk histories may illuminate the groups' reality and emotional life.

The method of having subjects tell stories of their own nation's past proved to be an apt procedure. Analysis of the stories revealed some conspicuous features of the Hungarian national identity.

11 Roots and perspectives of scientific narrative psychology

This is where our book comes to an end, but research on scientific narrative psychology has barely begun. The studies presented in Chapter 10 and the linguistic parsing modules of the various psychological constructs, for example mentalization or agency discussed in these studies, are still under development; similarly, the already completed and tested content analysis programs developed for scientific narrative psychology require further fine-tuning. There is a lot more technical work to be done, which affects fundamental questions in psychology and language technology, before the main historical issues and problems of cultural evolution raised in the first few chapters of this book can be addressed in concrete research projects. Nevertheless, we believe that we have accomplished our main goal. We started from the assumption that people construe themselves in and by stories in several important respects. In narratives they express how their experience and relationship to the social world is organized in the course of meaning construction, and how they create their identity. Moreover, we supposed that the qualities of this experience can give us important pieces of information concerning the behavioural adaptation of a storytelling person and the ways and chances of coping with different situations in his or her life too. So as to get a better understanding of these qualities of experience and ways of organizing experience, we have developed the method of the narrative psychological content analysis, which can reliably unravel psychologically relevant contents of meaning from the linguistic figures of narrative. In other words, we took seriously the relationship between language and human mental processes and between narrative and identity, and by analysing *narrative language* as a complex pattern carrying mental content we obtained scientific knowledge concerning the psychological processes of human social adaptation at both individual and group levels.

Instead of giving a summary of the theoretical positions and methods of scientific narrative psychology outlined throughout the chapters in this book, it may be useful to recapitulate the relation of narrative psychology to parallel approaches to narratives (see Table 11.1). Besides scientific narrative psychology, there are three distinct approaches in the field: cognitive studies of narratives, psychometric studies with narratives, and hermeneutic narrative psychology. Scientific narrative psychology shares the conviction with hermeneutic narrative psychology that narratives construct, transmit and reflect identity. In this sense, narratives have not only semantic or pragmatic, but also psychological meaning. However, these psychological meanings that we call identity states or identity qualities can be mapped in life histories or group histories not only by hermeneutic interpretation, but, to a large extent, quantitatively, by a system of computer programs developed for narrative psychological content analysis. Cognitive studies of narratives have achieved a very advanced stage in narrative comprehension. These studies focus on processing semantic and pragmatic information, but as opposed to scientific narrative psychology, are oblivious to psychological meaning and identity. They do not extend the results achieved by computer technology to studying identity processes. On the other hand, psychometric studies with narratives have a primary interest in psychological correlates of narrative language and narrative organization. They use computer technology for measuring word frequency and correlating it with personality variables, emotional states, and so on. Scientific narrative psychology's addition to this approach is a theoretical framework for the foundation of the relation between narrative language and psychological processes, as well as including complex narrative patterns and corresponding psychological dimensions in the computerized analysis.

Table 11.1 Relation of scientific narrative psychology to other approaches to narratives

Scientific narrative psychology	*Cognitive studies of narratives*	*Psychometric studies with narratives*	*Hermeneutic narrative psychology*
Quantitative methodology	Quantitative methodology	Quantitative methodology	Qualitative methodology
Narratives as vehicles of representations of individual and group experiences	Narratives as carriers of information	Psychological correlates of language use or impact of narrative organization on mental life	Meaning in social, cultural and textual context
Narrative composition of life stories reflects psychological states and identity qualities	Narrative structure is related to comprehension and memory organization	No interest in narrative composition and narrative structure	Case based interest in narrative composition
Using computer technology for identifying and measuring psychologically meaningful narrative components and patterns	Using computer technology to measure story organization and simulate story comprehension	Using computer technology for measuring word frequency	No measurement

It seems to be worthwhile summarizing the innovations of the narrative psychological content analysis. Narrative psychological content analysis differs from 'quantitative hermeneutics' and it is also radically different from any fashionable types of narrative analysis. As a consequence of postmodern thinking, the trend of qualitative analysis has developed in a broad sphere of empirical social sciences (Denzin and Lincoln 1994; Flick 2000; Hoshmand 2000; Polkinghorne 1997). From a scientific perspective, however, this is no more than a kind of theory-laden interpretation of empirical data, either in inductive or deductive manner.

Scientific narrative psychology, as with any other kind of narrative research, works with texts and stories which may come from personal documents, interviews, or even from literature, from cinematic art, from the fine arts, that is from professional authors. It can accommodate not only 'big' stories such as whole life histories or elicited stories of personal experiences (Freeman 2006), but also 'small stories', such as narratives used in conversations for creating and displaying the identities of the participants (Bamberg 2006; Georgakopoulou 2006; Schiffrin 1994). The narrative psychological content analysis, just as with any content analytic research, begins with qualitative decisions, which attribute some meaning to certain textual elements. In psychology, this meaning is usually psychological meaning. The analysis does not stop, however, at this qualitative phase. An important novelty of narrative psychological content analysis is that it treats the content analytical codes as values of psychological variables, which, in turn, will become quantifiable and statistically processible. Another remarkable novelty comes from the recognition of correspondences between narrative organization and psychological organization, namely from the fact that narrative features of self-narratives, such as the characters' functions, the temporal characteristics of the story, or the speakers' perspectives, will provide information about the features and conditions of self-representations. Similarly, the stories about the world will disclose the psychological features of social representations.

A further novelty of the narrative psychological content analysis is that its categories are based on textual features. These textual features, however complex they may be, can be identified in a more or less exact manner (László et al. 2002b, 2007). However, quantitative data gained by narrative psychological content analysis, i.e. the measured values of psychological variables, to whatever extent they are variables deduced from the theoretical connection of psychological and narrative variables, will be only of face validity. The external validity of the results may come from the application of control groups or by comparison with results obtained by other psychological methods of investigation.

Thus, scientific narrative psychology brings the postmodern idea of narrative construction back to the material world of psychological representation and the text. Although it attributes meaning to textual elements, this meaning is psychological meaning projected onto the theory of the evolution and operation of the psyche, which can be mapped not only by qualitative content analysis of the narrative discourse, but also by other techniques. Finally, narrative psychology, as a scientific mode of understanding, aspires to systematic data collection and a verifiable generalization of its results.

There are two conditions, which strongly support the empirical study of meaning construction in narratives in our days. Both are much discussed; however, their impact on scientific thinking is seldom touched upon. One of them is the process that we call globalization. More precisely, the consequence of globalization that cultural otherness and the behaviour which accompanies it, which has earlier been seen as esoteric or irrational, become our everyday experiences. They simply challenge the comfortable theses of our western-centric universalism. (Of course, irrational behaviour is not alien from western civilization either. The most prominent figures of the history of psychology – from Le Bon to Lewin or from Freud to Tajfel, and the list could well be continued – were busy with uncovering the psychological conditions of this irrationality.)

Another factor, as has happened many times in the history of science, is technological advance. Several recent results in information technology have created an opportunity to conduct computerized qualitative research on texts (see Denzin and Lincoln 1994; Miles and Huberman 1994). In the analysis of narratives, and in several other fields of inquiry, these eclectic tools prove to be much more effective than purely qualitative or purely quantitative methods. Existing and constantly developing complex computer programs can perform very rapid hypertext analysis too, which makes it possible to treat an entire corpus of text produced by a particular population as a huge database.

The scientific effect of technological innovations involves some special risks too. The easy and convenient use of huge databases may have the result that scientific research is conducted by precise and mechanical minds, and its creative nature becomes diminished. Whatever social phenomenon is studied, our investigations can never be governed solely by bottom-up theory building. The narrative psychological content analysis unifies the advantages of qualitative and quantitative research, because it should always be psychological theory based and also uses top-down rules which exploits computers' capacity to deal with complex linguistic forms. Thereby it provides structure for the unstructured aspects of narrative content. There are numerous types of narrative, and all of them can be further divided into subtypes in accordance with various approaches to social phenomena. It will always be the task of the researcher to find the best narrative and the best analytic tool for it, and this innovative activity should never be thrown at the mercy of complicated statistical heuristics.

Closely related to this issue is the view that technological progress makes it possible to establish not only new methods but also new models of humans. In the mid-twentieth century, development in cybernetics led to a switchboard model of the human mind in psychology and research was directed to associative relations and feedback. In the second half of the century, the computer became the central metaphor. The model of humans resembled more and more of an intelligent information processor. The limited processing and storage capacity of the early stage computers did not, however, allow modelling the whole richness of human psychological processes, particularly not the socially and culturally embedded processes of constructing and using meanings. Fourth generation computers already allow the handling of a large quantity of lifelike data, which can serve as a basis for constructing and empirically testing models that map at least some of the complexities of meaning. When it turns to stories and strives to reconstruct and explain the human psychology from the rich, but identifiable patterns of the structural characteristics of the narrative text, narrative psychology attempts to construct an empirically testable model of human beings who live with meanings.

Finally, we should stress again that scientific narrative psychology can be a tool which performs the task of the reconstruction in both historical and ontogenetic dimensions of the development of human psyche. We use the term *psyche* instead of *mind* or *cognition*, because cognition and meaning construction cannot be disentangled in historical and ontogenetic investigation of cultural processes. Meaning construction is embodied in emotion-laden *experiences* that are related to both individual and collective identity. Personal and collective narratives either from oral historical sources or in written form – since they carry organizational forms and phenomenal character of experiences – render historical and ontogenetic changes in identity construction accessible, and thereby enable a scientific study of cultural evolution.

Appendix

On Lin-Tag (www.mtapi.hu/Lin-Tag)

Linguistic pre-analysis of psychological narratives in Hungarian is performed by Lin-Tag, software developed by MorphoLogic Ltd. The program attempts to recognize linguistic markers relevant for psychological research by performing partial sentence parsing. The goal of the linguistic modules is to recognize and highlight those linguistic forms during text analysis that are relevant for a given narrative category and for the psychological content related to it. The following narrative categories are supported:

- Narrative perspective
- Approach–avoidance
- Functions of main characters
- Subjective time experience
- Self-reference
- Negation.

Of these categories the first three require deeper analysis, while for the others 'only' key words and expressions need to be highlighted.

For similar problems simple word form recognition tools are used in the English language literature; these also analyse the co-occurrences of these word forms. For the Hungarian language, this method is by no means sufficient. On the one hand, the occurrence of different forms of words cannot be simply listed (on an average a word may appear in several thousand different forms in a text), and on the other it is often not the word stems but the different linguistic forms that are important for analysis. While in English linguistic forms are expressed by means of word order and mostly separate words that belong to a phrase (isolating language), Hungarian uses various affixes to mark the grammatical relationship between often very remote words in the sentence. Therefore both word level analysis and the recognition of the grammatical relationship between words are indispensable for evaluating texts.

The process of program development is shown in Figure A.1. The Lin-Tag programs are built on HUMOR and HUMORESK, two software packages developed

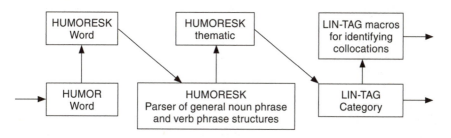

Figure A.1 The process of program development

by MorphoLogic Ltd. The HUMOR word analysis program performs a detailed analysis of Hungarian word forms. HUMOR breaks up word forms into functional pieces (morphemes) and assigns to them grammatical features that are necessary for later analysis (Prószéky and Kis 1999). For example, the word form 'almát' ('apple+ACC' or 'litter+his') is assigned the following description:

alma {N} = 'almá'+t {ACC} = 't'
'apple'
alom {N} = 'alm'+a {Pse3} = 'á'+t {ACC} = 't'
'litter'

Similarly, the word form 'legerosebbik' (strongest) is also analysed in two ways by the program, as a noun and as an adjective:

leg {SUP} = 'leg'+eros {Adj} = 'eros'+ebb {COMP} = 'ebb'+ik {HIGHL} = 'ik'+et {ACC} = 'et'
'strong'
leg {SUP} = 'leg'+ero {N} = 'ero'+s {SSUFF} = 's'+ebb {COMP} = 'ebb'+ik {HIGHL} = 'ik'+et {ACC} = 'et'
'strength'

Morphological analysis by itself is indispensable for content analysis, for in the case of the word form 'apát' (father+ACC or 'abbot'), for example, it does matter whether we are talking about a male parent in the accusative or a parish clerk in the nominative case. This is unambiguously decided by the parser in morphological analysis.

HUMORESK is a linguistic parser that can be applied for syntactic analysis (Prószéky et al. 2004). It is a suffix grammar based on case grammar that contains prohibitive rules too. It does not produce a complete sentence syntax, but it is suitable for the analysis of noun phrases and verb phrases. HUMORESK does not implement any revolutionary parsing algorithm. It performs a bottom-up text analysis; it assigns simplified feature arrays to each symbol, and the features are checked and inherited as the parsing tree is being built.

What is new in HUMORESK is the way rules are matched and formulated. The rules are described in the form of a finite set of patterns, so the system receives a lexicon for matching rules that is similar to the lexicon of morphological parsers. Each pattern is built up of underspecified elements, or symbols: for certain symbols only the labels marking syntactic roles are known, for others the stem or even the surface word form is also given.

For the above reasons HUMORESK cannot be clearly distinguished as a rule-based or a lexicon-based – or, using machine translation terminology, example-based – system: on the one hand, the data for analysis, that is, the primary component of the grammar is a rule whose elements are constrained, and on the other hand, it is a pattern (example) whose parts are not fully specified at the surface level of signal sequences.

HUMOR and HUMORESK are linked by an intermediary program, WORD AUTOMATON. This program produces a description from the output of HUMOR in a format that matches the feature categories of HUMORESK. The feature categories of HUMORESK may follow from the grammar, but there may be psychologically 'interesting' additions too. This is the point where psychological analysis begins. The *example of approach–avoidance* is used to illustrate the steps of writing a program in Lin-Tag. As the first step a bridge is built between the syntactic parser and Lin-Tag. This bridge, Tabs Table, describes psychological categories in grammatical terms. For instance, *approach* may be contained by the grammatical description of a verb: e.g. *jön* (come) or *ad+DAT* (give sg. to sy.), but it may be a verbal prefix or some adverb too. With the help of Tabs Table and on the basis of the grammar, Lin-Tag 'collects' all the expressions that belong to the approach category. In the next step so-called MACROS are created which filter out the elements from the categories of Tabs Table that do not correspond to the required contents, and they also complement the criteria of categorization. This is because it does matter from a psychological point of view whether approaching refers to the protagonist of the story, the self, or to some other character. This can be handled by a macro that considers only instances of approaching related to the self. The operation of Lin-Tag is shown in Figure A.2.

Linguistic operationalization of the programs

Linguistic typology may range languages into three groups (Greenberg 1974): the isolating languages consist of one-syllable words (e.g. Chinese); the agglutinative languages attach prefixes and suffixes to the words (e.g. Finnish, Estonian, Turkish, Hungarian); and finally we can distinguish the inflected languages, where the words themselves change through inflexion, such as in case of German, Italian, Polish or Russian languages. It is important to mention that languages cannot be placed unequivocally into these categories, they preferably belong to a certain group owing to their dominant characteristic features. The English language is more likely to be related to the isolating languages. On the contrary, the Hungarian language can be placed among the agglutinative languages, which means that the grammatical relations are represented by cumulative affixes; instead of

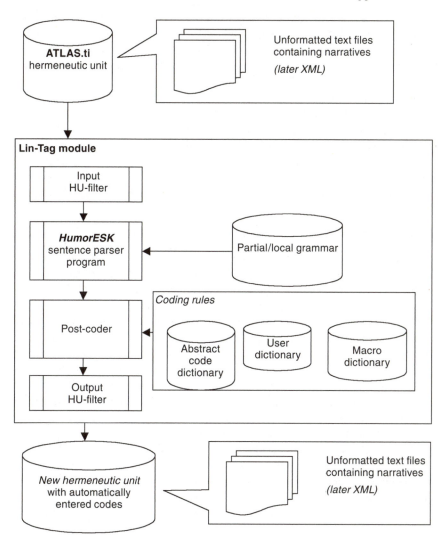

Figure A.2 Outlines of the operation of Lin-Tag

prepositions the language uses suffixes, that is it inflects. Therefore, considering the structure of the words, the Hungarian language is more difficult than most of the Indo-European languages. Hungarian words can be rather expanded: endings may appear successively; thus, in case of Hungarian, we keep count of more than ten thousand word-forms per word and the number of the feasible suffixed word-forms can be put at five billion (Kenesei 2004). (By comparison, all the word-forms of English language can be estimated at half a million.) With the help of the above mentioned method, that is with setting the possible word-forms of words as dictionary elements (lists), it is technically impossible to carry out and operate the Hungarian word-frequency analysing programs economically: they come up against difficulties – regarding the storing as well as access time – as far as the capacity of computers is concerned. Accordingly, such techniques should be applied, where the operation of the system is based on the analysis of morphologic units of the words. The aim of morphology is to break the words down to their components, to morphemes, and to disclose and label certain grammatical features of a component.

The linguistic operationalization of the narrative compositional features was based on morphology and on lexicalized local grammars, which grasp the targeted linguistic patterns (for similar efforts, see Webber 2004). As a demonstration, we will present the linguistic operationalization of the narrative perspective forms and of the control of spatial-emotional distance (approach–avoidance).

Linguistic operationalization of the perspective forms

This concept of a perspective in a self-narrative can be defined linguistically by taking into consideration those linguistic markers which have a role in a spatio-temporal location. There are two ways of locating spatially and temporally both the narrative content and the position. The narrator may carry out the location independently from his or her actual location. In this case the narrator uses specific terms referring to places (e.g. name of a town or a street) or dates (name of a month or day). Alternatively, the narrator may carry out the location by taking into consideration his or her actual location. In this dependent case, the narrator uses spatial (e.g. *there, here*) or temporal (e.g. *then, now*) deictic terms for spatio-temporal location. Both the independent and the dependent ways appear in a self-narrative, and both of them are able to define a particular spatial or temporal location. However, there are important differences between their uses. The terms used in an independent location are based on a well elaborated spatial and temporal system, while the deictic terms are related to a more robust spatial and temporal system, since they locate either distally or proximally the content and the position to each other. Another difference reflects their frequency in a self-narrative. Deictic terms appear much more frequently than terms referring to places and dates.

The linguistic operationalization of the three perspective forms consists of four groups of linguistic markers. The most frequently occurring group of linguistic markers are the temporal deictic markers, since this group consists of the markers of verb tense. The use of the present verb tense locates proximally the narrative content and the position to each other, while the use of the past verb tense locates them distally. Besides, there are several temporal adverbs which are able to locate either proximally or distally the narrative content and the position to each other (e.g. *most [now], akkor [then]*). The second group of linguistic markers consists of those spatial adverbs and demonstrative pronouns which also can be used in a proximal or a distal location (e.g. *itt [here], ez [this], ott [there], az [that]*). The third group of linguistic markers consists of specific terms which are related to one of the three perspective forms. Those terms which are used in a narrator independent way of location are related to the retrospective form since their meaning refers to a distal spatial or temporal location (e.g. *Budapest [Budapest], Január [January]*). Interjections are related to the experiencing form since in the case of these terms the content and the position are located proximally to each other (Wilkins 1995) (e.g. *hupsz [ops]*). Finally, there are a few verbs and several modifiers which are related to the metanarrative form since these terms either refer to a present mental act of a narrator (e.g. *emlékszem [I remember]*) or express the present stance of a narrator toward the narrative content (e.g. *valószíníleg [probably]*) respectively. The last group of linguistic markers consists of the sentence type. Clauses with the retrospective perspective form are always statements. However, clauses with the experiencing or metanarrative forms can be a statement, a question, an exclamation or an optative. A summary table of the linguistic codes of the narrative perspective algorithm is shown in Table A.1

The adopted perspective form in a narrative clause is identified by the co-presence of these linguistic codes. As an example, consider the next short excerpt from a hypothetical narrator who recounts a traffic accident.

(1) I took the road to the grocery store.
(2) I see a car running towards me!
(3) And I do not remember more, even now.

The narrator adopts retrospective perspective form in the first sentence, because of the past verb tense (VERB_PAST). In the second sentence, the narrator adopts experiencing perspective form, indicated by three linguistic markers: present verb tense (VERB_PRESENT), proximal spatial adverb (PROXLOC) and exclamation mark (PUNCMARK_!?). Finally, the narrator adopts metanarrative perspective form in the third sentence. It is also indicated by three markers: the occurrence of the verb of remember (SPEC_VERB), present verb tense (VERB_PRESENT), and proximal temporal adverb (PROXTIME).

Table A.1 Linguistic codes of the narrative perspective algorithm

Linguistic markers	Retrospective form	Experiencing form	Metanarrative form
Time deixis			
Tense	VERB_PAST	VERB_PRESENT VERB_OTHER	VERB_PRESENT
Temporal adverbs	DISTTIME	PROXTIME	PROXTIME
Space deixis			
Spatial adverbs	DISTLOC	PROXLOC	PROXLOC
Demonstrative pronouns	DISTLOC	PROXLOC	PROXLOC
Specific terms	—	SPEC_INT	SPEC_VERB SPEC_MOD
Sentence	PUNCMARK_.	PUNCMARK_!?	PUNCMARK_!?

Linguistic operationalization of the approach–avoidance dimension

The linguistic operationalization of the approach–avoidance motions consists of three groups of linguistic markers. The first group of linguistic markers consists of verbs referring to physical motions. The algorithm identifies the first and third person plural and singular verbs by sorting them into twelve auxiliary semantic categories. Since Hungarian is an affixing language, a surface morphological analysis is sufficient to identify the number and person of the verb. The categories are the following:

APPR_FARVD1 = predicative, first person verb referring to motion (e.g. go)
APPR_FARVD3 = predicative, third person verb referring to motion (e.g. runs)
APPR_FARVI1 = predicative, first person verb referring to 'moving something' (e.g. gave)
APPR_FARVI3 = predicative, third person verb referring to 'moving something' – approach (e.g. sends)
APPR_FARVS1 = predicative, first person verb attracting noun in accusative (e.g. know)
APPR_FARVS3 = predicative, third person verb, attracting noun in accusative (e.g. kissed)
AVOID_NEARVI1 = negative, first person verb, attracting noun in accusative (e.g. I did not kiss)
AVOID_NEARV3 = negative, third person verb, attracting noun in accusative (e.g. she does not know)
AVOID_FARVIX1 = predicative, third person verb referring to 'moving something' – avoid (e.g. lose)
AVOID_FARVIX3 = predicative, third person verb referring to 'moving something' – avoid (e.g. lost)
AVOID_NEXIST1 = negative, first person substantive verb (e.g. I was not)
AVOID_NEXIST3 = negative, third person substantive verb (e.g. he will not)

The second group of linguistic codes consists of nouns. Here the first person pronouns and their suffixed forms and another group of nouns which refer to significant others are taken into account. Persons regarded as significant others are those who play crucial role in the narrator's life story. Based on former studies (e.g. Péley 2002) family members, romantic partners and friends belong to this category. The tokens of this latter code are listed in dictionary files. However, in the course of the pilot analyses we recognized that in most of the cases these significant others are only labelled with pronouns, consequently, both the third and the first person pronouns and their suffixed forms are included in the analysis. The nouns are sorted into six categories depending on their semantic function. Examples of the categories are the following:

APPR_NEARNI1 = first person pronoun in dative (e.g. for me)
APPR_NEARNI3 = third person pronoun in dative or a significant other in dative (e.g. for mom)
APPR_NEARN1 = first person pronoun functioning as spatial adverb answering to WHERE TO? (e.g. to me)
APPR_NEARN3 = third person pronoun functioning as spatial adverb or a denominative answering to WHERE TO? (e.g. to her, to my friend)
APPR_NHOME1 = first person pronoun answering to WHERE? (e.g. at my house)
APPR_NHOME 3 = third person pronoun or an inflected noun refer to significant other answering to WHERE? (e.g. by dad)
AVOID_FARND1 = first person pronoun functioning as spatial adverb answering to WHERE FROM? (e.g. from me)
AVOID_FARND3 = third person pronoun functioning as spatial adverb or a denominative answering to WHERE FROM? (e.g. from her)
AVOID_FARVS1 = first person pronoun in accusative (e.g. me)
AVOID_FARVS3 = third person pronoun or a significant other in accusative (e.g. him)

The verbal and nominal codes build up the macros of APPROX and AVOID. The relation of verbs and nouns is defined by verbal prepositions which have to be provided by nominal structures. The predicative or negative form of the elements is substantial, because the negation of approach could denote avoidance, but it does not equal the negation of avoidance. The negation of avoidance does not definitely denote approach. Thus, the linguistic markers of approach and avoidance are text units consisting of co-present verbs and nouns.

Validity and reliability studies with the programs

Validity of the measures has been tested with three different techniques. First, for each module we carried out validity studies with a sample of eighty-three normal subjects stratified by age and gender. In this study subjects were asked to tell six critical life episodes. The short version of the Thematic Apperception Test and a ninety-four-item questionnaire were administered in the same session. The questionnaire included scales of standard identity and personality questionnaires, which targeted the same psychological constructs as the program modules did. Sample description is given in Table A.2.

Table A.2 Sample description

Gender	Young adults (18–35 years)	Adults (45+ years)
Female	33	17
Male	21	12

Second, we also used control groups with various mental disorders according to the DSM IV for some of the program modules. We had three groups of this kind: patients with major depression (20 subjects), borderline patients (22 subjects) and drug abusers (20 subjects). The results with groups of mental patients were used for Approx-Change, Self-reference and Negation modules.

Third, the validity of the Narrative perspective module was also tested by social perception experiments (Pólya et al. 2005).

Life episodes
Subjects told stories in the narrative interview about the following critical life episodes:
   FIRST MEMORY
Story about the earliest memory remembered by the subjects
   ACHIEVEMENT STORY
Story about an achievement, which the subject is proud of even today
   TERROR STORY
Story about a life event in which the subject experienced terror
   LOSS STORY
Story about a life event in which the subject experienced loss
   BAD RELATIONSHIP STORY
Story about a bad relationship of the subject's
   GOOD RELATIONSHIP STORY
Story about a good relationship of the subject's

According to the narrative interview technique, story episodes were told in the frame of a semi-structured life-interview. The interviewer raised the question for each life episode wherever it was thematically relevant in the interview.

Questionnaire

The ninety-four-item questionnaire contained the following subscales (the relevant modules are in parentheses):

Time Perception Scale (El-Meligi 1972) nine items (time modules)
Beck Depression Inventory (Beck et al. 1974) short version (negation, self-reference)
Big Five Questionnaire (Caprara et al. 1993), emotion control and impulse control for emotional stability subscales, twenty-four items (narrative perspective, approx-change, character functions)
Trait-Meta Mood Scale (Salovey et al. 1995), clarity subscale, eleven items (narrative perspectives, approx-change)
Experiences of Close Relationships (Brennan et al. 1998) Trust in partners subscale, thirty items (narrative perspective, approx-change)
Purpose to Life Scale (Antonovsky 1987), short version, thirteen items (all modules)

Reliability studies of the program modules

Reliability studies were performed in each case by comparing the results of automatic and manual coding. In each case a broad sample of texts (minimum 2,000 words) were used. Manual coding was performed by two independent coders with a minimum agreement of 0.87.

Validity studies of the program modules

Validity studies were performed by relating content analytic results obtained by a module in the stories relevant to the module to results obtained in the corresponding scales of the questionnaire and TAT variables. The number of subjects included in the statistical analysis changed because there was some minimal natural loss during the transcription of the interviews. In certain cases a story given by a subject was not amenable to narrative content analysis and had to be omitted. The number of subjects included in the statistical analysis is indicated in each case. As a demonstration, the results of the reliability and validity studies with the *narrative perspective* and the *spatial-emotional control* (approach–avoidance) programs will be presented below. (More details about the reliability and validity studies can be found in Ehmann et al. 2007; Hargitai et al. 2007; Pohárnok et al. 2007; Pólya et al. 2007.)

Studies with the narrative perspective module

Reliability of the perspective module

Two studies investigated the reliability of the perspective module. The first study analysed 130 self-narratives which consisted of 220 narrative clauses. The narrative interviews were taken from homosexual males and women participating in in-vitro fertilizing (IVF) treatment. The performance of the module was measured by two variables of recall and accuracy. As these two variables show, the module is most successful in identifying the retrospective form, followed by the experiencing and the metanarrative form (see Table A.3).

The second study analysed 130 self-narratives taken from the same sample. The length of these self-narratives were 15,696 narrative clauses which were coded manually and by the perspective module as well. The correlation coefficients

Table A.3 Performance of the self-narrative perspective module

Perspective forms	Recall (%)	Accuracy (%)
Retrospective form	88.1	96.7
Experiencing form	84.5	83.3
Metanarrative form	62.5	71.4

between two ways of coding reflect the module's performance. The correlation coefficient was r = 0.89, p < 0.01 in the case of a retrospective form, r = 0.85, p < 0.01 in the case of an experiencing form, and finally it was r = 0.63, p < 0.01 in the case of a metanarrative form.

In sum, the perspective module reliably codes the retrospective and experiencing forms, however the identification of the metanarrative form does not reach the 80 per cent level which was set as a performance criterion.

Validity study of the emotion regulating function of the narrative perspective module

Two studies were done to test the assumed psychological content of the narrative perspective. In these studies we used the relative frequency of each perspective form, which was calculated by dividing the summa perspectivizations by the number of the given perspective form.

The study was done with 83 subjects of the stratified sample (29 males and 54 females). Subjects whose stories consisted of fewer than four events were not considered. According to age distribution: young adults (18–35 years old: 50 persons, M = 23.02, SD = 3.90) and adults (45–60 years old: 33 persons, M = 51.65, SD = 3.82).

Dependent measures

Trait features of emotional experience were measured by questionnaires. The coherence of emotional experience was reflected by administering the Clarity factor of the Trait Meta-Mood Scale (Salovey et al. 1995), which reflects how clearly a person sees his or her feelings. The Purpose to Life Scale (Antonovsky 1987) was used to measure the sense of coherence construct. This construct

> is a global orientation that expresses the extent to which one has a pervasive, enduring though dynamic feeling of confidence that (1) the stimuli deriving from one's internal and external environments in the course of living are structured, predictable, and explicable; (2) the resources are available to one to meet the demands posed by these stimuli; and (3) these demands are challenges, worthy of investment and engagement.
>
> (Antonovsky 1987: 19)

Accordingly, the sense of coherence construct has three factors: comprehensibility, manageability and meaningfulness, respectively.

The stability of emotional experience was reflected by administering the Emotion stability factor of the Big Five Questionnaire (Caprara et al. 1993). This factor consists of two subscales. The emotional control subscale measures the capacity for coping with anxiety and emotions. The impulse control subscale measures the capacity for regulating irritability, discontent, and anger.

Results

We did not expect differences between genders in the frequency of perspective forms, and the results supported this expectation. However, there are reasons to assume that age yields certain differences. Since people often recall significant life events from the period of adolescence, it is likely that young adults recall relatively recent events, whereas older subjects report events more distant in time. Older subjects presumably had more opportunity to talk about the event, thereby shaping the meaning of the event. The experiencing narrative form is generally used when the shaping of the meaning of an event takes place; therefore we assumed that this perspective form occurs more often with young subjects. At the same time, older people are generally more sensitive to the emotional components of an event; therefore we expected a higher frequency of metanarrative perspective in this group. The results supported both expectations. Older subjects used less experiencing forms (two-tailed t-test $t = (81)2.04$, $p < 0.05$) and more metanarrative forms (two-tailed t-test $t = (81)2.54$, $p < 0.05$) than young subjects did (see Table A.4).

We did not expect frequency differences according to the themes of the episodes, and indeed, the results did not show any such differences. However, there are reasons to assume that narratives about positive life events may differ from narratives about negative life events in the way how they use perspective forms. Storytellers of positive events presumably tend to increase, whereas tellers of negative events tend to decrease the intensity of emotions involved in the event. Consequently, we may expect more metanarrative perspectives and less retrospective and experiencing perspectives with positive than with negative episodes. Table A.5 shows that the pattern of results conforms to this assumption, however the differences do not reach a significant level.

The characteristics of emotion regulation measured with questionnaires were correlated with the use of perspective forms (see Table A.6). We found several tendencies and significant results supporting the claim that use of particular perspective forms reflects particular forms of emotion regulation.

Table A.4 Relative frequency of the narrative perspective forms in the stratified normal sample

	Retrospective		Metanarrative		Experiencing	
	M	*SD*	*M*	*SD*	*M*	*SD*
Males (N = 29)	0.241	0.059	0.604	0.065	0.151	0.060
Females (N = 54)	0.237	0.070	0.614	0.075	0.149	0.051
18–35 years(N = 50)	0.246	0.064	0.595[a]	0.068	0.159[a]	0.051
45–60 years (N = 33)	0.226	0.069	0.634[b]	0.071	0.135[b]	0.056
Total (N = 83)	0.238	0.066	0.610	0.072	0.149	0.054

Note: a and b indices indicate that the difference is significant at least at $p < 0.10$ level

Table A.5 Relative frequency of narrative perspective forms in narratives of five different life episodes

Life episode	Retrospective		Metanarrative		Experiencing	
	M	SD	M	SD	M	SD
Achievement	0.232	0.101	0.621	0.127	0.146	0.086
Terror	0.253	0.113	0.601	0.118	0.146	0.094
Loss	0.246	0.113	0.606	0.115	0.149	0.092
Bad relationship	0.244	0.126	0.602	0.137	0.154	0.090
Good relationship	0.224	0.121	0.626	0.124	0.150	0.094

Table A.6 Correlations between the frequencies of perspective forms and the measures of coherence and stability of emotional experience

Emotion regulation		Retrospective		Metanarrative		Experiencing	
		M	SD	M	SD	M	SD
TMMS: Clarity factor	L	0.242	0.068	0.607	0.063	0.151	0.060
	H	0.236	0.066	0.613	0.079	0.147	0.050
Emotional control factor	L	0.254[a]	0.072	0.594	0.075	0.152	0.059
	H	0.228[b]	0.061	0.620	0.067	0.149	0.051
Impulse control factor	L	0.235	0.063	0.612	0.076	0.150	0.057
	H	0.241	0.069	0.610	0.068	0.149	0.052
Depression factor	L	0.250[a]	0.069	0.593[a]	0.069	0.154	0.051
	H	0.2223[b]	0.061	0.633[b]	0.070	0.144	0.058
Manageability factor	L	0.240	0.074	0.613	0.077	0.143	0.061
	H	0.237	0.061	0.608	0.068	0.155	0.048
Meaningfulness factor	L	0.257[a]	0.070	0.595	0.074	0.147	0.056
	H	0.230[b]	0.063	0.617	0.070	0.150	0.054
Comprehensibility factor	L	0.244	0.070	0.616	0.079	0.137[a]	0.058
	H	0.234	0.063	0.606	0.065	0.161[b]	0.048
Emotional lability factor	L	0.242	0.070	0.617	0.075	0.137a	0.056
	H	0.232	0.064	0.608	0.072	0.160b	0.050

Notes: a and b indices indicate that the difference is significant at least at p < 0.10 level
L = Low
H = High
TMMS: Trait Meta-Mood Scale

Low emotional intensity of the retrospective perspective is supported by results in the meaningfulness factor. Subjects with low depression (two-tailed t-test t(81) = 1.87, p < 0.10) and low meaningfulness (two-tailed t-test t(81) = 1.77, p < 0.10), that is subjects characterized by low emotional intensity use more retrospective perspectives than those who exhibit high values on these scales. However, it somewhat contradicts the expectations that subjects with high emotion control use less retrospective perspectives than those who exhibit low emotion control (two-tailed t-test t(81) = 1.76, p < 0.10).

The results also support the shaping role of the experiencing perspective. Subjects scoring high on the comprehensibility factor, who perceive events in a coherent structure, use more experiencing forms than subjects exhibiting low scores in this factor (two-tailed t-test t(81) = 2.08, p < 0.05). Similarly, subjects high in emotional lability use more experiencing perspectives than emotionally balanced subjects (two-tailed t-test t(81) = 1.84, p < 0.10).

Studies with the Approx-Change program

Three self-narratives (approximately 2000 words) were coded both manually and by the Approx-Change program. As can be seen in Table A.7, the program has a total of 54 per cent recall. The identification of APPROX expressions shows a higher level of recall, but lower accuracy, and it works less reliably in the case of AVOID expressions.

Validity tests of Approx-Change program in clinical and normal samples

Based on the results of our former studies (Pohárnok et al. 2007) it was presumed that a higher frequency of approach and avoidance expressions would appear in the self-narratives of patients with borderline personality disorder (BPD), as compared to the self-narratives of the normal sample. Both object relation theory (e.g. Kernberg 1975; Mahler et al. 1975) and attachment theory (e.g. Fonagy 1998; Holmes 2004) claim that BPD is principally characterized by ambitendencies of interpersonal behaviour and by unstable affect regulation. In the case of these patients the urge of avoidance due to the fear of engulfment and the wish for intimacy are activated simultaneously. This leads to unsuccessful regulatory attempts in relational regulation and affect regulation.

Table A.7 Reliability of the Approx-Change module

APPROX	Right score	Omission	False score	Total
Manual coding	46	—	—	46
Approx-Change module	28	18	31	28 (60%)
AVOID	Right score	Omission	False score	Total
Manual coding	27	—	—	27
Approx-Change module	12	15	5	12 (44%)

This hypothesis was tested in two samples of self-narratives (BPD N = 33, control N = 33 in the case of Good story with a significant other, and BPD N = 32, control N = 32 in the case of Bad story with a significant other). It was presumed that a greater proportion of approach and avoidance expressions would appear in the BPD group. The control and the BPD samples were matched according to the age of the participants and the number of words per story, and we applied an independent sample t-test to compare the means of approach and avoidance expressions in the two episodes.

As can be seen in Table A.8, there is a tendency in the differences between the two groups in the case of the Good story. Although the difference in the Avoid elements is statistically significant, there are no statistically significant differences in the total of approach and avoidance expressions. For the Bad story again, Avoid expressions differ significantly, whereas the differences in Approx expression only approach the significance level. Thus, the results with the Avoid expressions support our hypothesis, whereas the Approx results only partly do so.

Validity tests of the Approx-Change module in the stratified normal sample

The studies were done with the six life episode stories of the stratified normal sample (N = 83 mean). From the questionnaire we used the following subscales: To assess the quality of relational regulation the scale of *'Trust in partners'* of the **Experiences of Close Relationships** (Brennan et al. 1998) questionnaire was used. To assess the trait-like differences in self-regulation we used the subscales of *'Emotion control'* and *'Impulse control for Emotional Stability'* of the **Big Five Questionnaire** (BFQ, Caprara et al. 1993), the *'Clarity'* subscale of the **Trait-Meta Mood Scale** (Salovey et al. 1995) and the *'Manageability'* subscale of the **Purpose to Life Scale** (Antonovsky 1987).

First, we presumed that differences would appear in the total of approach and avoidance expressions between narratives involving negative emotional states (e.g. Loss story) and narratives involving positive emotional states (e.g. Good story). The statistical method of independent sample t-test was applied and we found that

Table A.8 Relative frequencies of APPROX and AVOID codes in the autobiographical episodes

Topic	APPROX		AVOID	
	M	*SD*	*M*	*SD*
Achievement (N = 78)	0.900	0.212	0.099	0.212
Fear (N = 77)	0.815	0.313	0.185	0.313
Loss (N = 78)	0.856	0.232	0.143	0.232
Bad (N = 66)	0.806	0.301	0.193	0.301
Good (N = 75)	0.853	0.247	0.146	0.247

the results met our expectations in the case of the Bad story and the Achievement story. We found the largest number of approach expressions in the Achievement stories and the largest number of avoidance expressions in the Bad stories. The results of the next paired t-tests, however, showed only non-significant differences between story-types (see Table A.9).

To account for these results, we assumed that the pattern of approach and avoidance is a deep-rooted feature of the organization of experiences – a trait-like characteristic feature – which appears independently from the emotional charge of a narrative. Besides this, we have to consider that the efficiency of the Approx-Change is responsible for the overall proportion of approach and avoidance expressions in the episodes: there is a smaller amount of recall in the case of avoidance expressions in all stories.

According to our second hypothesis the larger amount of APPROX and AVOID codes – the more frequent co-occurrence of approach and avoidance motions – demonstrates that the person who tells the story has difficulties with the adaptive affect regulation. These difficulties are presented in the more intense 'toward-away' motions in relation to the other and correlate with certain trait-like features of regulative mechanisms.

To test this hypothesis we analysed the Achievement and the Loss stories, because they involve opposite and well-defined affects. We created two equal groups of Achievement and Loss stories. One group contained the lowest (L) and the other contained the highest (H) amount of APPROX and AVOID codes. Then we compared the scores of the narrators' personality questionnaires in these two groups of stories.

Table A.9 Frequency of APPROX and AVOID codes and their co-occurrence (APPRAVOID) in the matched samples

Good story						
	APPROX $p = 0.078$ ($p < 0.10$)		AVOID $p = 0.029$ ($p < 0.05$)		APPRAVOID $p = 0.081$ ($p < 0.10$)	
Control (N = 33)	M 3.121	SD 2.583	M 0.515	SD 0.972	M 3.636	SD 2.804
BPD (N = 33)	4.090	3.521	0.969	1.310	5.060	4.022

Bad story						
	APPROX $p = 0.0699$ ($p < 0.10$)		AVOID $p = 0.033$ ($p < 0.05$)		APPRAVOID $p = 0.237$ ns.	
Control (N = 32)	M 4.281	SD 3.205	M 0.687	SD 0.965	M 4.968	SD 3.477
BPD (N=32)	4.093	3.401	1.343	2.057	5.437	4.641

As can be seen in Table A.10, participants who have lower scores on the scales of emotional and impulsivity control have larger amount of APPROX and AVOID codes, and have more frequent approach and avoidance expressions in their Achievement story. However, a smaller amount of APPROX and AVOID codes were found in the Achievement story of those participants who were able to understand and anticipate the stimuli influencing them, and manage these stimuli appropriately.

These results confirm our hypothesis, as the prevalence of approach and avoidance expressions implies more unstable and inadequate regulatory capacities, while their lower frequency suggests more optimal affect regulation. Those participants who have higher scores on the 'Trust in partners' subscale, both in the Loss stories and in the Achievement stories show a lower frequency of approach and avoidance expressions. It could be assumed that these persons are more successful in 'using' the reliable other for the support of their own affect regulation, thus they do not have to rely on their own unsuccessful regulatory capacities.

Table A.10 The relation between the total of approach and avoidance expressions in the Achievement and the Loss stories (APPRAVOID) and personality questionnaire scores

		Personality traits									
		Emotion control		Impulse control		TMMS: Clarity		PLS: Manageability		ECR: Trust	
		M	SD	M	SD	M	SD	M	SD	M	SD
Achievement APPRAVOID	L	39.433*	8.740	36.266*	6.073	47.100*	4.978	14.566*	2.699	44.900*	7.063
	H	29.714*	7.010	30.875*	7.579	40.666*	6.365	12.187*	2.948	39.500*	8.082
Loss APPRAVOID	L	38.034	8.033	36.862*	6.864	46.448	3.859	14.241	2.668	45.758*	6.588
	H	33.277	10.554	32.631*	7.197	43.000	7.615	12.947	3.865	40.157*	8.883

Note: The asterisk * means that there is a significant difference ($p < 0.05$) between the two groups.

References

Abelson, R.P. (1968) 'Psychological implication', in R.P. Abelson, E. Aronson, W.J. McGuire, T.M. Newcomb, M.J. Rosenberg and P.H. Tannenbaum (eds) *Theories of Cognitive Consistency: A sourcebook*. Skokie, IL: Rand McNally.

—— (1975) 'Does a story understander need a point of view?' Paper presented at the Workshop on Theoretical Issues in Natural Language Processing, MIT, Cambridge, MA, June.

—— (1976) 'Scripts in attitudes and decisions', in J.S. Carrol and J.W. Payne (eds) *Cognition and Social Behavior*. Hillsdale, NJ: Lawrence Erlbaum.

—— (1987) 'Artificial intelligence and literary appreciation: How big is the gap?', in L. Halasz (ed.) *Literary Discourse Aspects of Cognitive and Social Psychological Approaches*. Berlin: de Gruyter.

Abelson, R.P., Aronson, E., McGuire, W.J., Newcomb, T.M., Rosenberg, M.J. and Tannenbaum, P.H. (eds) (1968) *Theories of Cognitive Consistency: A sourcebook*. Skokie, IL: Rand McNally.

Abric, J.C. (2001) 'A structural approach to social representations', in K. Deaux and G. Philogéne (eds) *Representations of the Social*. Oxford: Blackwell.

Allport, G.W. (1935) 'Attitudes', in M. Murchison (ed.) *A Handbook of Social Psychology*. Worcester, MA: Clark University Press.

—— (1955) *Becoming: Basic considerations for a psychology of personality*. New Haven, CT: Yale University Press.

Antonovsky, A. (1987) *Unraveling the Mystery of Health*. San Francisco, CA: Jossey-Bass.

Asch, S. (1952) *Social Psychology*. New York: Prentice-Hall.

Assmann, J. (1992) *Das kulturelle Gedachtnis*. Munich: C.H. Beck.

Astington, J.W. (1990) 'Narrative and the child's theory of mind', in B.K. Britton and A.D. Pellegrini (eds) *Narrative Thought and Narrative Language*. Hillsdale, NJ: Lawrence Erlbaum.

Auerhahn, N.C. and Laub, D. (1998) 'Intergenerational memory of the Holocaust', in Y. Danieli (ed.) *International Handbook of Multigenerational Legacies of Trauma*. New York: Plenum.

Augustinos, M. (1990) 'The mediating role of representations on casual attributions in the social world', *Social Behaviour* 5: 49–62.

Bakhtin, M.M. (1981) 'Discourse in the novel', in M. Holquist (ed.) *The Dialogic Imagination: Four essays by M. M. Bakhtin*. Austin, TX: University of Texas Press.

—— (1984) *Problems of Dostoevsky's Poetics*. Minneapolis, MN: University of Minneapolis Press.

—— (1986) 'The problem of speech genres', in M.M. Bakhtin, *Speech Genres and Other Late Essays*. Austin, TX: University of Texas Press.

Bal, M. (1985) *Narratology: Introduction to the theory of narrative*. Toronto: University of Toronto Press.

Bamberg, M. (2006) 'Stories: Big or small? Why do we care?', *Narrative Inquiry* 16, 1: 139–147.

Bamberg, M. and Andrews, M. (2004) 'Introduction', in M. Bamberg and M. Andrews (eds) *Considering Counter-Narratives: Narrating, resisting. making sense*. Amsterdam: John Benjamins.

Bannister, D. (1966) 'A new theory of personality', in B.M. Foss (ed.) *New Horizons in Psychology*. Harmondsworth, UK: Penguin.

Barclay, C.R. (1996) 'Autobiographical remembering: Narrative constraints on objectified selves', in D.C. Rubin (ed.) *Remembering our Past*. Cambridge: Cambridge University Press.

Barclay, C.R. and Smith, T. (1992) 'Autobiographical remembering: Creating personal culture', in M.A. Conway, D.C. Rubin, H. Spinnler and W. Wagenaar (eds) *Theoretical Perspectives on Autobiographical Memory*. Dordrecht, Netherlands: Kluwer Academic.

Barthes, R. (1977) *Image, Music, Text*. New York: Hill & Wang.

Bartlett, F.C. (1923) *Psychology and Primitive Culture*. Cambridge: Cambridge University Press.

—— (1932) *Remembering: A study in experimental and social psychology*. Cambridge: Cambridge University Press.

Bauer, M. (1993) 'Resistance to change: a functional analysis of responses to technical change in a Swiss bank'. PhD thesis, London School of Economics.

—— (1996) *The Narrative Interview: Comments on a technique for qualitative data collection*. London: Methodology Institute, London School of Economics.

Baumeister, R.F. (1987) 'How the self became a problem: A psychological review of historical research', *Journal of Personality and Social Psychology* 52, 1: 163–176.

Beck, A,T., Rial, W.Y. and Rickerts, K. (1974) 'Short form of Depression Inventory: Cross-validation', *Psychological Reports* 34, 3: 1184–1186.

Ben Amos, D. (ed.) (1976) *Folklore Genres*. Austin, TX: University of Texas Press.

Bényei, T. (2002) 'Kiságy – monológok (Crib monologues)', *Élet és Irodalom* 46, 14: 25.

Berlyne, D.E. (1971) *Aesthetic and Psychology*, New York: Appleton-Century-Crofts.

Bettelheim, B. (1976) *The Uses of Enchantment: The meaning and importance of fairy tales*. London: Thames & Hudson.

Bibó, I. (1991) *Democracy, Revolution, Self-determination: Selected writings*. New York: Columbia University Press.

Billig, M. (1991) *Ideology and Opinions*. London: Sage.

Binet, A. and Henri, V. (1894) 'La mémoire des phrases (Mémoire des idées)', *Année Psychologique* 1: 24–59.

Bion, W.R. (1952) 'Group dynamics: A review', *International Journal of Psycho-Analysis* 33: 235–247.

—— (1961) *Experiences in Groups*. London: Tavistock.

Black, J.B. and Bower, G.H. (1980) 'Story understanding as problem solving', *Poetics* 9: 223–250.

Black, J.B., Turner, T.J. and Bower, G.H. (1979) 'Point of view in narrative comprehension, memory and production', *Journal of Verbal Learning and Verbal Behaviour* 18: 187–198.

Black, J.B., Galambos, J.A. and Read, S. (1984) 'Comprehending stories and social situations', in R. Wyer, T. Srull and J. Hartwick (eds) *Handbook of Social Cognition.* Hillsdale, NJ: Lawrence Erlbaum.

Block, N. (1980) *Readings in Philosophy of Psychology*, vol. 1. Cambridge, MA: Harvard University Press.

Blonsky, P.P. (1935) *Pamjati i myslenie.* Moscow: Ogiz-Szocegiz.

Bloom, W. (1992) *Personal Identity: National identity and international relations.* Cambridge: Cambridge University Press.

Bobrow, D.G. and Collins. A. (eds) (1975) *Representation and Understanding: Studies in cognitive science.* New York: Academic Press.

Bolton, D. (2003) 'Meaning and causal explanations in the behavioural sciences', in B. Fulford, K. Morris, J. Sadler and G. Stanghellini (eds) *Nature and Narrative: An introduction to the new philosophy of psychiatry.* Oxford: Oxford University Press.

Bonaiuto, M., Breakwell, G.M. and Cano, I. (1996) 'Identity processes and environmental threat: The effects of nationalism and local identity upon perception of beach pollution', *Journal of Community and Applied Social Psychology* 6, 3: 157–175.

Bonaparte, M. (1940) 'Time and the unconscious', *International Journal of Psycho-Analysis* 21: 427–468.

Bortolussi, M. and Dixon, P. (2003) *Psychonarratology: Foundations for the empirical study of literary response.* Cambridge: Cambridge University Press.

Boschan, P. (1990) 'Temporality and narcissism', *International Review of Psycho-Analysis* 17: 337–349.

Bourdieu, P. (1980) *Le Sens pratique.* Paris: Minuit.

Bower, G.H. (1976) 'Comprehending and recalling stories', American Psychological Association, Division 3, Presidential Address, Washington, DC, September.

Bower, G.H., Black, J.B. and Turner, T. (1979) 'Scripts in memory for text', *Cognitive Psychology* 11: 177–220.

Bradley, J. (1990) *TACT User Guide: Version 1.2.* Toronto: University of Toronto.

Branscombe, N. (2004) 'Social psychological antecedents of collective guilt.' Paper presented at the conference Collective Remembering, Collective Emotions and Shared Representations of History: Functions and dynamics, Aix-en-Provence, France, June.

Bransford, J.D. and Johnson, M.K. (1972) 'Contextual prerequisites for understanding: Some investigations of comprehension and recall', *Journal of Verbal Learning and Verbal Behaviour* 11: 717–726.

Breakwell, G.M. (1986) *Coping with Threatened Identities.* New York: Methuen.

—— (1993) 'Social representation and social identity', *Papers on Social Representations* 2, 3: 198–217.

Breakwell, G.M. and Canter, D. (1993a) 'Aspects of methodology and their implications for the study of social representations', in G.M. Breakwell and D. Canter (eds) *Empirical Approaches to Social Representations.* Oxford: Clarendon Press.

Breakwell, G.M. and Canter, D. (eds) (1993b) *Empirical Approaches to Social Representations.* Oxford: Clarendon Press.

Breakwell, G.M. and Lyons, E. (eds) (1996) *Changing European Identities: Social psychological analyses of social change.* Oxford: Butterworth-Heinemann.

Brennan, K., Clark, C.L. and Shaver, P.R. (1998) 'Self-report measurement of adult attachment: An integrative overview', in J.A. Simpson and W.S. Rholes (eds) *Attachment Theory and Close Relationships.* New York: Guilford Press.

Brewer, W.F. and Lichtenstein, E.H. (1981) 'Event schemas, story schemas and story grammars', in J. Long and A. Baddeley (eds) *Attention and Performance IX.* Hillsdale, NJ: Lawrence Erlbaum.

Brewer, W.F. and Nakamura, G.V. (1984) 'The nature and functions of schemas', in R.W. Wyer, Jr. and T.K. Srull (eds) *Handbook of Social Cognition*, vol. 1. Hillsdale, NJ: Lawrence Erlbaum.

Brockmeier, J. (2001) 'From the end to the beginning: Retrospective teleology in autobiography', in J. Brockmeier and D. Carbaugh (eds) *Narrative and Identity*. Amsterdam: John Benjamins.

Brockmeier, J. and Carbaugh, D. (eds) (2001) *Narrative and Identity*. Philadelphia, PA: John Benjamins.

Brockmeier, J. and Harré, R. (2001) 'Narrative: Problems and promises of an alternative paradigm', in J. Brockmeier and D. Carbaugh (eds) *Narrative and Identity*. Amsterdam: John Benjamins.

Brown, R.W. and Gilman, A. (1960) 'The pronouns of power and solidarity', in T.A. Sebeok (ed.) *Style in Language*. Cambridge, MA: MIT Press.

Bruner, E.M. (1986) 'Ethnography as narrative', in V.W. Turner and E.M. Bruner (eds) *The Anthropology of Experience*. Urbana, IL: University of Illinois Press.

Bruner, J. (1986) *Actual Minds. Possible Worlds*. Cambridge, MA: Harvard University Press.

—— (1987) 'Life as narrative', *Social Research* 54: 11–32.

—— (1990) *Acts of Meaning*. Cambridge, MA: Harvard University Press.

—— (1991) 'The narrative construction of reality', *Critical Inquiry* 18: 1–21.

—— (1996) *The Culture of Education*. Cambridge, MA: Harvard University Press.

Bruner, J. and Fleischer-Feldman, C. (1996) 'Group narrative as a cultural context of autobiography', in D.C. Rubin (ed.) *Remembering our Past*. Cambridge: Cambridge University Press.

Bruner, J. and Lucariello, J. (1989) 'Monologue as narrative of the world', in K. Nelson (ed.) *Narratives from the Crib*. Cambridge, MA: Harvard University Press.

Bühler, C. (1933) *Der menschliche Lebenslauf als psychologisches Problem* (*The Human Course of Life as a Psychological Problem*). Leipzig: Hirzel.

Butler, R. (1963) 'The life review: An interpretation of the reminiscence in the aged', *Psychiatry* 26: 65–76.

Cantor, J. (2004) ' "I'll never have a clown in my house!" Why movie horror lives on', *Poetics Today* 25: 283–304.

Caprara, G.V., Barbaranelli, C. and Borgogni, L. (1993) 'The Big 5 questionnaire: A new questionnaire to assess the 5 factor model', *Personality and Individual Differences* 15, 3: 281–288.

Carr, D.L. (1986) *Time, Narrative and History*. Bloomington, IN: Indiana University Press.

Castro, P. (2003) 'Dialogues in social psychology: Or, how new are new ideas?', in László, J. and Wagner, W. (eds) *Theories and Controversies in Societal Psychology*. Budapest: New Mandate: 32–55.

Castro, J. and Rosa, A. (2007) 'Psychology within time: Theorising about the making of sociocultural psychology', in J. Valsiner and A. Rosa (eds) *Cambridge Handbook of Sociocultural Psychology*. Cambridge: Cambridge University Press.

Cavalli-Sforza, L.L. and Feldman, M.W. (1981) *Cultural Transmission and Evolution: A quantitative approach*. Princeton, NJ: Princeton University Press.

Chiu, C., Krauss, R.M. and Lau, I.Y.M. (1998) 'Some cognitive consequences of communication', in S.R. Fussell and R.J. Kreuz (eds) *Social and Cognitive Approaches to Interpersonal Communication*. Hillsdale, NJ: Lawrence Erlbaum.

Churchland, P. (1995) *The Engine of Reason, the Seat of the Soul: A philosophical journey into the brain*. Cambridge, MA: MIT.

Codol, J.P. (1984) 'On the system of representations in an artificial social situation', in R.M. Farr and S. Moscovici (eds) *Social Representations*. Cambridge: Cambridge University Press.

Colby, B.N. (1973) 'A partial grammar of Eskimo folktales', *American Anthropologist* 75: 645–662.

Collingwood, R.G. (1947) *The Idea of History*. Oxford: Clarendon Press.

Condor, S. (2003) 'The least doubtful promise for the future?', in J. László and W. Wagner (eds) *Theories and Controversies in Societal Psychology*. Budapest: New Mandate.

Cosmides, L. and Tooby, J. (1992) 'Psychological foundations of culture', in J.H. Barkow, L. Cosmides and J. Tooby (eds) *The Adapted Mind*. New York: Oxford University Press.

Coyle, A. (1991) 'The construction of gay identity'. Unpublished PhD thesis, Department of Psychology, University of Surrey, Guildford.

Crossley, M.L. (2000) *Introducing Narrative Psychology: Self. trauma and the construction of meaning*. Buckingham: Open University Press.

Csabai, M., Erős, F. and László, J. (1998) 'Az észlelt kontroll szerepe az egészség szociális reprezentációnak szervezodésében' (The role of perceived control in social representation of health), *Pszichológia* 3: 353–375.

Csíkszentmihályi, M. and Beattie, O. (1979) 'Life themes: A theoretical and empirical exploitation of their origins and effects', *Journal of Humanistic Psychology* 19: 45–63.

Cullingford, R.D. (1978) *Script application: Computer understanding of newspaper stories* (Technical report 116). New Haven, CT: Department of Computer Science, Yale University.

Cupchik, G.C. (2004) 'The complementarity of emotion and cognition'. Paper presented at Ninth Congress of the International Society for the Empirical Study of Literature, Edmonton, Alberta, August.

Cupchik, G.C. and László, J. (1994) 'The landscape of time in literary reception: Character experience and narrative action', *Cognition and Emotion* 10: 297–312.

Dawkins, R. (1976) *The Selfish Gene*. Oxford: Oxford University Press.

—— (1982) *The Extended Phenotype*. Oxford: Oxford University Press.

D'Azevedo, W.L. (1962) 'Uses of the past in Gola discourse', *Journal of African History* 3, 1: 11–34.

De Fina, A. (2003) 'Crossing borders: Time, space and disorientation in narrative', *Narrative Inquiry* 13, 2: 367–393.

De Fina, A., Schiffrin, D. and Bamberg, M. (eds) (2006) *Discourse and Identity*. Cambridge: Cambridge University Press.

DeJong, G.F. (1979) 'Prediction and substantiation: A new approach to natural language processing', *Cognitive Science* 3: 251–273.

Dennett, D. (1991) *Consciousness Explained*. Boston: Little, Brown.

Denzin, N.K. (1992) *Symbolic Interactionism and Cultural Studies: The politics of interpretation*. Oxford: Blackwell.

Denzin, N.K. and Lincoln, Y.S. (1994) *Handbook of Qualitative Research*. London: Sage.

de Rosa, A. (1996) 'Reality changes faster than research: National and supranational identity in social representations of the European Community in the context of changes in international relations', in G.M. Breakwell and E. Lyons (eds) *Changing European Identities*. Oxford: Butterworth Heinemann.

de Rosa, A., Bigazzi, S. and Bocci, E. (2002) 'Forget – never forget: Emotional impact, iconic representational systems and social memory, in the reconstruction of the day who dramatically changed the personal and global risk perception'. Paper presented at Thirteenth EAESP General Meeting, San Sebastian, Spain, 26–29 June.

Dewey, J.A. (1922) *Human Nature and Conduct*. New York: Holt.

Dickins, T.E. (2004) 'Social constructionism as cognitive science', *Journal for the Theory of Social Behaviour* 34, 4: 333–352.

Di Giacomo, J.P. (1980) 'Intergroup alliances and rejections within a protest movement', *European Journal of Social Psychology* 10: 329–344.

Doise, W. (1976) 'Structural homologies, sociology and experimental social psychology', *Social Science Information* 15: 929–942.

—— (1993) 'Debating social representations', in G.M. Breakwell and D. Canter (eds) *Empirical Approaches to Social Representations*. Oxford: Clarendon Press.

Doise, W., Clémence, A. and Lorenzi-Cioldi, F. (1992) *Representations sociales et analyses de données*. Grenoble: Presses Universitaires de Grenoble.

Donald, M. (1991) *Origins of the Modern Mind*. Cambridge, MA: Harvard University Press.

Doosje, B., Branscombe, N.R., Spears, R. and Manstead, A.S.R. (1998) 'Guilty by association: When one's group has a negative history', *Journal of Personality and Social Psychology* 75, 4: 872–886.

Dufty, D.F., McNamara, D., Louwerse, M., Cai, Z. and Graesser, A.C. (2004) 'Automatic evaluation of aspects of document quality'. Available at http://portal.acm.org/citation.cfm?id=1026539, accessed 17 January 2008.

Dunbar, R.I.M. (1996) *Grooming, Gossip, and the Evolution of Language*. Cambridge, MA: Harvard University Press.

—— (2004) 'Social cognition as a constraint on social interaction', *Journal of Cultural and Evolutionary Psychology* 2, 3–4: 181–194.

Durkheim, E. (1947 [1893]) *The Division of Labour in Society*, 2nd edn. New York: Free Press.

Duveen, G.M. and Lloyd, B.B. (1993) 'An ethnographic approach to social representations', in G.M. Breakwell and D. Canter (eds) *Empirical Approaches to Social Representations*. Oxford: Clarendon Press.

Dyer, M.G. (1983) *In-depth Understanding*. Cambridge, MA: MIT Press.

Eco, U. (1994) *Six Walks in the Fictional Woods*. Cambridge, MA: Harvard University Press.

Ehmann, B. (2000) 'A számítógépes pszichológiai tartalomelemzés alkalmazási lehetőségei' (Perspectives of computerized content analysis). Unpublished PhD dissertation, ELTE (Eötvös Loránd University), Budapest.

Ehmann, B. and Erős F. (2002) 'Jewish identity in Hungary: A narrative model', in J. László and W. Stainton Rogers (eds) *Narrative Approaches in Social Psychology*. Budapest: New Mandate.

Ehmann, B., Garami, V., Naszódi, M., Kis, B. and László, J. (2007) 'Subjective time experience: Identifying psychological correlates by narrative psychological content analysis', *Empirical Culture and Text Research* 3: 14–25.

Elejabarrieta, F. (1994) 'Social positioning: A way to link social identity and social representations', *Social Science Information* 33: 241–253.

El-Meligi, A.M. (1972) 'A technique for exploring time experiences in mental disorders', in H. Yaker, H. Osmond and F. Cheek (eds) *The Future of Time*. London: Hogarth Press.

Elsbree, L. (1982) *The Rituals of Life: Patterns in narratives*. Port Washington, NY: Kennikat Press.

Erikson, E.H. (1959) 'Identity and the life cycle: Selected papers', *Psychological Issues* 1, 1: 5–165.

Erikson, E.H. (1968) *Identity: Youth and crisis*. New York: Norton.

Erős, F. and Ehmann, B. (1997) 'Jewish identity in Hungary: A narrative model suggested', in M. Hadas and M. Vörös (eds) 'Ambiguous Identities in the New Europe', *Replika* special issue: 121–133.

Erős, F., Ehmann, B. and László, J. (1998) 'The narrative organization of the social representation of democracy: A new approach to cross-cultural interview analysis'. Paper presented at Fourth International Conference on Social Representations, Mexico City, 25–28 August.

Faragó, K. (2001) *Térirányok, távolságok: Térdinamizmus a regényben* (*Spatial Directions, Distances: Spatial Dynamics in Novels*). Újvidék: Forum Könyvkiadó.

Farr, R.M. (1984) 'Social representations: Their role in the design and execution of laboratory experiments', in R.M. Farr and S. Moscovici (eds) *Social Representations*. Cambridge: Cambridge University Press.

Feyerabend: (1997) *Against Method: An outline of an anarchistic theory of knowledge*. London: Verso.

Fink, K. (1993) 'The bi-logic perception of time', *International Journal of Psycho-Analysis* 74: 303–312.

Fitzgerald, J.M. (1988) 'Vivid memories and the reminiscence phenomenon: The role of a self narrative', *Human Development* 31: 261–273.

—— (1996) 'Intersecting meanings of reminiscence in adult development and aging', in D.C. Rubin (ed.) *Remembering our Past*. Cambridge: Cambridge University Press.

Flick, U. (1995) 'Social representation', in J.A. Smith, R. Harré and L. Van Langhove (eds) *Rethinking Psychology*. London: Sage.

—— (2000) 'Episodic interviewing', in M.W. Bauer and G. Gaskell (eds) *Qualitative Researching with Text, Image and Sound*. London: Sage.

—— (2005) *An Introduction to Qualitative Research*, 3rd edn. London: Sage.

Fodor, J. (1975) *The Language of Thought*. Cambridge, MA: Harvard University Press.

Fónagy, I. (1989) *A költoi nyelv hangtanából* (*Phonetics of poetic language*). Budapest: Akadémiai Kiadó.

—— (1990) *Gondolatalakzatok, szövegszerkezet, gondolkodási formák* (*Thought Patterns and Text Structure*), *Linguistica Series Relationes 3*. Budapest: MTA Nyelvtudományi Intézete.

Fonagy, P. (1998) 'Prevention, the appropriate target of infant psychotherapy', *Infant Mental Health Journal* 19: 4–19.

Fonagy, P. and Target, M. (1997) 'Attachment and reflective function: Their role in self-organization', *Developmental Psychopathology* 9: 677–699.

Forgas, J.P. (ed.) (1981) *Social Psychology: Perspectives on everyday understanding*. London: Academic Press.

—— (ed.) (1998) *Feeling and Thinking: The role of affect in social cognition and behaviour*. New York: Cambridge University Press.

Fraser, J.T. (1981) 'Temporal levels and reality testing', *International Journal of Psycho-Analysis* 62: 3–26.

Freeman, M. (1993) *Rewriting the Self: History, memory, narrative*. London: Routledge.

—— (2006) 'Life "on holiday"? In defense of big stories', *Narrative Inquiry* 16, 1: 131–138.

Frenkel-Brunswick, E. (1936) 'Studies in biographical psychology', *Character and Personality* 5: 1–35.

Friedman, M.J. (1955) *Stream of Consciousness: A study of literary method*. New Haven, CT: Yale University Press.

Frye, N. (1957) *Anatomy of Criticism: Four essays.* Princeton, NJ: Princeton University Press.

Galli, I. and Nigro, G. (1987) 'The social representation of radioactivity among Italian children', *Social Science Information* 26, 3: 535–549.

Gardner, H. (1985) *The Mind's New Science: A history of the cognitive revolution.* New York: Basic Books.

Geertz, C. (1975) *The Interpretation of Cultures.* New York: Basic Books.

Genette, G. (1980) *Narrative Discourse.* Ithaca, NY: Cornell University Press.

Georgakopoulou, A. (2006) 'Thinking big with small stories in narrative and identity analysis', *Narrative Inquiry* 16, 1: 122–130.

Gergely, G., Nádasdi, Z., Csibra, G. and Biró, S. (1995) 'Taking the international stance at 12 months of age', *Cognition* 56: 165–193.

Gergen, K.J. (1971) *The Concept of Self.* New York: Holt, Rinehart & Winston.

—— (1973) 'Social psychology as history', *Journal of Experimental Social Psychology* 2: 278–287.

—— (1985) 'The social constructionist movement in modern psychology', *American Psychologist* 39: 226–275.

Gergen, K.J. and Gergen, M.M. (1983) 'Narratives of the self', in T.R. Sarbin and K.E. Scheibe (eds) *Studies in Social Identity.* New York: Praeger.

—— (1988) 'Narrative and the self as relationship', in L. Berkowitz (ed.) *Advances in Experimental Social Psychology*, vol. 21. San Diego, CA: Academic Press.

Gerrig, R.J. (1993) *Experiencing Narrative Worlds.* New Haven, CT: Yale University Press.

Giles, H. and Coupland, J. (1991) *Language: Context and consequences*, Pacific Grove, CA: Brooks/Cole.

Gilman, S. (1985) *Difference and Pathology: Stereotypes of sexuality, race and madness.* Ithaca, NY: Cornell University Press.

Goffman, E. (1959) *The Presentation of Self in Everyday Life.* Garden City, NY: Doubleday.

Goodman, N. (1981) 'Twisted tales: or, story, study, and symphony', in W.J.T. Mitchell (ed.) *On Narrative.* Chicago, IL: University of Chicago Press.

Goody, J. and Watt, I. (1963) 'The consequences of literacy', *Comparative Studies in Society and History* 5: 304–326.

Gottschalk, L.A. and Gleser, G.C. (1969) *The Measurement of Psychological States through the Content Analysis of Verbal Behavior.* Berkeley, CA: University of California Press.

Gottschalk, L.A. and Hambidge, G., Jr. (1955) 'Verbal behavior analysis: A systematic approach to the problem of quantifying psychological processes', *Journal of Projective Techniques* 19: 387–409.

Gottschalk, L.A., Gleser, G.C., Daniels, R.S. and Block, S.L. (1958) 'The speech patterns of schizophrenic patients: A method of assessing relative degree of personal disorganization and social alienation', *Journal of Nervous and Mental Disease* 127: 153–166.

Graesser, A.C. and Bower, G.H. (eds) (1990) *Inferences and Text Comprehension.* San Diego, CA: Academic Press.

Graesser, A.C. and Nakamura, G.V. (1982) 'The impact of schemas on comprehension and memory', in G.H. Bower (ed.) *The Psychology of Learning and Motivation*, vol. 16. New York: Academic Press.

Graesser, A.C., Golding, J.M. and Long, D.J. (1991) 'Narrative representation and comprehension', in R. Barr, M.L. Kamil, P. Mosenthal and P.D. Pearson (eds) *Handbook of Reading Research.* White Plains, NY: Longman.

Graesser, A.C., Pomeroy, V.J. and Craig, S.D. (2002) 'Psychological and computational research on theme comprehension', in M. Louwerse and W. van Peer (eds) *Thematics: Interdisciplinary Studies*. Amsterdam: John Benjamins.

Greenberg, J.H. (1974) *Language Typology: A historical and analytic overview*. The Hague: Mouton.

Greenwald, A.G. (1980) 'The totalitarian ego: Fabrication and revision of personal history', *American Psychologist* 35: 603–618.

Grize, J.B. (1989) 'Logique naturelle et representations sociales', in D. Jodelet, (ed.) *Les Représentations socials*. Paris: Presses Universitaires de France.

Gurin, P. and Markus, H. (1988) 'Group identity: The psychological mechanisms of durable salience', *Revue Internationale de Psychologie Sociale* 1, 2: 257–274.

Gyáni, G. (2003) *Posztmodern kánon* (*Postmodern Canon*). Budapest: Nemzeti Tankönyv Kiadó.

Győri, M., Lukács, Á. and Pléh, C. (2004) 'Towards the understanding of the neurogenesis of social cognition: Evidence from impaired populations', *Journal of Cultural and Evolutionary Psychology* 2, 3–4: 261–282.

Halász, L. (ed.) (1987) *Literary Discourse: Aspects of cognitive and social psychological approaches*. Berlin: de Gruyter.

Halbwachs, M. (1925) *Les Cadres sociaux de la mémoire*. Paris: Alcan.

—— (1941) *La Topographie légendaire des évangiles en Terre Sainte*. Paris: Presses Universitaires de France.

—— (1980) *Collective Memory*. New York: Harper.

Hamilton, D.L. (1981) *Cognitive processes in stereotyping and intergroup behaviour*. Hillsdale, NJ: Lawrence Erlbaum.

—— (2007) 'Agenda 2007: Understanding the complexities of group perception: Broadening the domain'. *European Journal of Social Psychology*, 37: 1077–1101.

Haraway, D.J. (1984) 'Primatology is politics by other means', in R. Bleier (ed.) *Feminist Approaches to Science*. London: Pergamon.

—— (1989) *Primate Visions: Gender, race, and nature in the world of modern science*. London: Routledge.

Hardy, B. (1968) 'Towards a poetics of fiction: An approach through narrative', *Novel* 2: 5–14.

Hargitai, R., Naszódi, M., Kis, B., Nagy, L., Bóna, A. and László, J. (2007) 'Linguistic markers of depressive dynamics in self-narratives: Negation and self-reference', *Empirical Culture and Text Research* 3: 26–38.

Harré, R. (1983a) 'Identity projects', in G. Breakwell (ed.) *Threatened Identities*. Chichester: Wiley.

—— (1983b) *Personal Being*. Oxford: Blackwell.

—— (1994) 'Emotion and memory: The second cognitive revolution'. Paper presented at the Collegium Budapest, 30 May.

—— (2002) *Cognitive Science: A philosophical introduction*. London: Sage.

Harré, R. and Gillett, G. (1994) *The Discursive Mind*. London: Sage.

Hartocollis, P. (1978) 'Time and affects in borderline disorders', *International Journal of Psycho-Analysis* 59: 157–163.

Harvey, J.H. and Martin, R. (1995) 'Celebrating the story in social perception, communication, and behavior', in J. Wyer, Jr. (ed.) *Knowledge and Memory: The real story – Advances in social cognition*, vol. 8. Hillsdale, NJ: Lawrence Erlbaum.

Hayek, F.A. (1967) *Studies in Philosophy, Politics and Economics*. London: Routledge & Kegan Paul.

—— (1969) *The Political Order of a Free People*. London: Routledge & Kegan Paul.

Heatherton, T.F. and Polivy, J. (1991) 'Development and validation of a scale for measuring state self-esteem', *Journal of Personality and Social Psychology* 60, 6: 234–239.

Heidegger, M. (1971) *Poetry, Language, Thought*. New York: Harper & Row.

Heider, F. (1958) *The Psychology of Interpersonal Relations*. New York: Wiley.

Heider, F. and Simmel, M. (1944) 'An experimental study of apparent behaviour', *American Journal of Psychology* 57: 243–259.

Hempel, G. (1942) 'The functions of general laws in history', *Journal of Philosophy* 39: 35–48.

Hermans, H.J.M. (1996) 'Voicing the self: From information processing to dialogical interchange', *Psychological Bulletin* 119: 31–50.

Herzlich, C. (1973) *Health and Illness: A social psychological analysis*. London: Academic Press.

Hewstone, M. (1986) *Understanding Attitudes to the European Community: A social psychological study in four member states*. Cambridge: Cambridge University Press.

Higgins, E.T. and Rholes, W.S. (1978) 'Saying is believing: Effects of message modification on memory and liking for the person perceived', *Journal of Experimental Social Psychology* 14: 363–378.

Hilton, D.J., Erb, H.-P., Dermot, M. and Molian, D.J. (1996) 'Social representations of history and attitudes to European unification in Britain, France and Germany', in G.M. Breakwell and E. Lyons (eds) *Changing European Identities*. Oxford: Butterworth Heinemann.

Hobsbawm, E. (1992) *Nations and Nationalism since 1780: Programme, myth, reality*, 2nd edn. Cambridge: Cambridge University Press.

Holmes, J. (2004) 'Disorganized attachment and borderline personality disorder: A clinical perspective', *Attachment and Human Development* 6, 2: 181–190.

Holsti, O.R. (1968) 'Content analysis', in G. Lindzey and E. Aronson (eds) *Handbook of Social Psychology*. Reading, MA: Addison-Wesley.

Hoshmand, L.T. (2000) 'Narrative psychology', in A.E. Kazdin, (ed.) *Encyclopedia of Psychology*. Washington, DC: American Psychological Association.

—— (2005) 'Narratology, cultural psychology, and counselling research', *Journal of Counseling Psychology* 52, 2: 178–186.

Hunt, M. and Hunt, B. (1977) *The Divorce Experience*. New York: New American Library.

Hunyady, G. (1998) *Stereotypes during the Decline and Fall of Communism*. London: Routledge.

Iser, W. (1978) *The Act of Reading*. Baltimore, MD: Johns Hopkins University Press.

Israel, J. and Tajfel, H. (eds) (1972) *The Context of Social Psychology: A Critical Assessment*. London: Academic Press.

Jahoda, G. (1963) 'The development of children's ideas about country and nationality: I. The conceptual framework', *British Journal of Educational Psychology* 33: 47–60.

Janet, P. (1928) *L'Evolution de la mémoire et de la notion du temp*. Paris: Alcan.

Jaspars, J.M.F. and Fraser, C. (1984) 'Attitudes and social representations', in R.M. Farr and S. Moscovici (eds) *Social Representations*. Paris: Presses Universitaires de France.

Jodelet, D. (1984) 'Représentations socials: Phénoménes, concepts et théorie', in S. Moscovici (ed.) *Psychologie sociale*. Paris: Presses Universitaires de France.

—— (1991) *Madness and Social Representations*. Hemel Hempstead: Harvester/Wheatsheaf.

Joffe, H. (1995) 'Social representations of AIDS: Towards encompassing issues of power', *Papers on Social Representations* 4, 1: 29–40.

Joffe, H.(1996) 'The shock of the new: A psycho-dynamic extension of social representational theory', *Journal for the Theory of Social Behaviour* 26, 2: 197–220.

Jones, E.E. and Davis, K.E. (1965) 'From acts to dispositions: The attribution process in person perception', in L. Berkowitz (ed.) *Advances in Experimental Social Psychology*, vol. 2. New York: Academic Press.

Jordan, N. (1953) 'Behavioral forces that are a function of cognitive organization', *Human Relations* 6: 273–287.

Jovchelovitch, S. (1995) 'Social representations and narrative: Stories of public life in Brazil'. Paper presented at the Small Meeting of the EAESP on The Narrative Organization of Social Representations, Budapest, 6–10 September.

—— (1996) 'Defence of representations', *Journal for the Theory of Social Behaviour* 26, 2: 121–135.

—— (2001) 'Social representations, public life and social construction', in K. Deaux and G. Philogene (eds) *Representations of the Social: Bridging theoretical traditions*. Oxford: Blackwell.

—— (2006) *Knowledge in Context: Representations. community and culture*. London: Routledge.

Just, M.A. and Carpenter, P.A. (1992) 'A capacity theory of comprehension: Individual differences in working memory', *Psychological Review* 99: 122–149.

Kaposi, D. (2003) ' "Narrativeless" – Cultural concepts and the fateless', *SPIEL* 21, 1: 89–105.

Karácsony, S. (1976) *A magyar észjárás (Hungarian Mentality)*. Budapest: Magveto.

Kelley, H.H. (1967) 'Attribution theory in social psychology', in D. Levine (ed.) *Nebraska Symposium on Motivation*, vol. 15. Lincoln, NE: University of Nebraska Press.

Kelly, G.A. (1955) *The Psychology of Personal Constructs*, vol. 1. New York: Norton.

Kenesei, I. (2004) *A nyelv és a nyelvek (Languages and the Language)*. Budapest: Akadémiai Kiadó.

Kernberg, O.F. (1975) *Borderline Conditions and Pathological Narcissism*. New York: Jason Aronson.

Kertész, I. (2006 [1975]) *Fateless*, trans. T. Wilkinson. London: Vintage.

Kézdi, B. (1995) *A negatív kód (The Negative Code)*. Pécs: Pannon Kiadó.

Kintsch, W. (1974) *The Representation of Meaning in Memory*. Hillsdale, NJ: Lawrence Erlbaum.

Kintsch, W. and van Dijk, T.A. (1978) 'Toward a model of test comprehension and production', *Psychological Review* 85: 363–394.

Klar, P., Roccas, R. and Liviatan, S. (2004) 'The pains of national identification: Looking at the ingroup's past and the present moral transgressions'. Paper presented at the conference Collective Remembering, Collective Emotions and Shared Representations of History: Functions and Dynamics, Aix-en-Provence, France, 16–19 June.

Klein, M. (1946) 'Notes on some schizoid mechanisms', *International Journal of Psycho-Analysis* 27: 99–110.

Kohut, H.M.D. (1971) *The Analysis of the Self*. Madison, WI: International Universities Press.

Kruglanski, A.W. (1975) 'The endogenous-exogenous partition in attribution theory', *Psychological Review* 82: 387–406.

Kutschera, F. von (1982) *Grundfragen der Erkentnistheorie*. Berlin: de Gruyter.

Labov, W. (1972) 'The transformation of experience in narrative syntax', in *Language in the Inner City*. Oxford: Blackwell.

Labov, W. and Waletzky, J. (1967) 'Narrative analysis: oral version of personal experience', in J. Helm (ed.) *Essays on the Verbal and Visual Arts*. Seattle, WA: American Ethnological Society. Reprinted in *Journal of Narrative and Life History* 7, 1–4: 3–38.

—— (1997) 'Oral versions of personal experience', *Journal of Narrative and Life History* 7:3–38.

Larsen, S.F. and László, J. (1990) 'Cultural-historical knowledge and personal experience in appreciation of literature', *European Journal of Social Psychology* 20, 5: 425–440.

László, J. (1986) 'Scripts for interpersonal situations', *Studia Psychologica* 28, 2: 125–136.

—— (1987) 'Understanding and enjoying', in L. Halasz (ed.) *Literary Discourse: Aspects of cognitive and social psychological approaches*. Berlin: de Gruyter.

—— (1990) 'Images of social categories vs. images of literary and nonliterary objects', *Poetics* 6: 1–15.

—— (1997) 'Narrative organisation of social representations', *Papers on Social Representations* 6, 2: 155–172

—— (1999) *Cognition and Representation in Literature: The psychology of literary narratives*. Budapest: Akadémiai Kiadó.

—— (2003) 'History, identity and narratives', in J. László and W. Wagner (eds) *Theories and Controversies in Societal Psychology*. Budapest: New Mandate.

László, J. and Cupchik, G.C. (1995) 'The role of affective processes in understanding literary narratives', *Empirical Studies of the Arts* 13: 25–37.

László, J. and Farkas, A. (1997) 'Central-Eastern European collective experiences', *Journal of Community and Applied Social Psychology* 7: 77–87.

László, J. and Larsen, S.F. (1991) 'Cultural and text variables in processing personal experiences while reading literature', *Empirical Studies of the Arts* 9: 23–34.

László, J. and Pólya, T. (2002) 'The role of the narrative perspective in the cognitive-cultural context', in C. Graumann and W. Kallmeyer (eds) *Perspective and Perspectivation in Discourse*. Amsterdam: John Benjamins.

László, J. and Pólya, T. (2007) 'Level of abstraction versus objectivity-subjectivity in Linguistic Inter-group Bias: Victim/perpetrator relations in a changing Europe – Prejudice escalation and prejudice reduction'. Paper presented at Second Warsaw-Jena Conference, Warsaw, 13–15 April.

László, J. and Thomka, B. (eds) (2001) *Narratív pszichológia (Narrative Psychology)*. Budapest: Kijárat.

László, J. and Viehoff, R. (1993) 'Literarische Gattungen als kognitive Schemata', *SPIEL*, 12, 1: 230–251.

László, J., Kiss, G., Kovács, A., Sallay, H. and Ehmann, B. (1998) *A családi szocializáció szerepe a fiatalkori munkanélküliség helyzetéhez való alkalmazkodásban* (The Role of Family Socialization in Coping with Juvenile Unemployment), Budapest: Scientia Humana.

László, J., Ehmann, B. and Imre, O. (1999) 'Social representations of history and national identity'. Paper presented at the Twelfth General Meeting of the EAESP, Oxford, July.

László, J., Ehmann, B. and Imre, O. (2002a) 'Les représentations sociales de l'histoire: La narration populaire historique et l'identité nationale', in S. Laurens and N. Roussiau (eds) *La Mémoire sociale. Identités et représentations sociales*. Rennes, France: Université de Rennes.

László, J., Ehmann, B., Péley, B. and Pólya, T. (2002b) 'Narrative psychology and narrative psychological content analysis', in J. László and W. Stainton Rogers (eds) *Narrative Approaches in Social Psychology*. Budapest: New Mandate.

László, J., Ehmann, B., Pólya, T. and Péley, B. (2007) 'Narrative psychology as science', *Empirical Culture and Text Research* 3: 1–13.

Latour, B. (1988) *The Pasteurization of France*. Cambridge, MA: Harvard University Press.

Lawson, D.E. (1963) 'The development of patriotism in children: A second look', *Journal of Psychology* 55: 279–286.

Leach, E. (1976) *Culture and Communication: The Logic by which Symbols are Connected*. Cambridge: Cambridge University Press.

Lee, B. (1997) *Talking Heads: Language, metalanguage and the semiotics of subjectivity*. Durham, NC: Duke University Press.

Lehnert, W.G., Dyer, M.G., Johnson, P.N., Yang, C.J. and Harley, S. (1983) 'BORIS – An in-depth understander of narratives', *Artificial Intelligence* 20, 1.

Leslie, A.M. (1987) 'Pretense and representation: The origins of "theory of mind"', *Psychological Review* 94: 412–426.

—— (1991) 'The theory of mind impairment in autism: Evidence for a modular mechanism of development', in A. Whiten (ed.) *Natural Theories of Mind: Evolution, development, and simulation of everyday mindreading*. Oxford: Blackwell.

Lévi-Strauss, C. (1992) *Tristes Tropiques*. New York: Penguin.

Levy-Brühl, L. (1910) *Les fonctions mentales dans les sociétés inférieures*. Paris: Alcan.

—— (1926) *How natives think*. London: Allen & Unwin.

Lewin, K. (1948) 'Some social-psychological differences between the United States and Germany (1936)', in *Resolving Social Conflicts: Selected papers in group dynamics*. New York: Harper & Row.

—— (1951) *Field Theory in Social Sciences*. New York: Harper.

Linde, C. (1993) *Life Stories: The creation of coherence*. New York: Oxford University Press.

Liu, J.H. and Hilton, D.J. (2005) 'How the past weighs on the present: Social representations of history and their impact on identity politics', *British Journal of Social Psychology* 44: 537–556.

Liu, J.H. and László, J. (2007) 'A narrative theory of history and identity: Social identity, social representations, society and the individual', in G. Moloney and I. Walker (eds) *Social Representations and Identity: Content, process, and power*. Basingstoke: Palgrave-Macmillan.

Liu, J.H. and Liu, S.H. (2003) 'The role of the social psychologist in the "Benevolent Authority" and "Plurality of Powers" systems of historical affordance for authority', in K.S. Yang, K.K. Hwang, P.B. Pedersen and I. Daibo (eds) *Progress in Asian Social Psychology: Conceptual and Empirical Contributions*. Westport, CT: Praeger.

Liu, J.H., Wilson, M.W., McClure, J. and Higgins, T.R. (1999) 'Social identity and the perception of history: Cultural representations of Aotearoa/New Zealand', *European Journal of Social Psychology* 29: 1021–1047.

Liu, J.H., Goldstein-Hawes, R., Hilton, D.J., Huang, L.L., Gastardo-Conaco, C., Dresler-Hawke, E., et al. (2005) 'Social representations of events and people in world history across twelve cultures', *Journal of Cross-Cultural Psychology* 36, 2: 171–191.

Lucius-Hoene, G. and Deppermann, A. (2002) *Rekonstruktion narrativer Identität*. Opladen, Germany: Leske & Budrich.

Lyons, E. and Sotirakopoulou, K. (1991) 'Images of European Countries'. Paper presented at British Psychological Society Social Psychology Section Annual Conference, University of Surrey, September.

Lyons, J. (1995) *Linguistic Semantics*. New York: Cambridge University Press.

Lyotard, J.F. (1984) *The postmodern condition: A report on knowledge*, trans. G. Bennington and B. Massumi. Minneapolis, MN: University of Minnesota Press.

Maas, A., Salvi, D., Arcuri, L., and Semin, G.R. (1989) 'Language use in intergroup context: The linguistic intergroup bias', *Journal of Personality and Social Psychology* 57: 981–993.

Maas, A., Milesi, A., Zabbini, S. and Stahlberg, D. (1995) 'The linguistic intergroup bias: Differential expectancies or in-group protection?', *Journal of Personality and Social Psychology* 68: 116–126.

Maas, A., Ceccarelli, R. and Rudin, S. (1996) 'Linguistic intergroup bias: Evidence for in-group-protective motivation', *Journal of Personality and Social Psychology* 71: 512–526.

McAdams, D.P. (1985) *Power, Intimacy, and the Life Story: Personological inquiries into identity*. New York: Guilford Press.

—— (1993) *The Stories We Live by: Personal myths and the making of the self*. New York: William Morrow.

—— (2001) 'The psychology of life stories', *Review of General Psychology* 5, 2: 100–122.

McAdams, D.P., Hoffman, B.J., Mansfield, E.D. and Day, R. (1996) 'Themes of agency and communion on significant autobiographical scenes', *Journal of Personality* 64: 339–377.

McClelland, D.C., Atkinson, J.W., Clark, R.A. and Lowell, E.L (1953) *The Achievement Motive*. New York: Appleton-Century-Crofts.

McGuire, W.J. (1993) 'The poly-psy relationship: Three phases of a long affair', in S. Iyengar and W.J. McGuire (eds) *Explorations in Political Psychology*. Durham, NC: Duke University Press.

McGuire, W.J. and McGuire, C.V. (1988) 'Content and process in the experience of the self', in L. Berkowitz, (ed.) *Advances in Experimental Social Psychology: Social psychological studies of the self – Perspectives and programs*, Vol. 21. San Diego, CA: Academic Press.

MacIntyre, A. (1981) *After Virtue: A study in moral theory*. Notre Dame, IN: University of Notre Dame Press.

McLean, K.C. and Pasupathi, M. (2006) 'Collaborative narration of the past and extraversion', *Journal of Research in Personality* 40, 6: 1219–1231.

McLean, K.C. and Pratt, M.W. (2006) 'Life's little (and big) lessons: Identity statuses and meaning-making in the turning point narratives of emerging adults', *Developmental Psychology* 42, 4: 714–722.

MacLuhan, M. (1968) *The Gutenberg Galaxy: The making of typographic man*. Toronto: University of Toronto Press.

McNair, D.M., Lorr, M. and Droppleman, L.F. (1981) *Manual: Profile of mood states*. San Diego, CA: Education and Industrial Testing Service.

Mahler, M., Pine, B. and Bergman, A. (1975) *The Psychological Birth of the Human Infant*. New York: Basic Books.

Main, M. and Hesse, E. (1990) 'Parents' unresolved traumatic experiences are related to infant disorganized attachment status: Is frightened and/or frightening parental behavior the linking mechanism?', in M.T. Greenberg, D. Cicchetti and E.M. Cummings (eds) *Attachment during the Preschool Years: Theory, research and intervention*. Chicago, IL: University of Chicago Press.

Mancuso, J.C. and Sarbin, T.R. (1983) 'The self-narrative in the enactment of roles', in T. R. Sarbin and K.E. Scheibe (eds) *Studies in Social Identity*. New York: Praeger.

Mandl, H., Stein, N.L. and Trabasso, T. (eds) (1984) *Learning and Comprehension of Text*. Hillsdale, NJ: Lawrence Erlbaum.

Mandler, J.M. and Johnson, N.S. (1977) 'Remembrance of things parsed: Story structure and recall', *Cognitive Psychology* 9: 111–151.

Marková, I. (2003) *Dialogicality and Social Representations*. Cambridge: Cambridge University Press.

Markus, H. and Kitayama, S. (1991) 'Culture and the self: Implications for cognition, emotion, and motivation', *Psychological Review* 98: 224–253.

Marshack, A. (1972) *Roots of Civilization: The cognitive beginnings of man's first art. symbol, and notation*. New York: McGraw-Hill.

Martindale, C. (1975) *Romantic Progression: The psychology of literary history*. New York: Wiley.

—— (1990) *The Clockwork Muse: The predictability of artistic change*. New York: Basic Books.

Martindale, C. and West, A.N. (2002) 'Quantitative hermeneutics', in M. Louwers and W. van Peer (eds) *Thematics: Interdisciplinary studies*. Amsterdam: John Benjamins.

Mátrai, L. (1973) *Élmény és mu (Art and Experience)*. Budapest: Gondolat.

Matte-Blanco, I. (1988) *Thinking, Feeling and Being*. London: Routledge and the Institute of Psycho-Analysis.

—— (1989) 'Comments on "From symmetry to asymmetry" by Klaus Fink', *International Journal of Psycho-Analysis* 70: 491–498.

Mead, G.H. (1934) *Mind, Self, and Society*. Chicago, IL: University of Chicago Press.

Mérei, F. (1949) 'Group leadership and institutionalisation', *Human Relations* 2: 23–39.

—— (1984) *Lélektani Napló I: Az utalás lélektana (Psychological Diary I: The psychology of allusion)*. Budapest: Muvelodéskutató Intézet.

—— (1989) *Társ és csoport (The Other and the Group)*. Budapest: Akadémiai Kiadó.

Mészáros, Á. and Papp, O. (2006) 'A kauzális kohésió vizsgálata az Intex számítógépes eszközzel' (A study of causal cohesion by Intex algorithms). Paper presented at Fourth Magyar Számítógépes Nyelvészeti Konferencia, Szeged, Hungary, 7–8 Deember.

Michotte, A.E. (1963) *The Perception of Causality*. London: Methuen.

Middleton, D. and Brown, S.D. (2005) *The Social Psychology of Experience: Studies in remembering and forgetting*. London: Sage.

Miles, M.B. and Huberman, A.M. (1994) *Qualitative Data Analysis: An expanded sourcebook*, 2nd edn. Thousand Oaks, CA: Sage.

Miller, J. (1984) 'Culture and the development of everyday social explanation', *Journal of Personality* 46: 961–978.

Mink, L.O. (1978) 'Narrative form as cognitive instrument', in R.H. Canary and H. Kozicki (eds) *The Writing of History: Literary form and historical understanding*. Madison, WI: University of Wisconsin Press.

Mintz, I. (1971) 'The anniversary reaction: a response to the unconscious sense of time', *Journal of the American Psychoanalytic Association* 19: 720–735.

Moliner, P. (1995) 'A two-dimensional model of social representations', *European Journal of Social Psychology* 25: 27–40.

Moscovici, S. (1973) 'Foreword', in C. Herzlich (ed.) *Health and Illness: A social psychological analysis*. London: Academic Press.

—— (1976 [1961]) *La Psychoanalyse, son image et son public*, 2nd edn. Paris: Presses Universitaires de France.

—— (1984) 'The phenomenon of social representations', in R.M. Farr and S. Moscovici (eds) *Social Representations*. Cambridge: Cambridge University Press.

—— (1986) 'The Dreyfus Affair, Proust and social psychology', *Social Research* 53, 1: 23–56.

—— (1988) 'Notes towards a description of social representations', *European Journal of Social Psychology* 18: 211–250.

—— (1994) 'Social representations and pragmatic communication', *Social Science Information* 33, 2: 163–177.

Moscovici, S. and Hewstone, M. (1983) 'Social representations and social explanations: From the "Naive" to the "Amateur" scientist', in M. Hewstone (ed.) *Attribution Theory: Social and functional extensions.* Oxford: Blackwell.

Moscovici, S. and Vignaux, G. (2000) 'Le concept de thémata', in C. Guimelli (ed.) *Structures et transformations des representations socials.* Neuchâtel, Switzerland: Delachaux & Niestlé.

Muhr, T. (1991) 'ATLAS.ti: A prototype for the support of text interpretation', *Qualitative Sociology* 14: 349–371.

Mulkay, M. (1985) *The Word and the World: Explorations in the form of sociological analysis.* London: Allen & Unwin.

Murray, H.A. (1938) *Explorations in Personality.* New York: Oxford University Press.

Neisser, U. (1976) *Cognition and Reality.* San Francisco, CA: Freeman.

Nelson, K. (1993) 'The psychological and social origins of autobiographical memory', *Psychological Science* 4: 7–14.

Newell, A. and Simon, H.H. (1972) *Human Problem Solving.* Englewood Cliffs, NJ: Prentice-Hall.

Nora, P. (1989) 'Between memory and history: Les Lieux de mémoire', *Representations* 26: 7–25.

Oatley, K. (1992) *Best Laid Schemes: The psychology of emotions.* New York: Cambridge University Press.

Ochs, E. and Capps, L. (2001) *Living Narrative.* Cambridge, MA: Harvard University Press.

Olson, D.R. (1977) 'From utterance to text: The bias of language in speech and writing', *Harvard Educational Review* 47: 257–258.

Páez, D., Valencia, J., Marques, J. and Vincze, O. (2004) 'Collective memory and social identity: social sharing of the past and social identity in Spain'. Paper presented at the conference Collective Remembering, Collective Emotions and Shared Representations of History: Functions and Dynamics, Aix-en-Provence, France, 16–19 June.

Pasupathi, M. (2001) 'The social construction of the personal past and its implications for adult development', *Psychological Bulletin* 127: 651–672.

Pataki, F. (2001) *Élettörténet és identitás (Life Story and Identity).* Budapest: Osiris.

Péley, B. (2002) 'Narrative psychological study of self and object representations with young deviant people', in J. László and W. Stainton Rogers (eds) *Narrative Approaches to Social Psychology.* Budapest: New Mandate.

Pennebaker, J.W. (1993) 'Putting stress into words: Health, linguistic and therapeutic implications', *Behavior Research and Therapy* 31, 6: 539–548.

Pennebaker, J.W. and Banasik, B. (1997) 'On the creation and maintenance of collective memories: History as social psychology', in J.W. Pennebaker, D. Paez, and B. Rimé (eds) *Collective Memory of Political Events: Social psychological perspectives.* Mahwah, NJ: Lawrence Erlbaum.

Pennebaker, J.W. and Francis, M.E. (1996) 'Cognitive, emotional, and language processes in disclosure', *Cognition and Emotion* 10: 601–626.

Pennebaker, J.W. and King, L.A. (1999) 'Linguistic styles: Language use as an individual difference', *Journal of Personality and Social Psychology* 77: 1296–1312.

Pennebaker, J.W., Mayne, T.J. and Francis, M.E. (1997a) 'Linguistic predictors of adaptive bereavement', *Journal of Personality and Social Psychology* 72, 4: 863–871.

Pennebaker, J.W., Páez, D. and Rimé, B. (eds) (1997b) *Collective Memory of Political Events: Social psychological perspectives.* Mahwah, NJ: Lawrence Erlbaum.

Pennebaker, J.W., Francis, M.E. and Booth, R.J. (2001) *Linguistic Inquiry and Word Count (LIWC) LIWC.* Mahwah, NJ: Lawrence Erlbaum.

Pennebaker, J.W., Mehl, M.R. and Niederhoffer, K.G. (2003) 'Psychological aspects of natural language use: Our words, our selves', *Annual Review of Psychology* 54: 547–577.

Pennebaker, J.W., Páez, D. and Deschamps, J.C. (2006) 'The social psychology of history: Defining the most important events in the last 10, 100, and 1000 years', *Psicología Política* 32: 15–32.

Pennington, N. and Hastie, R. (1992) 'Explaining the evidence: Testing the story model for juror decision making', *Journal of Personality and Social Psychology* 62: 189–206.

Piaget, J. and Weil, A.M. (1951) 'The development in children of the idea of homeland, and of relations with other countries', *International Social Science Bulletin* 3: 561–578.

Pinker, S. (1997) *How the Mind Works?* New York: Norton.

Pléh, C. (2003a) 'Thoughts on the distribution of thoughts: Memes or epidemies', *Journal of Cultural and Evolutionary Psychology* 1, 1: 21–51.

—— (2003b) 'Decomposition and reassembling of the self: Possibilities of meeting cognitive and social constructions', in J. László and W. Wagner (eds) *Theories and Controversies in Societal Psychology.* Budapest: New Mandate.

Pléh, C., László J., Síklaki, I. and Terestyéni, T. (1983) 'What is the point in points without a grammar (A comment on Wilensk's paper)', *Behavioral and Brain Sciences* 4: 607–608.

Pohárnok, M., Naszódi, M., Kis, B., Nagy, L., Bóna, A. and László, J. (2007) 'Exploring the spatial organization of interpersonal relations by means of computational linguistic analysis', *Empirical Culture and Text Research* 3: 39–49.

Polkinghorne, D.E. (1988) *Narrative Knowing and the Human Sciences.* Albany, NY: State University of New York Press.

—— (1997) 'Reporting qualitative research as practice', in W.G. Tierney and Y.S. Lincoln (eds) *Representation and the Text: Re-framing the Narrative Voice.* Albany, NY: State University of New York Press.

Pólya, T. (2007) *Identitás az élettörténetben (Identity in Life Story).* Budapest: New Mandate.

Pólya, T., László, J. and Forgas, J.P. (2005) 'Making sense of life stories: The role of narrative perspective in communicating hidden information about social identity and personality', *European Journal of Social Psychology* 35: 785–796.

Pólya, T., Kis, B., Naszódi, M. and László, J. (2007) 'Narrative perspective and the emotion regulation of a narrating person', *Empirical Culture and Text Research* 3: 50–61.

Popper, K. (1957) *The Poverty of Historicism,* London: Routledge.

Potter, J. and Wetherell, M. (1987) *Discourse and Social Psychology: Beyond attitudes and behaviour.* London: Sage.

Prince, G. (1973) 'A grammar of stories: An introduction', *Poetics* 14: 177–196.

—— (1990) 'On narrative studies and narrative genres', *Poetics Today* 11, 2: 271–282.

Progoff, I. (1975) *At a Journal Workshop.* New York: Dialogue House.

Prohászka, L. (1936) *A vándor és a bújdosó (The Wanderer and the Refugee).* Budapest: Egyetemi Nyomda.

Propp, V. (1968) *The Morphology of Folk Tales*. Austin, TX: University of Texas Press

Prószéky, G. and Kis, B. (1999) *Számítógéppel – emberi nyelven. Intelligens szövegkezelés számítógéppel (Computer and Human Language: Intelligent text processing with computer)*. Budapest: Szak Kiadó.

Prószéky, G., Tihanyi, L. and Ugray. G. (2004) 'Moose: A robust high-performance parser and generator', in *Proceedings of the Ninth Workshop of the European Association for Machine Translation*. Valletta, Malta: Foundation of International Studies.

Purkhardt, S.C. (1993) *Transforming Social Representations: A social psychology of common sense and science*. London: Routledge.

Rainer, T. (1978) *The New Diary*. Los Angeles, CA: J. P. Tarcher.

Ricoeur, (1965) *De l'interpretation: Essai sur Freud*. Paris: Fayard.

—— (1981) *Hermeneutics and the Human Sciences*. Cambridge: Cambridge University Press.

—— (1984–1989) *Time and Narrative*, vols 1–4. Chicago, IL: University of Chicago Press.

—— (1991) 'L'identité narrative', *Revues de Sciences Humaines* 221: 35–47.

Rorty, R. (2004) 'Analytic philosophy and narrative philosophy'. Lecture II, Pécs, 4 May.

Rose, D. (1997) 'Television madness and community care', *Journal of Community and Applied Social Psychology* 8: 213–228.

Rosenberg, S. and Jones, R. (1972) 'A method for investigating and representing a person's implicit theory of personality: Theodor Dreiser's view of people', *Journal of Personality and Social Psychology* 22, 3: 372–386.

Ross, L. and Nisbett, R.E. (1991) *The Person and the Situation*. New York: McGraw-Hill.

Ross, L., Bierbauer, G. and Hoffman, S. (1976) 'The role of attribution processes in conformity and dissent: Revisiting the Asch situation', *American Psychologist* 31: 148–157.

Rowett, C. and Breakwell, G.M. (1992) *Managing Violence at Work: Workbook*. Slough: NFER-Nelson.

Rubin, D.C. (1995) *Memory in Oral Traditions*. Oxford: Oxford University Press.

—— (ed.) (1996) *Remembering our Past*. Cambridge: Cambridge University Press.

Rumelhart, D.E. (1975) 'Notes on a schema for stories', in D.G. Bobrow and A. Collins (eds) *Representation and Understanding: Studies in cognitive science*. New York: Academic Press.

Ryan, M.L. (1981) 'Introduction: On the why, what and how of generic taxonomy', *Poetics* 10: 109–126.

Salovey, P., Mayer, J.D., Goldman, S.L., Turvey, C. and Palfai, T.P. (1995) 'Emotional, attention, clarity, and repair: Exploring emotional intelligence using the Trait-Meta-Mood Scale', in J.W. Pennebaker (ed.) *Emotion, Disclosure, and Health*. Washington, DC: American Psychological Association.

Sarbin, T.R. (1986a) 'The narrative as a root metaphor for psychology', in T.R. Sarbin (ed.) *Narrative Psychology: The storied nature of human conduct*. New York: Praeger.

—— (ed.) (1986b) *Narrative Psychology: The storied nature of human existence*. New York: Praeger.

Schafer, R. (1980) 'Narration in the psychoanalytic dialogue', *Critical Inquiry* 7: 29–53.

Schaller, M. and Conway, L.G. (1999) 'Influence of impression-management goals on the emerging contents of group stereotypes: Support for a social-evolutionary process', *Personality and Social Psychology Bulletin* 25: 819–833.

Schank, R.C. (1975) 'The structure of episodes in memory', in D.G. Bobrow and A.N. Collins (eds) *Representation and Understanding*. New York: Academic Press.

Schank, R.C. (1986) *Explanation Patterns*. Hillsdale, NJ: Lawrence Erlbaum.

Schank, R.C. and Abelson, R.P. (1977) *Scripts, Plans, Goals, and Understanding*. Hillsdale, NJ: Lawrence Erlbaum.

—— (1995) 'Knowledge and memory: The real story', in R.S. Wyer, Jr. (ed.) *Knowledge and Memory: The real story*. Hillsdale, NJ: Lawrence Erlbaum.

Schiffrin, D. (1994) *Approaches to Discourse*. Cambridge, MA: Blackwell.

Scholes, R. (1980) 'Language, narrative and anti-narrative', in W.J.T. Mitchell (ed.) *On Narrative*. Chicago, IL: University of Chicago Press.

Schütze, F. (1977) 'Die Technik des narrativen interviews in Interaktionsfeldstudien'. Unpublished manuscript, University of Bielefeld, Germany.

Searle, J.R. (1998) *Mind, Language and Society*. New York: Basic Books.

Seifert, C.M., Dyer, M.G. and Black, J.B. (1986) 'Thematic knowledge in story understanding', *Text* 6: 393–425.

Semin, G.R. (2000) 'Agenda 2000–Communication: Language as an implementational device for cognition', *European Journal of Social Psychology* 30: 595–612.

Semin, G.R. and Fiedler, K. (1988) 'The cognitive functions of linguistic categories in describing persons: Social cognition and language', *Journal of Personality and Social Psychology* 54: 558–568.

—— (1991) 'The linguistic category model, its bases, applications and range', in W. Stroebe and M. Hewstone (eds) *European Review of Social Psychology*, vol. 2. Chichester: Wiley.

Shils, E. (1981) *Tradition*. Chicago, IL: University of Chicago Press.

Shklovsky, V. (1965 [1917]) 'Art as technique', in L.T. Lemon and M.J. Reis (eds) *Russian Formalist Criticism*. Lincoln, NE: University of Nebraska Press.

Silberztein, M. (2006) Nooj, http:// www.nooj4nlp.net, accessed 17 January 2008.

Silvermann, I. and Eales, M. (1992) 'Sex differences in spatial abilities: Evolutionary theory and data', in J.H. Barkow, L. Cosmides and J. Tooby (eds) *The Adapted Mind: Evolutionary psychology and the generation of culture*. New York: Oxford University Press.

Singer, J.A. and Salovey: (1993) *The Remembered Self: Emotion and memory in personality*. New York: Free Press.

Snow, C. P. (1993) *The Two Cultures*. New York: Cambridge University Press.

Spence, D.P. (1982) *Narrative Truth and Historical Truth. Meaning and interpretation in psychoanalysis*. New York: Norton.

Sperber, D. (1985) 'Anthropology and psychology: Towards an epidemiology of representations', *Man* 20: 73–89.

—— (1990) 'The epidemiology of beliefs', in C. Fraser and G. Gaskell (eds) *The Social Psychological Study of Widespread Beliefs*. Oxford: Clarendon Press.

—— (1996) *Explaining Culture: A naturalistic approach*. Oxford: Blackwell.

Sperber, D. and Wilson, D. (1986) *Relevance: Communication and cognition*. Oxford: Blackwell.

Stainton Rogers, W. (1991) *Explaining Health and Illness*. Hemel Hempstead: Harvester-Wheatsheaf.

—— (1996) 'Critical approaches to health psychology', *Journal of Health Psychology* 1, 1: 556–559.

Stein, N.L. and Glenn, C.G. (1979) 'An analysis of story comprehension in elementary-school children', in R.O. Freedle (ed.) *New Directions in Discourse Processing: Advances in discourse processes*, vol. 2. Norwood, NJ: Ablex.

Stein, N.L. and Policastro, M. (1984) 'The concept of a story: A comparison between children's and teacher's viewpoints', in H. Mandl, N.L. Stein, and T. Trabasso (eds) *Learning and Comprehension of Text*, Hillsdale, NJ: Lawrence Erlbaum.

Stephenson, N., Breakwell, G.M. and Fife-Schaw, C.R. (1993) 'Anchoring social presentations of HIV protection: The significance of individual biographies', in P. Aggleton, P. Davies and G. Hart (eds) *AIDS: Facing the second decade*. London: Falmer.

Stephenson, G.M., László, J., Ehmann, B., Lefever, R.M.H. and Lefever, R. (1997) 'Diaries of significant events: Socio-linguistic correlates of therapeutic outcomes in patients with addiction problems'. *Journal of Community and Applied Social Psychology* 7: 389–411.

Stern, D.N. (1989) 'Crib monologues from a psychoanalytic perspective', in K. Nelson (ed.) *Narratives from the Crib*. Cambridge, MA: Harvard University Press.

—— (1995) *The Motherhood Constellation: A unified view of parent-infant psychotherapy*. New York: Basic Books.

Sternberg, M. (1978) *Expositional Modes and Ordering in Fiction*. Baltimore, MD: Johns Hopkins University Press.

Stich, S.P. (1983) *From Folk Psychology to Cognitive Science*. Cambridge, MA: MIT Press.

Stone, P.J., Dunphy, D.C., Smith, M.S. and Ogilvie, D.M. (1966) *The General Inquirer: A computer approach to content analysis*. Cambridge, MA: MIT Press.

Sutton-Smith, B. (1976) 'The importance of the storytaker: An investigation of the imaginative life', *The Urban Review* 8: 82–95.

Szondi, L. (1956) *Lehrbuch der Experimentellen Triebdiagnostik*, vol. 1. Bern: Hans.

Tajfel, H. (1970) 'Experiments in intergroup discrimination', *Scientific American* 223, 5: 96–102.

—— (1972) 'Experiments in a vacuum', in J. Israel and H. Tajfel (eds) *The Context of Social Psychology: A critical assessment*. London: Academic Press.

—— (ed.) (1978) *Differentiation between Social Groups*. London: Academic Press.

—— (1981) *Human Groups and Social Categories: Studies in social psychology*. Cambridge: Cambridge University Press.

Tajfel, H., Nemeth, C., Jahoda, G., Campbell, J.D. and Johnson, N.B. (1970) 'The development of children's preference for their own country: A cross-national study', *International Journal of Psychology* 5: 245–253.

Tajfel, H., Billig, M.G., Bundy, R.P. and Flament, C. (1971) 'Social categorization and intergroup behaviour', *European Journal of Social Psychology* 1, 2: 149–178.

Tarde, G. (1895) *Les Lois de l'imitation*. Paris: Alcan.

Taylor, C. (1979) 'Interpretation and the science of man', in P. Rabinow and W.A. Sullivan (eds) *Interpretive Social Sciences*. Berkeley, CA: University of California Press.

Terr, L. (1984) 'Time and trauma', *Psychoanalytic Study of the Child* 39: 633–665.

Thomas, W.I. and Znaniecki, F. (1918–1920) *The Polish Peasant in Europe and America*. Chicago, IL: University of Chicago Press.

Thorndyke, P.W. (1977) 'Text and context: Explorations in the semantics and pragmatics of discourse', *Journal of Pragmatics* 1: 211–232.

Tocqueville, A. (1969 [1935]) *Democracy in America*, edited by J.P. Mayer, trans. G. Lawrence. Garden City, NY: Anchor.

Tomasello, M. (1999) *The Cultural Origins of Human Cognition*. Cambridge, MA: Harvard University Press.

Tomasello, M., Carpenter, M., Call, J., Behne, T. and Moll, H. (2005) 'Understanding and sharing intentions: The origins of cultural cognition', *Behavioral and Brian Sciences* 28: 675–735.

Trabasso, T., Secco, T. and Van Den Broek, P. (1984) 'Causal cohesion and story coherence', in H. Mandl, N.L. Stein and T. Trabasso (eds) *Learning and Comprehension of Text*. Hillsdale, NJ: Lawrence Erlbaum.

Tulving, E. (1972) 'Episodic and schematic memory', in E. Tulving and W. Donaldson (eds) *Organization of Memory*. New York: Academic Press.

Turner, J.C. (1975) 'Social comparison and social identity: Some prospects for intergroup behaviour', *European Journal of Social Psychology* 5: 5–34.

Turner, J.C., Hogg, M.A., Oakes, P.J., Reicher, S.D. and Wetherell, M. (1987) *Rediscovering the Social Group: A self-categorization theory*. Oxford: Blackwell.

Turner, R. (1968) 'The self-conception in social interaction', in C. Gordon and K.J. Gergen (eds) *The Self in Social Interaction: Classic and contemporary perspectives*, vol. 1. New York: Wiley.

Uspensky, B.A. (1974) *The Poetics of Composition: Structure of the artistic text and the typology of compositional form*. Berkeley, CA: University of California Press.

Vala, J. (1992) 'Towards an articulation of social identity and social representations'. Paper presented at First International Conference on Social Representations, Ravello, Italy, 3–5 October.

Van Peer, W. and Chatman, S. (eds) (2001) *New Perspectives on Narrative Perspective*. Albany, NY: State University of New York Press.

Vaughan, G.M. (1964) 'The development of ethnic attitudes in New Zealand schoolchildren', *Genetic Psychology Monographs* 7: 135–175.

Vincze, O., Tóth, J. and László J. (2007) 'Representations of the Austro-Hungarian Monarchy in the history books of the two nations', *Empirical Text and Culture Research* 3: 62–71.

Vygotsky, L.S. (1971) *The Psychology of Arts*. Cambridge, MA: MIT Press.

—— (1978) *Mind in Society: The development of the higher psychological processes*. Cambridge, MA: Harvard University Press.

—— (1981) 'The genesis of higher mental functions', in J.V. Wertsch (ed.) *The Concept of Activity in Soviet Psychology*. Armonk, NY: M.E. Sharpe.

Wagenaar, W.A., van Koppen, P.J. and Crombag, H.F.M. (1993) *Anchored Narratives: The psychology of criminal evidence*. Hemel Hempstead: Harvester-Wheatsheaf.

Wagner, W. (1993) 'Can representations explain social behavior? A discussion of social representations as rational systems', *Papers on Social Representations* 2: 236–249.

—— (1995) 'Description, explanation and method in social representation research'. *Papers on Social Representations* 4: 156–176.

—— (1998) 'Social representations and beyond: Brute facts, symbolic coping and domesticated worlds', *Culture and Psychology* 4, 3: 297–329.

Wagner, W. and Hayes, N. (2005) *Everyday Discourse and Common Sense*. Basingstoke: Palgrave Macmillan.

Wagner, W., Elejabarrieta, F. and Lahnsteiner, I. (1995) 'How the sperm dominates the ovum: Objectification by metaphor in the social representation of conception', *European Journal of Social Psychology* 25, 6: 671–688.

Wagner, W., Duveen, G., Farr, R., Jovchelovitch, S., Lorenzo-Chioldi, F., Markova, I. and Rose, D. (1999) 'Theory and method of social representation', *Asian Journal of Social Psychology* 2: 95–125.

Webber, B. (2004) D-LTAG: Extending lexicalized TAG to discourse', *Cognitive Science* 28: 751–779.

Weintraub, W. (1981) *Verbal Behavior: Adaptation and psychopathology*. New York: Springer.

—— (1989) *Verbal Behaviour in Everyday Life*. New York: Springer.

Wertsch, J.V. (2002) *Voices of Collective Remembering*. Cambridge: Cambridge University Press.

White, H. (1981) 'The value of narrativity in the representation of reality', in W.J.T. Mitchell (ed.) *On Narrative*. Chicago, IL: University of Chicago Press.

Whorf, B.L. (1956) *Language, Thought, and Reality*. Cambridge, MA: MIT Press.

Wilensky, R. (1978) 'Why John married Mary: Understanding stories involving recurring goals', *Cognitive Science* 2, 3: 235–266.

—— (1983) 'Story grammars vs. story points', *Behavioral and Brain Sciences* 6: 579–623.

Wilkins, D.P. (1995) 'Expanding the traditional category of deictic elements: Interjections as deictics', in J.F. Duchan, G.A. Bruder and L.E. Hewitt (eds) *Deixis in Narrative: A cognitive science perspective*. Hillsdale, NJ: Lawrence Erlbaum.

Wilkinson, B. (1997) 'Feminist psychology', in D. Fox and I. Prilleltensky (eds) *Critical Psychology: An introduction*. London: Sage.

Wimmer, H. and Perner, J. (1983) 'Beliefs about beliefs: Representations and constraining functions of wrong beliefs in young children's understanding of deception', *Cognition* 13: 103–128.

Winograd, T. and Flores, F. (1987) *Understanding Computers and Cognition: A new foundation for design*. New York: Addison-Wesley.

Wittgenstein, L. (1961) *Philosophical Investigations*. Oxford: Blackwell.

Worth, S. (1972) *Through Navajo Eyes: An exploration in film communication and anthropology*. Bloomington, IN: Indiana University Press.

Wundt, W. (1916) *Elements of Folk Psychology: Outlines of a psychological history of the development of mankind*, trans. E.L. Schaub. London: Allen & Unwin.

Wyer, R.S., Adaval, R. and Colcombe, S.J. (2002) 'Narrative-based representations of social knowledge: Their construction and use in comprehension, memory, and judgment', in M.P. Zanna (ed.) *Experimental Social Psychology*, Amsterdam: Academic Press.

Zajonc, R.B. (1969) 'Cognitive theories in social psychology', in G. Lindzey and E. Aronson (eds) *Handbook of Social Psychology*, vol. 1. Reading, MA: Addison-Wesley.

Zerubavel, Y. (1994) 'The historic, the legendary, and the incredible: Invented tradition and collective memory', in J.R. Gillis (ed.) *Commemorations: The politics of national identity*. Princeton, NJ: Princeton University Press.

Zhang, H. and Hoosain, R. (2005) 'Action of themes during narrative reading', *Discourse Processes* 40, 1: 57–82.

Index